"Pat has been over the target since the beginning when he let everyone know about Dominion voting system internet connections in Detroit. He has continued to expose the stolen election ever since. Listen to what he has to say. You'll learn something the fake news media doesn't want you to know!"

—Mike Lindell, *CEO My Pillow, Inc.*

"There are only a handful of people who relentlessly pursued the truth regarding the 2020 Election. Patrick Colbeck takes the "GOLD" in this masterful work - meticulous details on our voting systems along with solutions for the future."

—Liz Harris, *AZ Grassroots Leader*

"Elections belong to the people not the government"

—Mark Finchem, *AZ State Representative*

"Pat Colbeck has painstakingly worked to investigate the corruption surrounding the 2020 election. His knowledge of the subject and dedication to cleaning up our elections is an asset to anyone wanting a better understanding of what transpired in 2020. He is a dedicated patriot, and his work reflects his passion for honesty and transparency."

—Christina Bobb, *Former DHS Executive Secretary and USMC Judge Advocate*

"Almost immediately after the 2020 general election, Senator Colbeck and I began collaborating and investigating election irregularities. He traveled the country talking with people, listening to their accounts of how this particular election was so out of the norm, and collecting evidence. This book, like his website, letsfixstuff.org, are organized to enable Americans everywhere to connect the dots and understand with clarity what really happened in the 2020 Election."

—Phil Waldron, *Col USA (Ret)*

"Pat Colbeck witnessed fraud in the 2020 election firsthand. He's worked tirelessly exposing it ever since. His work will go a long way to prevent it from ever happening again."

—Liz Harrington

THE 2020
COUP

THE 2020 COUP

What Happened. What We Can Do.

PATRICK COLBECK

THE 2020
COUP

Published by
McHenry Press
www.McHenryPress.com
*"Publishing books in the land of the free
and the home of the brave."*

Library of Congress Control Number: 2022907098

Paperback ISBN: 978-1-955043-65-6

Typeset by Art Innovations (http://artinnovations.in/)
Cover design by Debbie Lewis

Printed in the United States of America

*This book is dedicated to
#MeddlingKids everywhere devoting themselves
to the relentless pursuit of the truth
behind what happened during the 2020 election.*

"We have put together and you guys did it for the President Obama's administration before this… we have put together I think the most extensive and inclusive voter fraud organization in the history of American politics."

—JOE BIDEN

on "Pod Save America" Podcast uploaded on October 24, 2020

Media translation courtesy of Reuters who asserted in an October 29, 2020 story that it was a "slip of the tongue." He meant to say "voter protection program".

Contents

Prologue

was there. I was in Detroit at the TCF Center on election night for more than twenty-four hours straight. I witnessed firsthand the late-night delivery of ballots without any chain of custody. As a certified Microsoft Small Business Specialist, I witnessed firsthand evidence that the tabulators which reportedly counted 174,384 votes in a race decided by 154,188 were indeed connected to the internet. I was one of the numerous poll challengers barred from reentry to the Absentee Vote Counting Board as they spoiled and replicated military ballots without the requisite bipartisan oversight. I was there when they put pizza boxes over the windows to keep anyone from witnessing this process even from a distance. I was there when the Wayne County Board of Canvassers refused to certify the election. I testified before the State Board of Canvassers. I've read the media reports sharing the official narrative of what happened. They pushed propaganda not facts. They promoted how elections were supposed to work not how they did. I listened to reports of election officials asserting that the 2020 general election was the most secure election in history. If this was the most secure election in history, I shiver at the thought of what was happening in previous elections.

We were told by elected and election officials that there is no evidence of election fraud. When pressed with evidence of election fraud, these same officials pivoted to say the evidence was not widespread. When widespread evidence of election fraud was shown, they asserted that it wasn't significant enough to change the results of the election. It was significant, as you will discover in this book.

When I spoke publicly about what I witnessed on national television and radio, people from all over the country began to share their evidence with me. My home became a virtual library of election fraud evidence, which I shared with elected officials. The evidence was virtually ignored in my home state of Michigan until an old friend of mine in Arizona, Rep. Mark Finchem, contacted me. He asked me to share my testimony in Arizona. This opened the door for me to testify in Michigan before my former stomping ground in the Michigan Senate. I prayed with witnesses who, fearful of the backlash they and their family would receive as a result, were in tears moments before they were to testify before the Michigan House Oversight Committee. I was later approached by Mike Lindell, who included my testimony in his documentary called *Absolute Proof*. A few months after that, he asked me to talk about election system internet connections at his livestream Cyber Symposium event in August 2021 in South Dakota. I have testified to what I observed in whatever forum would listen, from groups of twenty-five people huddled together in a barn to thousands of Americans assembled in an orchard in northern Michigan.

Since November 3, 2020, I have been actively knitting together the evidence which I have received into a picture of how the coup was executed. My investigations necessarily focus on Michigan, but, as you will see, there are common threads between Michigan and what was observed in other states. My professional background is that of a systems engineer. I love to connect the dots between components within complex systems. The coup was indeed one of these complex systems. The challenge before us is to how to present the evidence of a complex coup in a simple manner without diluting the substance of the evidence. In this book, I present the evidence of this complex system in as simple of a manner as possible. Ultimately, you will be the judge as to whether I have succeeded in this charge or not.

My bet is that you have not yet seen the vast majority of the evidence which I present. Why? Because those behind the coup are desperately working to ensure you don't see it.

This is not a book meant to vent sour grapes as some will inevitably seek to portray it. As a Republican State Senator, I called for an investigation into the 2016 election after reports of fraudulent activities in Detroit. In case you may have forgotten, Trump was not only declared the victor nationally in 2016, he was also declared the winner in Michigan by a narrow margin of 10,704 votes. I didn't call for an investigation of the 2016 election results on the basis of which candidate was declared the winner. I called for an investigation to ensure the integrity of our elections. The same is true in the wake of the 2020 election.

The 2020 election was not a typical battle between Democrats and Republicans at the polls. It was not about Biden versus Trump. It was between those who seek to "fundamentally transform" America and those who seek to preserve all that is noble, true, excellent and praiseworthy about America. In many ways, it is a spiritual battle between good and evil for the very notion of truth itself.

As you will see in this book, there is a price to be paid in today's America for the pursuit of the truth. There is a price to be paid for simply exercising one's constitutional rights to free speech, freedom of assembly, and freedom to seek redress for grievances. Freedom truly is not free.

Introduction

The November 2020 general election remains a hotly contested topic.

Skepticism is rampant.

On one hand there are those who are skeptical that there was any election fraud at all during the 2020 election. They feed off media stories that declare any assertions of election fraud as unsubstantiated or refer to anyone suggesting the possibility of election fraud as conspiracy theorists.

On the other hand, there are those who are skeptical that Joe Biden earned the most votes in the history of the Republic. How could a lackluster candidate who could only rally a few dozen supporters at his "rallies" defeat, by a wide margin, Donald Trump, whose campaign rallies regularly featured tens of thousands of supporters?

There is skepticism on both sides. America is divided.

The aim of this book is to unite America by appealing to everyone's yearning to know the truth. Sadly, this appears to be a unique approach in our public square today. Our major news outlets in particular use their platforms to promote division not unity. Their constitutional right to freedom of the press is being used to sow propaganda not facts.

If you want to be manipulated, by all means, continue to watch or read stories by your favorite cable news network or social media stream. If you want to be informed, this book will provide eye-opening, factual information you will likely not have heard on the major news outlets.

In this book, we go beyond simply sharing a bunch of facts. We organize these facts in a systematic breakdown of the 2020 election to make them easier to absorb. We hope to appeal to skeptics on both sides of the election integrity debate.

After a primer on election integrity, we will then employ the scientific method. We present a theory for how the election may have been stolen. We then proceed to map the known facts to this theory and present our findings.

No exaggerations.

No unsupported assertions of fact.

The difference between what is known and what is unknown will be highlighted not blended. For those of you old enough to remember Joe Friday in the *Dragnet* TV series, this book will feature just the facts. We want to unite America around an increasingly rare concept: the truth.

Buckle up, it's time to explore the important question: Was America the victim of a coup?

CHAPTER 1

Most Secure Election in History?

On November 13, 2020, the Cybersecurity and Infrastructure Security Agency, also known as CISA, issued a joint statement from Elections Infrastructure Government Coordinating Council and the Election Infrastructure Sector Coordinating Executive Committees featuring the now well-known assertion: "The November 3rd Election was the most secure in American history."[1]

On November 17, 2020, the director of CISA, Christopher Krebs, was fired from his post. Afterward, he doubled down on his assertion that the 2020 election was indeed secure. Despite such assurances, those who witnessed election fraud filed hundreds of affidavits to the contrary. These affidavits open the affiants to felony perjury charges if not truthful.

Yet election fraud skeptics persist in their assertion that this was the most secure election in history. They refer to the claims of affiants as "unsubstantiated" or "technically incomprehensible." This perspective is echoed by most major media outlets.

On the rare occasion that one of these outlets does issue a report on the topic of election fraud, the report almost always labels anyone claiming evidence of election fraud as a conspiracy theorist or simply a liar.

What were the specific claims that earned affiants such labels? Viewers are left to wonder as the mainstream media never delves into the substantive details of fraud but only assert that the 2020 election was the most secure election in history.

It is difficult not to draw parallels with the Ministry of Truth from George Orwell's classic novel *1984*.

In summary, one side of the election fraud debate believes that the integrity of our elections is beyond reproach. The other side believes that the integrity of our elections has been compromised. To complicate matters, discussion of election fraud has been discouraged in the public square. In fact, there are government officials who assert that the very act of questioning the integrity of our elections itself undermines the integrity of our government.

Should we allow our citizens to question the integrity of our elections? Is our government so fragile that it cannot withstand citizens exercising their constitutional rights to free speech and to petition the government for a redress of grievances?

This begs the question, does election integrity even matter?

CHAPTER 2

Why Election Integrity Matters

n January 2017, DHS designated the infrastructure to administer elections in America as critical infrastructure. That means that our election system is a critical component of our national infrastructure right along with our access to electricity, water, and food. It is a critical component of our national infrastructure for a reason.

We are a republic.

We elect representatives to serve us on our behalf. Our representatives are bound to protect the rights enshrined in our Constitution.

What happens when our elections become selections? What happens when our leaders are selected by enemies to the principles enshrined in our Constitution? What happens when people who serve someone other than the American people are placed in positions of authority within our government?

Our Constitution is gone

Our Bill of Rights is gone

Government of, by, and for the people is gone

This is why any attack on our election system by enemies foreign or domestic should be considered an act of war.

Those who serve in the United States military take the following oath: "I do solemnly swear that I will support and defend the Constitution of the United States against all enemies, foreign and domestic; that I will bear true faith and allegiance to the same."

The priority of our military service personnel is not to support and defend the land. It is to support and defend the Constitution of the United States. They swear an oath to support and defend a set of words written on parchment. They swear allegiance to a set of principles agreed upon by we the people. These principles represent the supreme law of the land in America. Without these principles, without the rule of law, America is simply a plot of land on a map.

Treason against the United States is defined in Article III Section 3 of our Constitution as "levying war against them or in adhering to their enemies, giving them aid and comfort".

Foreign or domestic enemies do not need to use force of arms to lay claim to that plot of land on a map; they can eliminate America simply by stealing an election.

Elections can therefore be viewed as a battleground.

In most cases, the battle is between the competing ideologies of political parties. They are often a battle between competing thoughts on how to achieve the objectives cited in the Preamble of our US Constitution. In some cases, however, elections are a battle between those who seek to undermine these objectives and those who seek to preserve these objectives. In some cases, elections are a battle for the very preservation of the principles that bind us together in our Constitution.

What happens when an election results in a divided, not united, states?

What happens when injustice replaces justice?

What happens when domestic tranquility is replaced by domestic turmoil?

What happens when the general welfare of our citizens is degraded not elevated?

What happens when the blessings of liberty are eroded not secured?

What happens when all this has come to pass at the hands of enemies either foreign or domestic?

Our America of the people, by the people, and for the people has been destroyed. This is why the theft of our elections represents an existential threat to the preservation of America. This is why our military service personnel take an oath to support and defend a set of principles as their first priority. Because election security is a matter of national security.

CHAPTER 3

Security Threats to Our Election System

ELECTION INFRASTRUCTURE COMPONENTS

Let's delve into a discussion of the security threats to our election system. Rather than provide you with a list of the risks that I have discovered on my own, I believe it would be quite revealing to hear from people who investigated these risks prior to the 2020 general election and who now assert that it was the most secure election in American history.

An investigative news story by NBC News that aired on January 10, 2020,[1] provided a stark summary of the hacking risks for voting systems connected to the internet.

CYNTHIA MCFADDEN: We've heard it at congressional hearings for years.

MR. HICKS: Our voting machines are not connected to the internet.

KEVIN SKOGLAN: We knew that wasn't true.

CYNTHIA MCFADDEN: Cybersecurity expert Kevin Skoglan wanted to prove it so he and nine other independent

security consultants created their own search engine looking
for election systems online

KEVIN SKOGLAN: We found over 35 had been left online
and we continue to find more.

[. . .]

CYNTHIA MCFADDEN: Skoglan's team found ES&S vot-
ing systems online in at least some of the precincts in 11 states
including the battleground states of Florida, Michigan and
Wisconsin.

If you were able to get inside these systems, could you do
more than perhaps mess up the preliminary results could you
actually get deeper into the system.

KEVIN SKOGLAN: Absolutely. And that's my biggest concern.

On July 28, 2020, three months before the November 3 election,
the Cybersecurity & Infrastructure Security Agency (CISA), the agency responsible for understanding, managing, and reducing the risk to
our cyber and physical infrastructure, released what they referred to as
a Critical Infrastructure Security and Resilience Note,[2] which included
a list of election components vulnerable to cyber and non-cyberattacks.
These components are the fundamental building blocks of our election
system. Let's look at what CISA identified as vulnerable components.

Voter Registration Database

The first of these vulnerable building blocks is the voter registration
database. Voter registration is an ongoing process to create new records,
update existing records, and remove outdated records. Voter registration databases receive data automatically and indirectly from a variety of
sources, including other government agencies and organizations that aid
in the registration process. The databases contain information on whether people are entitled to vote, where they can vote, and on what unique

ballot style they will vote, based upon voter geographical placement within multiple layers of political and taxing districts. The management of voter registration databases are the responsibility of each state. These databases are typically managed by the secretary of state for each state. These databases are used to enter, store, and edit voter registration information. Security risks include servers that host the database and online portals that provide access. Since these databases are connected to the internet, they pose serious security risks due to the ability for them to be hacked.

Pollbooks

Another vulnerable building block of the election system are pollbooks. Pollbooks are precinct-specific extracts of the statewide voter registration files. Poll workers use the information in the pollbooks to determine whether or not a voter is eligible to vote. It contains information used to validate the identity of a prospective voter. When voters vote in person at the polls, poll workers use this information to decide whether or not the voter is eligible to receive a ballot to cast at that precinct. Poll workers also use this information to validate the identity of an absentee voter before allowing the absentee ballot to be tabulated. Pollbooks may be either networked or non-networked. Networked pollbooks are electronic pollbooks with a connection to an external database such as the statewide voter registration file. Non-networked pollbooks are either paper pollbooks or digital files saved on local computers. Either way, poll workers use pollbooks to validate the identify and eligibility of prospective voters. Poll workers are also empowered to view, edit, and modify voter records via the pollbooks. Pollbook integrity is critical. The information which they contain determines whether a voter receives a ballot or doesn't.

Ballot Preparation

Ballots are another key election infrastructure component with security vulnerabilities. Modern ballots are much more sophisticated than a piece of paper with checkboxes next to names. Today's ballots are sophisticated paper and/or digital documents. In fact, in some cases, ballots are replaced by Direct-Recording Electronic (DRE) voting machines.

Ballot preparation is a complicated process of overlaying political geographies with the contests and candidates specific to each district and then translating those layouts into unique combinations of ballot data. Ballot preparation data takes multiple forms such as ballot images (both paper and electronic), the data files necessary to build ballot images, audio files for special use ballots, and specific files for export to external systems such as websites or Uniformed and Overseas Citizens Absentee Voting Act (UOCAVA)-focused digital systems. Ballot preparation also generates the data necessary for tabulating votes within a voting machine and aggregating tabulated votes within a jurisdiction or state. This process is usually completed in an election documents and records management system (EDRMS), which is special software designed to manage documents and records throughout the document lifecycle, from creation to destruction. Access to the information in such systems would enable anyone attempting to subvert the integrity of an election with the information necessary to create ballots independently of election officials. Of course, ballots are also where voters record their votes. Vote tallies are generated from the information on ballots therefore their integrity is very important to protect.

Voting Machines

Another class of election infrastructure components that are at risk are voting machines. Voting machine systems consist of the technology and processes used to cast and, in some cases, generate voter ballots of all types (paper-based or digital systems such as DRE voting). Voting machines often feature ballot marking capabilities that assist in providing an audit trail although DRE systems are noteworthy for their lack of paper audit trail. Electronic voting machines feature hardware and software components which must be certified as "secure" prior to use in an election. The Federal Election Assistance Commission provides a list of certified voting system configurations. Election equipment is supposed to be delivered in a configuration consistent with a certified configuration. The process of preparing electronic voting machines includes loading the ballot files created during ballot preparation onto the voting machines' software. Voting machines are held in storage in the custody of election officials, but after delivery they are placed at voting locations for use during early voting and on Election Day. Voting machines are the most visible form of technology that voters interact with during the voting process.

Tabulation Systems

Tabulators are critical election infrastructure components with significant security vulnerabilities. At the precinct-level, tabulators are used to read a ballot, convert the ballot image to votes, and add the vote data on a given ballot to the running tally of votes stored in a digital table. Precinct-level vote tallies are then aggregated by centralized vote tabulation systems at the municipal, county, and state levels. Collectively, these systems help determine and communicate the results of an election. If tabulators are compromised, they can shift votes from one candidate to another. These vote shifts can change the results of an election.

Official Websites

Official websites are additional critical components of election infrastructure used by election officials to communicate information to the public, including how to register to vote, where to vote, and to convey election results. Sometimes election websites are hosted on government-owned infrastructure, but they often are hosted by commercial partners. Whether hosted by the government, commercially, or privately, websites can be areas of vulnerability as they often feature network connections to election results databases.

Storage Facilities

Physical buildings, such as storage facilities, polling places, and election offices, are also critical infrastructure components which need to be secured. Storage facilities may be located on public or private property and may be used to store election and voting system infrastructure before Election Day. Polling places (including early voting locations) are where individuals cast their votes. They may be physically located on public or private property. Election offices are where election officials conduct official business. These offices can be in public libraries, municipal buildings, private homes, and public areas for jurisdictions without a dedicated workspace.

Summary

Today's modern electronic voting system has quite a few moving parts. The more complex the system, the more vulnerable it is to exploitation. Furthermore, many election officials do not have the technical expertise regarding information technology to mitigate the risks to these systems. Of particular concern is the trend toward increasing network connectivity between election components. The centralization of our election system by networking components together makes it easier for fewer and fewer bad actors to subvert the integrity of the election system. Manual systems featuring paper ballots eliminate many of the security vulnerabilities inherent with electronic voting systems. Election officials, poll workers, and poll challengers can see, touch, and feel paper-based election systems. They can secure these systems by observation. In contrast, it is very difficult for these same individuals to monitor electronic communications.

CONSEQUENCES OF ELECTION INFRASTRUCTURE SECURITY BREACHES

The consequences of security breaches according to CISA fall into the following three impact categories: confidentiality, integrity, and availability impacts. The most significant of these, of course, pertain to the integrity of the election results.

The integrity of our election systems can be subverted in a variety of ways. While election integrity has always been a concern, our modern electronic voting systems make it easier than ever to effect large scale changes with minimum effort. Key election records such as our statewide voter registration file, the pollbooks, the ballot itself, and the subsequent vote tallies have all been digitized in our modern election system. Each of these records are connected in what can be described as our election record chain of custody.

Each record in the election record chain of custody can be thought of as a link. The first link is the statewide voter registration file. The statewide voter registration file contains a list of everyone eligible to vote and includes information necessary to verify the identity of voters such as their drivers license signature. The next link is that of the pollbook. The pollbooks are simply precinct-specific extracts of the statewide voter registration file used by poll workers to verify the identity of a given voter prior to processing a ballot cast in that voter's name. That makes ballots the next link in the election record chain of custody. The ballot, of course, contains the intended votes of a voter. The final link in the chain of custody is the vote tally. The vote tally should simply be the sum of all the votes cast on valid ballots.

If you break any single link in the chain, you break the integrity of the entire election. For example, if you have an incorrect birthdate in the statewide voter registration file, it will propagate to an incorrect birthdate in the pollbooks. If an incorrect birthdate is in the pollbook, someone may receive a ballot despite not having met the minimum age requirement to vote. If an ineligible voter casts a ballot, the subsequent vote tally is compromised.

In a modern electronic voting system, each of the above handoffs is digitized. Whereas data transfers or modifications of these records could be easily monitored by any citizen when our elections were driven by paper records, the monitoring of our digital election records is often restricted to a select few. In this light, the push to digitize our election system has severely impaired transparency. As transparency dissolves, so does the integrity of our elections.

How could these links be compromised? Let's start by looking at the statewide voter registration database. Nefarious actors can add, delete, or modify voter registration data in statewide voter registration files. Such actions can enable what are called phantom voters or result in the denial of voting rights to individuals otherwise qualified to vote. The seeding of the statewide voter registration file with "phantom voters" yields a "slush fund" of voters that could be fraudulently assigned to ballots.

If the statewide voter registration file has been corrupted, any poll-books generated from this database will also be corrupted. This corruption of voter data can go both ways. If bad actors were to access electronic pollbooks, the pollbooks could be used to push fraudulent data to the statewide voter registration file. Furthermore, pollbooks could be accessed real-time by bad actors to reveal who has not yet voted or tap into a voter slush fund. These voter slush funds can be used by clandestine ballot factories to match manufactured ballots to low propensity voters. This match-making exercise helps to avoid an abundance of embarrassing "you already voted" remarks by poll workers when a low propensity voter actually shows up at a voting precinct in person to vote.

Ballot integrity can also be compromised. Some modern voting systems use what is referred to as DRE or Direct-Recording Electronic voting machines. Without significant transparency provisions that would compromise the principle of a secret ballot, voters have no substantive assurance that the votes they cast on a voting machine touch screen are actually what has been recorded in the vote tally. Even when paper ballots are used, they can be manipulated to compromise the integrity of the election record chain of custody. Something as simple as the formatting of paper ballots can be used to manipulate election results. Ballot formatting can be manipulated to trigger scanner errors. These scanner errors in turn will trigger manual or automated adjudication processes. These adjudication processes can then be used to shift votes between candidates. Absentee ballots are particularly vulnerable to this method of subversion as the control over how a vote is cast when there is a scanner error is turned over to poll workers not the voter.

The end game of all this electronic record manipulation is the vote tally. The consequence of a compromised vote tally is the selection of a compromised public official. Vote tallies can be manipulated in a variety of ways. Bad actors can program tabulators to automatically shift a percentage of votes from one candidate to another when the tabulator reads a scanned ballot image and allocates votes in a vote tally database. The tabulation databases themselves can be directly manipulated to replace actual vote tallies with alternative vote tallies. Bad actors who have access to vote tallies before election precincts close can use that information to know if they need to stuff the ballot box with more ballots than anticipated.

If election components are connected to each other on local networks or via internet connections, pollbook ballot tallies and tabulator ballot counts are vulnerable to being re-synchronized with each other to cover any discrepancies between the number of voters and the number of votes cast. If bad actors wish to give the appearance of a secure election, the total number of voters handed ballots per the pollbook records must reconcile with the number of ballots stored in ballot containers as well as the total number of votes in the final statement of votes.

This is just a small sample of the way security breaches can affect elections.

For those who assert that the 2020 general election was the most secure election in history, ask yourselves which of the security concerns raised by CISA, a federal agency, were addressed between the release of the aforementioned CISA Critical Infrastructure Security and Resilience Note on July 28, 2020, and November 3, 2020.

While the federal government has the authority to identify and mitigate any national security threats to our election system, the US Constitution clearly specifies that state governments are responsible for the conduct of our elections. It is each state's responsibility to ensure that elections are conducted in a secure manner.

In Michigan, one of the 2020 battleground states, the Michigan Election Security Advisory Commission was also tasked with the identification and mitigation of election threats. Their report, issued in October of 2020, identified several significant election security risks. On the topic of the voter registration system, they cited issues with security credential management and a lack of monitoring of suspicious activities. On the topic of post-election audits, they cited a lack of transparency about the process and asserted that the current post-election audit standards did not satisfy the constitutional right of Michigan citizens to conduct an audit of statewide election results. They also cited the threats posed by misinformation or disinformation campaigns, election night reporting risks, and the risks inherent in submitting electronically unofficial election results to county clerks. The report noted that connecting tabulators to the internet or other external networks creates significant risks to the integrity of the election.

For those who assert that the 2020 general election was the most secure election in history, which of the concerns raised in the October report by the Michigan Election Security Advisory Commission were addressed prior to November 3?

Does anyone truly believe that any of these concerns were addressed at all prior to the election?

If not, is it fair to say that there were significant threats to election integrity that were not addressed prior to the November 3, 2020, election?

CHAPTER 4

Investigative Tools

The security assessments by CISA and the State of Michigan merely highlighted the risks to our election system. Risks are simply bad things that *could* happen.

How do we know if any of these bad things *did* actually happen? How would we know if there were any security breaches?

ACCESS TO INFORMATION

Identifying election fraud is all about access to data. The best way to know if there were any security breaches would be to serve as an election official such as a clerk or secretary of state. In such a position, you should be able to request, observe, and analyze any election data pertinent to your respective jurisdiction. In essence, you would have access to all of the components identified by CISA as security risks.

If you are not an election official, you can still assist election officials by serving as a poll worker. While you would typically not have the authority to access election information beyond that available at your assigned duty station, you would be able to observe the overall conduct of the election. Poll workers are able to identify process anomalies and bring them to the attention of election officials.

If you are unable to observe the election process as a poll worker, the next best role would be that of a poll challenger. Poll challengers have access to basic election information specific to the pollbooks and ballots provided the poll workers do not interfere with such observations. In order to discourage such interference, certified poll challengers typically have their poll challenger duties protected under the law. One could also serve as a poll watcher, but there are typically no such protections under the law.

The aforementioned roles apply to monitoring election processes as they are executed.

With so many people monitoring the execution of our elections, is it even possible to conceal the theft of thousands of votes from all the observers? Wouldn't you need thousands of corrupt election officials?

On November 1, 2006, software developer Clinton Eugene Curtis, a programmer who worked for Yang Enterprises, testified before the US House Judiciary Committee about how he created software to rig an election in Florida:

Attorney Cliff Arnebeck called Clint Curtis before the Committee, for the purpose of determining if the vote-counting process of the 2004 U.S. General Election in Ohio could have been manipulated by a computer.
ARNEBECK: Mr Curtis, are there programs that can be used to secretly fix elections?
CURTIS: Yes.
ARNEBECK: How do you know that to be the case?
CURTIS: Because in October of 2000 I wrote a prototype for present Congressman Tom Feeney, at the company I work for in Oviedo, Florida, that did just that.
[...]
REP. JERROLD NADLER: We've been told, I've been told, that people who assume that lots of the election results, a large

fraction of the election results in this state may have been affected by computerware fraud in the computer are paranoid, because in order to do that you would have to have access to thousands of machines, and that would be readily detectable. Is that true?

CURTIS: It depends on the technology used. If you did a central tabulation machine that fed in, all you would have to do is set a flag. If you set a flag, the central tabulation machine would then flip your vote.

REP. JERROLD NADLER: So if you, so one person putting in bad code in a central tabulation machine could affect thousands and thousands, or tens of thousands, of votes?

CURTIS: Right. And you could activate it.

But wait, you might be thinking, our elections feature county officials, sometimes referred to as county boards of canvassers, who would ensure that the election results are accurate prior to certification, right?

REP NADLER: And would that program that you designed be something that elections officials that might be on county boards of elections could detect?

CURTIS: They'd never see it.

Let's assume that our election officials, poll workers, poll challengers, and poll watchers never see any election fraud prior to certification of the vote. Many times, fraud may not be observed on election day, but suspicions arise after the election has concluded. How could citizens get access to information that would assist in further investigations?

Ask

The vast majority of clerks are just as passionate about election integrity as my fellow "meddling kid" investigators are. The first step in any jurisdiction where fraud is suspected is to simply *ask* the pertinent clerk for information. Even if they do not have it readily available, there is a pretty good chance they could obtain it. When I was a Michigan state senator, I received numerous requests for information. Sometimes I had direct access to the information. Sometimes I had to put in a request to the agency which did have access to the information. In either case, I took my role as public servant seriously. I didn't forget who worked for whom. It has been my experience that most clerks look at their duties the same way. Give them an opportunity to assist you in your investigation. If they refuse to assist you in response to any reasonable request, well, I guess you know where they stand on election integrity.

FOIA

If you are unable to receive the data you need via a simple request, your next option is to submit a Freedom of Information Act (a.k.a. FOIA) request. The Freedom of Information Act gives citizens the right to access most public records for what is a typically a nominal fee defined in statute. If access is wrongfully denied, citizens are authorized to bring suit to compel disclosure and may be awarded damages and reasonable attorney fees.

It is not difficult to issue a FOIA request, but you need to be very precise as to what you are seeking, or you will generally receive the bureaucratic runaround. In fairness to government officials, it can be very difficult to read the minds of those requesting the data, so specificity is indeed recommended. I have personally issued and supported many FOIA requests.

Here are some examples of my FOIA requests:

Example 1: State of Michigan Request
Cost: $1,563.27
Information Request: In a spreadsheet compatible electronic format (csv or Excel), provide a list of all voters said to have voted in Michigan during the 2020 general election.

For each voter identified, include the following information:
- Full name (First, Middle, Last)
- Full address in compliance with United States Postal Service addressing standards (Street Address, Municipality, State, Zip code)
- Date of birth (Year as a minimum)
- Voting precinct
- County of residence
- Method of voting (At polling place or Absentee)

If the method of voting is Absentee, include the following additional information:

- Permanent absentee voter status (Yes or No)
- Means by which absentee ballot application was submitted (electronically, mail, in-person, other (specify how))
- Organization who received ballot application (e.g. MI Secretary of State, Clerk's office)
- Address where ballot application was received
- Date of receipt of Absentee ballot application
- Address application was sent to
- Address application was received by (if different then address application was sent to)
- Date when absentee ballot for 2020 general election was sent to voter
- Date when absentee ballot for 2020 general election was received
- Address where absentee ballot for 2020 general election was received

List may be broken down into multiple electronic files featuring one million records or less each but should not exceed 1 unique file per county (maximum number of files would be 83).

Why is this list of voters important? This information is extremely valuable when it comes to evaluating the integrity of elections. It provides auditors with a list of people to contact in order to verify whether or not they truly voted during the 2020 election. If someone listed as a voter testifies that they did not actually vote, that is a very clear indicator of fraud. Furthermore, there are laws which require the retention of these records. Under MCL 168.509q, voting history must be retained for a five-year period. Under USC 52, Section 20701, all election records must be maintained for at least 22 months after the election. Failure of election officials such as the Secretary of State to retain such records is a violation of the law and could be used as grounds for decertifying an election.

According to the Michigan Secretary of State, 5,579,317 ballots were cast in the 2020 general election. On March 3, 2021, the Michigan Auditor General was tasked with assessing the integrity of Michigan's statewide voter registration file referred to as the Qualified Voter File (QVF). In their March 4, 2022, report,[1] they reported that 5,533,818 votes were cast yielding a clear discrepancy with the figures provided by the Michigan Secretary of State. Despite this difference of 45,499 votes (more than the reported 2016 margin of victory in Michigan of 10,704 votes), the Auditor General made the amazing claim that the integrity of the QVF was "effective." Not only would most observers note that such a discrepancy indicates that the integrity was "not effective," it would also indicate that there are 45,499 violations of state and federal statute which need to be investigated by law enforcement. My FOIA request for a list of those who voted in the 2020 General Election will enable every day citizens to evaluate once and for all whether or not the QVF integrity was truly "effective".

Example 2: City of Detroit Request
Cost: $0 (because it is supposed to be open to public)
Information Request: Pursuant to MCL 168.764b, each clerk in the State of Michigan shall maintain a list open to the pub-

lic that contains the names and addresses of all authorized
assistants appointed by the clerk who are available to collect
absent voter ballots on or before election day in the City of
Detroit.

Please provide the names and addresses of individuals authorized by the Clerk for the City of Detroit to perform such duties
in support of the 2020 general election per MCL 168.764b as
of November 3, 2020.

Why is this list of authorized assistants important? Ballot harvesting is illegal in Michigan, but there is a loophole that allows ballot harvesting for "authorized assistants." Under MCL 168.764b, each clerk
in the State of Michigan must maintain a list open to the public that
contains the names and addresses of all authorized assistants appointed
by the clerk to collect absentee ballots on behalf of their jurisdiction.
If video footage of ballot harvesters were to be released as a result of an
investigation, it is important to know before the release of said footage
who was truly authorized to be a ballot harvester and who was not. Also,
it provides the ability to canvass the authorized assistants to make sure
that they met all of the statutory requirements of an authorized assistant
prior to engaging in ballot harvesting.

In response to my FOIA request, I was initially provided with a list
of authorized assistants with redacted addresses. Redacted addresses are
not sufficient to validate the identity of an authorized assistant. Since
this is not compliant with the referenced statute, I had to appeal this
submittal. The city of Detroit replied to my appeal by submitting the
unredacted list. Persistence pays off.

Due to the legal implications of failure to comply with FOIA requests, it is recommended that such requests be made by written record.
Most government entities support the submittal of FOIA requests via

email. I recommend that you enable a delivery and read receipt when requesting digitally. Certified mail is another option.

Please note that not all government information is subject to a FOIA request.[2] Prior to submitting your FOIA requests, you will save yourself some heartache by first checking your state's FOIA laws. In short, the FOIA process is not for the faint of heart. It can also be expensive. Despite this, it is often the best option available to citizen investigators.

Subpoena

Sometimes FOIA requests are not successful or simply not an option due to the type of information requested. In such cases, the last resort is to issue a subpoena for the information. Subpoenas can be issued by either judges or legislatures in support of investigations. Subpoenas have much broader authority than FOIA requests. They are often not subject to the FOIA exemptions cited previously. While failure to respond to FOIA requests often results in civil fines, failure to respond to subpoena requests results in criminal charges that may lead to jail time as well as fines.

RECOUNTS

Often, the first reaction when election fraud is suspected is to call for a recount. Can an election be stolen in a manner that a recount would not detect? The answer is yes, as Mr. Curtis' continues his testimony:

> REP NADLER: And if you had a recount with no paper trail, would that be revealable by seeing a discrepancy between what the central tabulator showed and what the individual machines would show.
> CURTIS: Not if I wrote it. I would make it match.

So what good is a recount then?

Let's look at what a recount does tell you and what it doesn't.

A recount tells you:

- How many ballots were stored by the clerk
- How many votes were cast in the stored ballots
- The variance between the certified ballot count and number of ballots stored
- The variance between the certified vote tally and the vote tally from the ballots stored

A recount doesn't tell you:

- How many ballots were fraudulently "stuffed" into a ballot box
- How many ballots were fraudulently removed from a ballot box
- How many ineligible voters fraudulently cast ballots
- What caused the variance between the certified and recount results

Clearly, recounts are lacking in the ability to determine whether election fraud was committed.

What else can we do to determine if fraud was committed?

AUDITS

Conduct an audit. The premise of an audit is simple: Did you do what you said you would do? An audit is simply a verification that you did what you were supposed to do. There are several kinds of audits, which I mention below.

Fake Audits

There are attempts, whether intentional or out of ignorance, to make people believe that a recount of ballots is an audit, but that's not true. We've already addressed the shortcomings of a recount, but the assertion that a recount is an audit is repeated so often that it merits further discussion.

Let's look at an audit example with which many Americans may be familiar: an IRS audit. When the IRS audits someone, do they ask the taxpayer to check their math on their 1040 Form? No. That would be analogous to a recount. During a tax audit, the IRS asks the taxpayer to provide a paper trail which validates the entries on their 1040 Form. It is this paper trail that is analyzed to either validate or invalidate the entries on the 1040 form. If the 1040 entries are not supported by a paper trail, the IRS has the authority to reject your return and levy fines until properly prepared.

Elections should be no different. We need to press beyond recounting ballots and ensure that the paper trail for each ballot passes the sniff test.

Risk Limiting Audits

In addition to falsely calling a recount an audit, some election officials attempt to pass off what are called risk limiting audits as forensic audits, but are they?

According to Prof. Phil Stark of UC Berkeley, the man who coined the term "risk limiting audits," who was interviewed in the 2020 HBO documentary *Kill Chain: The Cyber War on America's Elections,* a risk limiting audit is simply a "hand count of everything." In other words, it is a recount. The only paper trail in a risk limiting audit comes in the form of paper ballots.

What makes risk limiting audits unique from a typical recount is that risk limiting audits are supposed to tell you when it's OK to stop counting ballots based upon the statistical significance of further counting.

Forensic Audit

A true election audit simply verifies that the election processes that people were *supposed* to follow were *actually* followed. If you anticipate the need to go to court after an election, you will need to conduct a *forensic* audit, which is simply an audit with sufficient rigor to be admissible in a court of law.

Such an audit would go beyond recounting the ballots and evaluate whether election processes were followed. Investigations into election fraud need to go beyond superficial observations such as "how many votes do the ballots show" to investigations of how did those ballots get into the ballot box in the first place?

In order to conduct an effective audit, it is important to start with an understanding of how an election is supposed to work. Election processes are defined in law by the legislature. These election laws are supplemented by detailed election procedures defined by election officials, such as the secretary of state. While there are some common threads between states, election processes can vary significantly between states. Suffice it to say, elections are much more complex than marking a vote on a ballot and counting the number of marks for a given candidate. This can make the conduct of a true audit of election processes much more involved than a simple recount.

The election records subject to examination in such an audit would feature the components identified by CISA in their July 2020 report.[3] The targets at risk of attacks per their assessment include the following election components:

- Voter registration database
- Electronic and paper pollbooks
- Ballot preparation
- Voting machine systems
- Vote tabulation and aggregation systems
- Official websites
- Storage facilities
- Polling places
- Election offices

Particular emphasis should be applied to the statewide registered voter database, pollbooks, ballots, and the all-important vote tallies. As previously mentioned, these records are the basic building blocks of the election record chain of custody.

By focusing upon the election record chain of custody, we can simplify the execution of a true audit. The chain of custody is analogous to the paper trail required in an IRS audit. Election records are modified during an election via a sequence of data transfers starting with the data being stored in the statewide voter registration file. During the preparation for an election, election officials transfer voter roll data to precinct-specific pollbooks. The data in these pollbooks is then used by poll workers and election officials to determine whether or not a voter is eligible to cast a ballot. If a voter is eligible to cast a ballot, the voter transfers their candidate preferences to the ballot. Once a voter casts their ballot, there is no way to trace that ballot back to the voter because Americans value ballot secrecy. No one has a right to know how any citizen casts their vote. There are generally no identifying marks on a ballot that would indicate which voter cast that ballot. Once a ballot is cast, the voter's preferences on a ballot are then transferred to a precinct-specific tabulation center where the vote results for all election contests are counted. These precinct-specific vote tallies are added up at the municipal, county, state, and national levels to determine which candidate received the most votes. It is these aggregated vote tallies that drive people to stay up and watch well into the wee hours of the morning after an election to see who won.

The processing of these election records features critical handoffs which must be monitored to ensure the integrity of any election. If the information in the state voter registration database differs from that contained in the pollbooks for a given election, it indicates that there is an issue with the integrity of one of these records. If these discrepancies occur before an election, they need to be reconciled prior to allowing any affected voters to cast a ballot else that ballot is likely fraudulent. If these discrepancies occur after an election, it is an indication that either election processes were not followed effectively during the election, or someone is attempting to prevent discovery of election fraud. If the number of votes cast per the pollbook does not equate to the number of ballots in the ballot box, the precinct is out of balance. Out of balance precincts indicate that election processes were not followed thereby giving cause for election officials not to certify an election. If the vote tallies indicate more votes being cast for a given candidate than ballots in the ballot box, this is another indicator that election processes were not followed thereby giving cause for election officials not to certify an election. When the statewide voter registration file, pollbooks, ballots and vote tallies are consistent with one another and logs of the data transfers show that the integrity of the chain of custody has been maintained, we can have significant confidence that an election was conducted with integrity. Without such indications, however, we should not have confidence that an election was conducted with integrity.

The integrity of the results depends upon the integrity of each handoff of data in the election record chain of custody. To secure the integrity of the election record chain of custody, individual election records must be secured at all times. A variety of security measures are needed to reduce the risk of tampering with election results.

The most important security measure pertains to personnel. There is no substitute for ensuring that our elections are run by people of exceptional ability and personal integrity. To protect against the absence of these qualities in our election officials, our elections feature additional safeguards regarding personnel. These safeguards include statutory requirements for balanced political party representation in election staffing as well as provisions that allow for poll challengers and poll watchers to observe all aspects of the election process. Transparency is our best defense against fraud.

Physical security measures are also important. Physical security measures include locked rooms or locked storage containers. These locked compartments are used to secure election equipment and paperwork from unauthorized access. Serialized, tamper-proof seals are also used. These seals provide visible indications that physical election records have not been tampered with during transfer from point A to point B or since being placed in secure storage.

Electronic voting systems require additional security safeguards. These complicated systems featuring hardware, software and networking components need to be tested, certified, and physically secured. When electronic voting equipment is not in use, unplugging the equipment in conjunction with physical security measures does provide a significant degree of security although many devices include battery backup that impair this security. When electronic voting systems are in use, however, security verification for electronic equipment becomes significantly more complicated. It involves an assessment of credential management practices, hardware configurations, software configurations, firewalls, peripherals, and network configurations as a minimum. Our primary concern is that the election data managed by the electronic voting system is stored and transferred in a secure manner.

Physical election data transfers can be observed by poll challengers and election officials. Electronic data transfers cannot often be observed at all during an election. Secure data transfers can be accomplished via supervised physical transfer of removable storage devices in the case of non-networked devices. For networked devices, secure data transfers become more complicated. For devices featuring wireless or hardwired connections to other electronic devices, security risks are typically reduced but by no means eliminated through the use of virtual private network connections. Transparent, verifiable, electronic logs of data transfers are essential elements of any attempt to ensure that the chain of custody has been secured.

How do we ensure the integrity of each of these data transfers? Conduct an audit. See Appendix B for a template that could be used to scope the work for full forensic audit of an election.

SUMMARY

Ultimately, the only way to demonstrate that an election was secure is to perform an assessment of whether all election processes were followed or not. Recounts don't do that. Risk limiting audits don't do that. Only a forensic audit of all the records in the election record chain of custody does that. Audits are the only way to determine if an election was truly secure or not.

CHAPTER 5

The Theory

Back to our salient question. Was America the victim of a coup? Did foreign or domestic enemies of the United States of America subvert the integrity of the 2020 election or not?

As demonstrated previously, the answers to this question are significant. The consequences of subverting an election are immense. The process of getting straight answers needs to be systematic, methodical, and factual.

Prudence, indeed, will dictate that established election results should not be questioned for light and transient causes. Therefore, we will now proceed to apply the scientific method to the question: Was America the victim of a coup?

Let's start by posing a theory as to how the election *may* have been stolen. To do so, we will attempt to shift our perspective from one seeking to protect our elections to that of someone seeking to subvert our elections. We will review all the security risks identified so far and convert them into a plausible theory as to how someone would go about stealing an election. We will then test this theory by citing factual evidence pertinent to this theory. Then it will be up to you, the reader, to determine whether or not the evidence supports the theory.

Posing a theory is not as easy as it might seem. Many Americans have been programmed to assume that our elections are immune to tampering. In order to protect the faith of our citizens in our government institutions, government officials tend to classify any assertions of election system vulnerabilities as misinformation or conspiracy theories. Other Americans fail to fathom the idea that there are people in the world who are committed to stealing an election—and many of these people have the resources to do so. Americans don't like to think that way. We tend to believe most people in the world are inherently good. In the past, America has learned the hard way that that simply is not true.

On December 7, 1941, 2,403 Americans lost their lives in the Main Attack on Pearl Harbor in Hawaii. On September 11, 2001, 2,977 people died in New York, Pennsylvania, and Washington, DC.

These were acts of war. We need to recognize that there are bad people in the world that seek to harm America. Once we understand that fact, it behooves us to examine how these bad people might seek to harm America.

Make no mistake, any attempt to undermine the integrity of our election system is an act of treason or war.

The question before us is how would someone wage war upon the United States through our election system? What strategy would be used? To answer this question, we will review the writings of the fifth century BC military strategist Sun Tzu. His book *Art of War* contains time-tested maxims on military strategy that are taught in military academies around the world to this very day. These maxims yield significant insights as to how any enemy of the United States would seek to attack our election system. Based upon my experience, I believe that the following maxims in particular merit close attention:

"Every battle is won or lost before it is ever fought"
"You can be sure of succeeding in your attacks if you only attack places which are undefended"

"According as circumstances are favorable, one should modify one's plans."
"Attack is the secret of defense; defense is the planning of an attack."

We have used these maxims as the foundation of our theory as to how the 2020 election may have been hijacked. This theory features the following four strategic phases:

- Preparation Phase: Create or expand weaknesses in our election system
- Main Attack Phase: Exploit single greatest weakness, mail-in ballots, to stuff the ballot box with fraudulent votes
- Backup Attack Phase: Leverage networked electronic voting systems to modify the vote tally directly in order to ensure victory
- Defense Phase: Make sure that no one discovers the fraud, communicates the fraud or overturns the fraudulent election results.

Within each of these strategic phases, we will look for evidence of a specific set of tactics being employed that seek to achieve the goal of each phase. These tactics can be organized into the following basic groups: process execution anomalies, election record anomalies and influence operations. Process execution anomalies include changes to processes, violations of the law, or training-related tactics. Election record anomalies refer to unusual conditions of key election records such as the statewide voter registration database, pollbooks, ballots or vote tallies. The term *influence operation* traces its roots to military planners. Influence operations refer to attempts to achieve a specific behavioral objective while concealing such attempts from the general public.

There is a lot to unpack about election fraud. It helps to keep it organized. Without this structure, it is difficult to see how the different factoids and news stories all fit together. Strategy provides the big picture. Tactics connect the big picture to the evidence. And together strategy and tactics paint a complete picture of how the election may have been stolen.

Let's start painting this picture together.

PREPARATION

"Every battle is won or lost before it is ever fought"
—SUN TZU

The first phase in any military campaign often involves preparation. In military parlance, this is often referred to as "shaping the battlefield." Battlefields are shaped to best suit your own objectives and tactics while impairing the objectives and tactics of your enemy.

The goal of the preparation phase in any attempt to subvert the integrity of an election would be to create weaknesses in the election system or enhancing existing weaknesses. The preparation phase for any campaign to subvert our elections would likely be measured in years, not months, before the first ballot is cast.

The term *campaign* is not only used frequently in military circles. It is also used frequently in reference to elections. Much as there is typically a code of conduct in the execution of military campaigns, there is also a code of conduct for the execution of political campaigns. These codes of conduct are not always followed by both sides in a conflict. In the aftermath of World War II, the Nuremburg Court sought to hold combatants accountable for what were deemed to be war crimes. There are legal mechanisms in place to address malfeasance regarding elections as well. Much as in war, though, accountability for such malfeasance during elections is important both for justice to be served as well as a future deterrent.

Holding people accountable for such malfeasance during political campaigns can be difficult. This difficulty stems from a basic observation. Both legitimate and subversive political campaigns have the same objective—victory at the ballot box. The difference between a legitimate political campaign and a subversion campaign lies in exactly how that objective is achieved. A legitimate campaign plays by the established rules to ensure a level playing field for all. A subversion campaign either ignores the rules or changes the rules to tilt the playing field in favor of one or more candidates. By their very nature, effective subversion campaigns are often difficult to detect...but they can be detected via a structured investigation of their tactics.

Process Anomalies

Process anomalies would likely be the primary emphasis during the preparation phase of any campaign to subvert our elections. In order to detect these process anomalies, it is critical that investigators first understand how elections are supposed to be conducted. This requires a solid understanding of the following process standards as a minimum:

- U.S. Constitution
- Federal election law statutes[1]
- State Constitution
- State election law statutes
- State election procedures

In the era of electronic voting systems, a significant amount of election oversight is outsourced to private vendors which are not often prone to direct oversight by poll watchers, poll workers or often even our duly elected election officials. In this light, investigators also need a working understanding of the following as well:

- Election Assistance Commission Certification Procedures
- Election Assistance Commission VSTL Standards
- Election Assistance Commission VVSG Requirements
- Contracts between Election Officials and Electronic Voting System Vendors

Once investigators have a solid understanding of how elections are supposed to work, they will have a firm foundation from which to evaluate changes to election processes which may be intended to create or exploit weaknesses in the integrity of elections.

Some of the most obvious changes to look for involve constitutional amendments, statutory revisions, or election procedure changes by election officials. Remember, a subversion campaign doesn't play by the rules. These changes would likely be intended to make it more difficult for those who do play by the rules to detect any malfeasance.

One also needs to be aware of another key tactic that can be employed during preparation known as *lawfare*. Using lawfare tactics, bad actors can attempt to change laws or election procedures via the courts. Of course, this is a perversion of the separation of powers within a constitutional republic, but it happens more often than one may think. This tactic can be very useful when the legislature and/or executive branch are controlled by the opposing political party. Lawfare provides bad actors with the ability to skip what is often a messy, resource-intensive effort to pass legislation or pursue ballot petitions. Often all that is necessary is for them to file a lawsuit which claims that a particular law (e.g., Civil Rights) has been violated by other laws or election procedures. The court or other party would then use the filing as the impetus to change certain interpretations of a given law or drive changes to election procedures. The net result is a change in election processes via the judicial branch without ever getting the permission of the legislative or executive branch.

Any subversion campaign would likely also seek to hinder transparency. There are many ways to accomplish this objective. For starters, investigators should be wary of any attempts to promote any election activities not readily observed by the general public. Mail-in voting is probably the best example of such an activity. The US Postal Service is not meant to be a secure transaction system. Even less secure than the US Postal Service, however, are drop boxes. Drop boxes have been introduced in many communities as an alternative to the Postal Service. Despite often being accompanied by security provisions in statute, these statutory requirements are not consistently adhered to.

There are issues with voting by mail that go beyond the security of our mail system or drop boxes. Unlike poll-based voting, key elements of the voting process, such as the validation of the voter identity or the handling of ballot scanning errors, are handled by third parties or without the presence of the actual voter.

Another way to hinder transparency would be to implement procedures or technology so complex or labor-intensive that specialized vendors are required to execute these procedures often without any oversight by elected officials or the general public. Electronic voting systems are a perfect example of such a mechanism.

Any scheme to subvert our election would also be keen to minimize the number of bad actors required. One way to accomplish this objective is to centralize the management of election operations. In contrast, parties interested in election security would decentralize the management of election records to make it more difficult for a few bad actors to mess with the results. The electoral college is an example of how to decentralize the management of presidential elections. Without the electoral college, one state with corrupt election practices would be capable of stealing the presidential election. The electoral college serves as a firewall that prevents the spread of corrupt election results to other states.

To put this in context, let's talk about the scale of fraud needed to subvert an election. In a decentralized election, one would need a bad actor in all jurisdictions where vote manipulation would be needed. In Michigan, there are over 4,700 precincts, 83 counties and 1 state elections bureau. To affect a broad-based theft of a statewide election, almost 5,000 agents would be required. Each one of these agents would be a potential failure point or whistleblower.

In contrast, a fully centralized election could conceivably concentrate the number of bad actors to a single individual. How would one centralize an election? The most obvious way to do so would be to implement electronic voting systems capable of communicating with one another. If any of the components of these electronic voting systems were accessible via network connections at any time between the certification of the electronic voting systems and the certification of the vote, then it is conceivable that all it takes is a single individual with an IV drip of their favorite caffeinated beverage to convert any election into a selection. One should be very wary of any evidence of voting systems being connected to the internet any time between the certification of the electronic voting system configuration and the certification of the vote. Furthermore, if any single device on a network, even a printer, is connected to the internet, every data repository and data transfer on that network is vulnerable to subversion.

In addition to enabling the centralization of election management, the use of electronic voting systems also makes it inherently difficult to monitor transfers of digital election data. This makes the transparency of basic election processes, such as tallying the vote, problematic to say the least.

Any time there is a discussion of security and computerized systems, the security of account credentials needs to be addressed. Lax account credential management practices enhance data management risks by enabling bad actors to modify or delete election records or the logs corresponding to these actions. The sharing of administrative credentials across multiple personnel or multiple organizations is a major red flag. Not only does it provide bad actors with an opportunity to access the system, shared credentials help cover the tracks of these bad actors.

The watchlist so far contains some pretty basic items. There should be no surprises. Let's ratchet up the sophistication a notch and look at election theft from the perspective of someone attempting to truly engineer the election outcome.

How would an engineer approach the problem of controlling the outcome of an election?

Any sophisticated attempt to control election outcomes would likely be preceded by patents, design manuals, or technical whitepapers featuring electronic voting systems. This groundwork would likely be tied to the design of digital controllers able to adjust election outcomes with minimal risk of discovery.

Digital controllers are used to control the temperatures in homes, the cruising speeds of cars, or keep a plane on track towards its destination. Is it really that difficult to believe that there are people in the world that would seek to use electronic voting systems to control the outcome of elections? If so, what would that look like?

The simplest type of controller design is simply an open-loop controller. An open-loop controller would change the vote tally based upon a predetermined formula such as allocating every fifth vote to your preferred candidate. In an open-loop controller, there would be no need to monitor the vote tally status or other election metrics. Subsequently, there would be no need to connect electronic voting machines to the internet to change votes in this manner. Someone need only identify a formula by which votes would be shifted from one or more candidates to another. This formula could be embedded into software or hardware any time prior to tabulation of votes. Program execution can be limited to specific timing windows to avoid detection during public accuracy tests. Of course, this fraud is one of the rare examples that could actually be detected by a hand recount of ballots, but what if there was no incentive to perform a recount because the expected candidate still won the precincts they were expected to win?

In a statewide election, there are red precincts and blue precincts. Solid red precincts typically yield margins of victories of 10% or better for Republicans. Solid blue precincts typically yield margins of victories of 10% or better for Democrats. If Republicans or Democrats were to fraudulently "shave" 3-5% from the victory margins in the "easy win" precincts for the opposition, the cumulative vote differentials would likely be sufficient to tip the scales in a statewide race without raising any suspicions by the opposition. After all, the red precincts still went red. There would be no need for a recount or audit of these precincts. If there were a push for a hand recount, any such recount would likely be preceded by legal actions such as injunctions that would cause delays until a clandestine "repositioning" of physical ballots could be orchestrated.

Recounts of scanned ballot images as opposed to physical ballots would not be sufficient to detect this fraud. Ballot images are simply electronic files. If there were a fake ballot image repository embedded on a storage device or there were an internet connection allowing the import of ballot images to the ballot image storage device, ballot images could be inserted or deleted to ensure that the fraudulent vote tally would not be detected by a recount of ballot images. Open-loop controllers in precinct tabulators could be used to perform this "shaving" exercise.

The significant limitation of open-loop controllers is that a successful outcome depends heavily upon an accurate prediction of voter turnout and how many votes would be needed to steal the election. This risk can be mitigated using another type of control method referred to as a closed-loop or feedback control system. A closed-loop controller would be able to adjust the shifting of votes based upon variables such as voter turnout. Unlike open-loop controllers, closed-loop controllers that depend upon external data such as the statewide vote tally would need to receive that data somehow. This is yet another reason that any connection of voting equipment to the internet prior to certification of the election would be suspect.

Let's see what we need to be on the lookout for regarding our key election records during the preparation phase.

Record Anomalies

During the preparation phase, the integrity of the state voter registration file should be the center of attention. Are there any anomalies in the statewide voter registration file? These anomalies might be more voters than residents in a given jurisdiction or a large number of names in common across multiple states or failure to demonstrate the chain of custody for changes to the registered voter file. Election fraud schemes benefit significantly from having a list of low-propensity voters in the statewide voter registration file. Phantom voters could be seeded into this database from a variety of sources. Most news stories regarding phantom voters involve claims of dead people voting but the sources of names and addresses for phantom voters can come from a variety of sources including creation of voters from thin air. Any failure to demonstrate the maintenance of chain of custody for additions, modifications or deletions to the statewide voter registration file should be reasons for concern.

While the statewide voter registration file is of primary concern during this phase, ballot anomalies should not be ignored. Have ballot specifications been defined? Do these specifications make it easy for a bad actor to replicate a ballot? One should look for large orders of test ballots or blank ballots beyond what would likely be necessary for public accuracy test or spoil and duplicate rates. These extra ballots would be a red flag as they could be used to cast extra votes if not accounted for with a disciplined chain of custody. Best practice would dictate that ballots should be printed on paper that features security features like those found in paper currency. Orders of ballots printed on secure paper would not even be necessary, though, if the ballots were allowed to be printed on standard paper stock. In this case, a bad actor could create a ballot factory if they had access to blank ballot images and ordered standard paper from their favorite office supply store. The existence of ballot factories would be a significant red flag.

One should also be wary of late ballot changes that might result in a large number of incorrect ballots to already be in circulation at time of election.

Other questions to consider: Are the ballots serialized and tracked by lot? Who is monitoring the status of the printed ballots? How?

Influence Operations

Influence operations represents another group of tactics to look for during the preparation phase. Is there any indication of domestic or foreign agents interfering with any aspect of our election processes? If identified, this should be of grave concern to Americans of all political persuasions. One also needs to look for any personnel anomalies such as suspect contracts or a lack of balance in poll worker political affiliations.

Be wary of any attempts to prevent poll challengers from examining the election processes prior to Election Day. Any promotion of tactics designed to interfere with the duties of poll challengers or canvassers should be investigated.

An old adage of seasoned investigators is to follow the money. Election fraud is no different. Often financial transactions can be indicators of relationships that promote election fraud. Are there any financial transactions related to the conduct of the election that are out of the ordinary?

Federal law requires the retention of all physical and electronic election records for a minimum of twenty-two months after an election. Be wary of provisions in legal documents that could be used to slow down or prevent any investigations into potential election fraud.

Another subject that needs to be addressed is one that is very difficult to sort through at times: disinformation. Disinformation can take many forms and serve many different purposes. Sometimes it is intended to steer public thinking to adopt a particular narrative. At other times, it can be used to push a particular behavior. While sometimes, it is simply meant to discredit substantive investigation into election fraud.

Influence operations would likely feature fifth columnists. They are often a source of significant disinformation. The term "fifth columnist" refers to a group of clandestine supporters of an enemy that seek to sabotage efforts within a given faction. They masquerade as advisors or supporters of one group yet secretly work on behalf of another group.

Ultimately, any subversion of the election would need to be done in a manner that earns the support of the majority of Americans. Since fraudsters are making up their own election results, it makes sense that these results should be designed to reflect plausible talking points. These talking points become the equivalent of an alibi. Disinformation campaigns could be used to promote this alibi.

Summary

The net result of the preparation phase would be the creation of new weaknesses or the enhancement of any existing weaknesses in the election processes. The more effort expended during the preparation phase, the less effort is needed to successfully execute subsequent phases. A successfully executed preparation phase would ensure that the election battle was won before the other side even knew there was a battle going on.

MAIN ATTACK

"You can be sure of succeeding in your attacks if you only
attack places which are undefended"

—*SUN TZU*

Once the battlefield has been prepared, the next phase would likely be to launch the main attack. This main attack would exploit the weaknesses created or expanded during the preparation phase. What is one of the greatest security weaknesses in our election process? Mail-in voting.

The likely goal of this phase would be simple: cast and/or shift a sufficient number of absentee ballot votes to secure victory in a manner that minimizes the risk of detection. The number of ballots needed is determined by the projected voter turnout and the vote margins that would fit a plausible post-election narrative.

The main attack phase would start with the casting of the first absentee votes and ends with the closure of polls. If the preparation phase has been successful, main attack phase anomalies should be fairly difficult to detect. Process execution and election record anomalies, however, would likely still be evident to some degree.

Process Anomalies

If we assume that the stated election processes would ensure a secure election if executed properly (a bit of a stretch), the key things to look for during the main attack phase are examples of non-compliance with these processes. One should look for poorly trained poll workers or poor communications to election officials. Are the current election laws and procedures being enforced?

Investigators need to pay close attention to suspected breaches in the election record chain of custody. When data is transferred from point A to point B, has the chain of custody been maintained? Looking for any signs of concealment of fraudulent data transfers is a top priority.

Of particular concern would be evidence of network connectivity especially internet connectivity. In addition to putting the election record chain of custody at significant risk it would also enable digital spies. Digital spies provide intelligence that would enable bad actors to know whether or not the election is going according to plan. The earlier that this intelligence can be communicated, the more likely it is that any deviations from the plan could be rectified in a stealthy manner (yet another reason that early voting is a bad idea).

With or without internet connections, however, electronic data transfers are inherently more difficult to monitor than physical data transfers. Physical data transfers can generally be witnessed by poll challengers and poll watchers. Electronic data transfers cannot generally be witnessed by third-party observers unless the logs are reviewed as part of a post-election audit. A clear indicator of election fraud would be the modification or deletion of these electronic logs. These logs are the primary means of verifying the chain of custody for any electronic data transfers.

One also needs to pay close attention to the hardware and software configurations for electronic voting systems. Are they compliant with the certified configurations? Have they been secured from tampering both physically and digitally?

Now let's look at the processing of our weak link in our elections: mail-in ballots. The Achilles heel of mail-in ballot processing security is that the majority of the process is handled by third parties. If phantom voters were loaded into the statewide voter registration file, the stage is set for the issuance of fraudulent mail-in ballots. Remember the election record chain of custody. The statewide voter registration bone is connected to the pollbook bone which is connected to the ballot bone which is connected to the vote tally bone. If any link in this chain of custody is compromised, the entire election is compromised. Applications for mail-in ballots on behalf of phantom voters could be fraudulently submitted online. When the post office receives the mail-in ballots, they would be sent to friendly addresses or loaded with non-existent addresses that will be flagged as "return to sender." Sympathetic post office workers could then collect flagged ballots and distribute them to designated ballot mills where the ballots would be filled out and put into the associated ballot envelope. These ballot envelopes with ballot inside would then be dropped off at an appropriate drop box. The statewide voter registration file would show the voter as an eligible voter. The poll-books would show valid ballot envelopes and ballots. Once received by the clerk from the drop boxes, the ballots would be processed along with all the other ballots. There would be no need for corrupt local election officials. Election officials could dot the *I*s and cross the *T*s for all their election processes and still preside over a fraudulent election. Canvassing would be the most effective mechanism for discovering such fraud. Unfortunately, canvassing would typically only be executed well after the election results were certified.

Once fraudulent votes have been cast during the main attack phase via mail, the wheels of subversion would have already been set in motion. If voter turnout projections are accurate, all that is left to do is make sure that no one discovers the fraud as the ballots are received and processed. In this light, careful attention should be paid to ensure that voter identities are verified prior to processing any mail-in ballot.

Record Anomalies

Now it's time to look at what anomalies to look for in specific key election records in the chain of custody. Let's start with the statewide voter registration file. The integrity of the statewide voter registration file is of particular concern. If the information has been corrupted, all the election records downstream of the registered voter file including the election results would likely be corrupted as well. Any manipulation of the statewide voter registration file needs to be accompanied by a clear chain of custody including a record of who modified which record, how it was modified and when. These logs are invaluable references in support of any post-election audit.

Since pollbooks are simply precinct-specific extracts of the state-wide voter registration file, if the statewide voter registration file is corrupt, the pollbooks will be corrupt. This is concerning because pollbooks are used by poll workers to determine whether or not a given in-person voter or remote voter are eligible to cast a ballot. In this role pollbooks act as important election security firewalls. Once a poll worker determines that a voter is eligible to cast a vote as a result of being registered to vote, it is incumbent upon that poll worker to verify the identity of the voter. If either the eligibility or the identity of the voter has not been verified, their ballot should not be cast. Any indications of ballots being cast prior to certifying the eligibility or identity of a voter would be a huge red flag. Once a ballot has been approved for counting, there is no way to connect a given ballot to a given voter. At that point, all one can do is look for discrepancies between the number of voters issued ballots per the pollbook and the number of ballots cast. If these numbers do not match in a given precinct, that precinct is "out of balance." Out of balance precincts indicate serious breaches to the election record chain of custody and could be used as grounds for not certifying an election. Even if a precinct is balanced, however, one might detect fraudulent pollbook data after the election by examining who has voted per the pollbook. Are there unnatural patterns such as more voters than registrants? One should also look for evidence of pollbook internet connectivity. Remote access to pollbooks or the state voter registration database would enable someone to stuff the ballot box and stay in sync with the pollbook ballot count.

We've covered the first two links in the election record chain of custody pertaining to the statewide voter registration file and pollbooks. Ballots are the next link in the chain. Ballot-specific fraud indicators to look for include:

- Test ballots found with regular ballots
- Blank ballots not accounted for
- Unsecured ballots

- Absentee ballots do not have any folds
- Sequential ballots processed in tabulators
- Large batches of ballots dropped in drop boxes

Of particular concern regarding ballots is the act of ballot harvesting. Ballot harvesting is the collection and submittal of absentee ballots by third parties rather than by voters themselves. Ballot harvesting is illegal in most states. Why? Chain of custody integrity is one of the major reasons ballot harvesting is concerning. One could classify the United States Postal Service as an "approved ballot harvester" for mail-in ballots. Ostensibly, the Postal Service has built-in mechanisms to mitigate the risk of fraud including mail tracking systems and an Inspector General with broad investigative and enforcement authority. There are no such security precautions with generic ballot harvesters. Drop boxes provide ballot harvesters with a clandestine means of injecting multiple ballots into the election system.

Ballot harvesters go hand in hand with another election theft red flag known as ballot factories. Ballot factories can be centralized into a single large processing center or distributed among many smaller centers. They can take on a variety of forms, but they all share the objective of converting blank ballots into completed ballots. Blank ballots can be provided from an unsecured stash of official ballots or could be printed on standard stock paper using images of ballots obtained by the fraudsters. These ballots could then be completed manually by hand using a cadre of bad actors or the votes could be printed directly onto the ballot in an automated manner. Any evidence of voting system–specific printing equipment and ballot shipments would be indicative of an automated ballot factory. Close examination of ballots would likely reveal anomalies indicating fraud. Look for shortcuts taken when completing the ballots, such as large percentages of straight ticket voting or sloppy ballot markings indicating speed-induced errors. Look for machine-based precision or repeated patterns in the markings. This is an obvious indicator of fraud. Also, it should go without saying, but if you notice mail-in ballots without folds, the ballots are likely fraudulent.

The last link in the election record chain of custody is perhaps the most important: the vote tally. In the main attack phase, the primary mechanism for fraud would likely be stuffing the ballot boxes with fraudulent mail-in ballots, but there are other mechanisms to look out for. The release of unofficial vote tallies before the precinct-level results are certified is a common practice among election officials. Please understand that this practice is of significant benefit to those intent upon election fraud not simply those impatient to know who is winning the election. If the choice is between election security and speed, my vote goes to election security. Be on guard for tabulation equipment with network connections. If unofficial results are to be released, these releases should not be limited to a select few. They should also be accompanied by a disciplined chain of custody so that these vote tally submittals can be correlated with other election records during any audit of election returns. As results are communicated, look for results inconsistent with historical results for a given jurisdiction. If a given party typically wins a given precinct by 10% but only wins by 5%, it may be indicative of an open-loop controller being used to adjust the allocation of votes. A hand count of the ballots would be able to confirm if the reported tallies are accurate, but a hand count would likely not be requested as long as the party of the victory didn't change. One should also be on the lookout for undocumented precincts where votes may be tallied without poll challenger oversight. Of course, one should also look for inconsistencies between vote tallies reported at the precinct, municipality, county, and state levels. If they don't add up, there is likely a breach in the vote tally chain of custody.

Influence Operations

Influence operations are not likely to play a significant role in the main attack phase. Mail-in ballot fraud is designed to be undetected. A well-executed attack would enable those behind the fraud to "lay low" and simply execute the plan. In this light, there is no need for any significant influence operations. One should be wary, however, of any attempts to interfere with poll challenger oversight of election processes.

Summary

The net result of this phase would be the insertion or shifting of votes in a manner that has minimal risk of detection. The primary tactics used in this phase revolve around the subversion of the mail-in voting process. If pre-election voter turnout forecasts voter turnout are accurate, those behind the election fraud will have been successful and likely would not leave anyone with any reason to believe election fraud played any significant role whatsoever in the election. If the pre-election forecasts are not accurate, though, a backup plan would be needed.

BACKUP ATTACK

"According as circumstances are favorable, one should modify one's plans."

—SUN TZU

For anything as important as an election, it is reasonable to assume that significant effort would go into devising a backup attack should the main attack fail to achieve the results needed. The backup attack would likely exploit the same weakness exploited during the main attack phase: mail-in voting. What is unique about this phase from the main attack phase is the degree of risk a bad actor would be willing to take. In this phase, the risk of losing the election supersedes the risk of discovery. The desire for concealment is no longer the primary driver, victory is.

The likely goal of this phase is simple. Victory at all costs. The duration of this phase would be from the closure of the polls until the election is certified.

Process Anomalies

Many of the same tactics used during the main attack phase would also be used in the backup attack phase. What's different in this stage is the willingness to pursue higher risk tactics as well. These tactics are bolder, sloppier, and increasingly desperate. Consequently, one should pay close attention to anomalies in election records during this phase.

Record Anomalies

Particular attention should be paid to election record anomalies during the backup attack phase. It is likely that election record anomalies will be more pronounced and obvious during this phase.

Vote tallies should be the center of attention. Election integrity watchdogs should be on the lookout for anomalies in election night reporting such as large jumps in votes for a given candidate, vote ratio anomalies, negative vote increments in cumulative vote reports or percentage of precincts reporting anomalies. Vote tally reports may yield digital controller fingerprints. One should look for inconsistencies between top of the ticket races and down ballot races, open-loop control injections at county level, and closed-loop control to fine tune records.

Another indicator of fraud would be vote tally increments that exceed capacity of tabulators. This may be an indicator of the direct manipulation of election results databases.

When it comes to ballot anomalies, there are a variety of anomalies to watch out for. For starters, be wary of ballot deliveries after the polls have been closed. Any such deliveries need to be supported by iron clad explanations supported by chain of custody evidence. Ensure that all ballots are secured. When ballots are not actively being processed, ensure that they are secured in official ballot containers. Be on guard for mail-in ballots without any folds. Make sure that any ballots marked as "provisional" are not counted until there is incontrovertible evidence that they were cast by an eligible voter.

The list of eligible voters should be static on election day. Same day voter registration practices introduce a measure of chaos into this equation, but a static list of eligible voters should be the rule not the exception. Be on guard for large numbers of "new voters" not captured in the pollbooks. Be wary of attempts to update the state voter registration file directly on election day. Pollbook anomalies happen when there is a complete disregard for key election processes such as voter identity validation before allowing a ballot to be cast. A disciplined chain of custody is critical. Pollbooks don't only serve as a means of validating the identity of a voter before they cast their ballot, they also are the repository for the precinct-specific process issues that occurred during the processing of ballots. Pollbook journals are very helpful to canvassers considering whether or not to certify election results. Be wary of any attempts to interfere with the capture of challenges from certified poll challengers in the pollbook. Also, be wary of any adjustments to the pollbook after election day processing has been completed. Connectivity of pollbooks to the internet should also be a matter of significant concern as it would enable someone to stuff the ballot box while staying in sync with the voter count in the pollbook.

Influence Operations

There would likely be significant effort expended to cover up intensified fraud activities during the backup attack phase. Influence operations would likely proliferate misinformation and use overt intimidation tactics to prevent oversight of election processes by poll challengers. Sympathetic media outlets would likely provide cover for any such subversion activities.

Summary

The net result of this phase would be the insertion or shifting of votes in a manner that achieves the desired election outcome regardless of the risk. Efforts to exploit weaknesses in the integrity of mail-in voting processes would be intensified during the tabulation of votes. Electronic voting systems would likely be leveraged to ensure some measure of consistency between the pollbooks, ballots, and vote tallies. Influence operations would be ramped up to ensure that any intensified process subversion would be undetected.

DEFENSE

"Attack is the secret of defense;
defense is the planning of an attack."

—SUN TZU

Last but not least is the defense phase. In the wake of a successful main attack phase and backup attack phase, resources would then be employed to ensure the persistence of such success. The election theft coup will have been successful, now it would be necessary to consolidate the ground taken. The likely goal of this phase would be to prevent anyone from overturning any fraudulent election results.

This phase starts with the certification of the vote and lasts until the last voice expressing concerns with election fraud has been pummeled into silence. The defense phase is when the election fraud cover-up kicks into high gear. Influence operations take center stage.

Process Anomalies

In spite of influence operations taking center stage, there are still likely to be significant process anomalies that will need the cover provided by the influence operations. The certification of the vote is the first of these processes to which close attention must be paid. There will likely be significant pressure for certification officials to simply rubber stamp the election and move on without a thorough audit of election results.

Upon certification, the evidence of election fraud from previous phases will likely result in cries for recounts and audits. Recounts will likely be promoted as audits as a means of giving the appearance of rigor to investigations into election concerns. If the recount narrative fails, fake audits would likely be pursued. In most cases these "audits" would not even suffice as recounts. The devil is in the details, but most people won't even look beyond the headlines at the actual audit results. Significant effort would be likely be expended to prevent any substantive audit of the election record chain of custody.

Record Anomalies

During the defense phase, there would be a concerted effort to prevent access to or destroy any records that would be subject to discovery via subpoena or post-election audits. Under USC Title 52 Section 20701, however, *all* election records must be preserved for twenty-two months after an election. Section 20702 makes it a felony to destroy such records. Any violation of the chain of custody for election records in the wake of the election is a major red flag.

Influence Operations

Media and political talking points can exert significant influence on an unsuspecting public. Be wary of standard media narratives and/or censorship of election fraud narratives. There is a reason why one of the first targets in any coup is the media. Seizure of TV stations, radio stations, newspapers, and phone exchanges are a high priority. Why? They need to legitimize their victory by convincing the people that the election results are genuine. To do that they will actively censor anyone questioning the results and label their assertions as conspiracy theories. Citizens at large will be subject to carefully constructed talking points dutifully repeated over all media channels. The only views that will be tolerated are those which promote the narrative that the election was the most secure election in history.

How can one differentiate between the truth and propaganda? Be wary of misleading headlines. Always go beyond the headlines to the source data. Be wary of reports which fail to provide links to the source data used for their story so that interested viewers are able to come to their own conclusions. Be wary of reports that fail to present both sides of an issue in an unbiased manner.

Lawfare is another major influence in defending a stolen election. It involves the issuance of nuisance lawsuits or injunctions designed to interfere with any investigations into election fraud. Contracts and laws drafted in the preparation phase are fully leveraged to obstruct any attempts to examine election records in the defense phase. Intimidation is another facet of lawfare. If intimidation is successful, there is no need to file an actual lawsuit. Filing a lawsuit increases the risk of discovery of information that bad actors would seek to hide. There are less risky and less expensive ways to intimidate would be investigators. These options include threatening their livelihood via disbarment, loss of business license, loss of sponsors or the issuance of cease-and-desist orders.

Be wary of fifth columnists in bodies responsible for election oversight. One way to ensure that no substantive action is taken to investigate election fraud is to ensure that any organization with the authority and/or interest in investigating election fraud receives counsel that would discourage such investigation.

Any exploit as significant as the theft of an election would most certainly be followed by a race to take credit for the theft. Do you think for a moment that anyone brazen enough to steal a nationwide election in the United States would keep it to themselves? Not likely. Be on the lookout for those attempting to take credit for the crime of the century. Of course, they won't call it that.

Summary

The net result of the defense phase would be a successful cover-up of any anomalies that may have raised suspicion of fraud during the riskier backup attack phase. Records would be deleted. Fake audits would be conducted. The voices of poll challengers citing concerns with election integrity would be silenced. Influence operations would take center stage.

Theory Review

To re-cap, our theory as to how one would go about stealing an election features four phases:

- Preparation: Create and expand weaknesses in election system

- Main Attack: Exploit most significant weakness – mail-in voting
- Backup Attack: Inject additional votes as needed to ensure victory
- Defense: Prevent anyone from overturning the election results

So how would someone ensure victory in a presidential election using this battle plan?

Let's focus upon what happens to our key election records during each phase.

- Preparation Phase
  - Identify the number of electoral college votes needed
  - Estimate the voter turnout
  - Create a voter database that includes likely candidate disposition
  - Calculate the votes needed to win based upon turnout
  - Calculate the number of fraudulent votes needed in each state
  - Identify states most vulnerable to insertion of fraudulent votes
  - Identify a pool of fraudulent or low-propensity voters in state voter registration database they could allocate to ballots
  - Develop voter allocation algorithms to ensure that the allocation of voters to ballots does not raise any red flags
  - Develop vote adjustment algorithms that ensure victory
  - Implement methods for obtaining blank ballots
  - Prepare ballot factories
  - Manufacture absentee ballots

- Allocate absentee ballots and envelopes to fraudulent or low-propensity voters
- Create contingency election results databases
- Main Attack Phase
  - Distribute manufactured ballots to ballot harvesters
  - Ballot harvesters deposit absentee ballots in drop boxes or clerk offices.
  - Leverage internet connections to monitor actual vote returns and individual voter status on election day
- Backup Attack Phase
  - Order additional fraudulent ballots if early returns project a shortfall for desired vote margin
  - Adjust election results directly by swapping out actual election results database with a contingency election results database
  - Inject absentee ballots into counting boards that would support updated vote tallies
  - Update pollbooks to reflect injected ballot counts
- Defense Phase
  - Prevent access to election records
  - Destroy election records

As you have likely come to realize from the information presented thus far, our election system is quite complex. This complexity provides anyone intent upon subverting an election with quite a few opportunities to do so if we are not vigilant. Our election system is designated as a critical component of our nation's infrastructure. It is incumbent upon us to ensure that this designation is more than mere lip service.

CHAPTER 6

The Evidence

We have now posed a theory about how an election might be stolen. Does the evidence discovered to date surrounding the 2020 election support this theory?

Now it is time to address the following assertions of skeptics who say:

"There is no evidence"

"There is no credible evidence"

"There is no widespread evidence"

"There is no significant evidence"

Let's zero in on the assertion that there is no significant evidence. What constitutes "significant evidence"? Presumably any evidence that points to the possibility of activity impacting enough votes to change the election results.

According to the official election results, Michigan has the largest vote gap to account for in any of the battleground states. Michigan had 8,105,524 registered voters in the 2020 election. The Michigan Secretary of State reported that 5,579,317 votes were cast.[1]

In order to be significant enough to change the results of the presidential race in Michigan, any fraud identified would need to account for the 2.78% or 154,188 vote margin of victory reported for Joe Biden.

The gap in PA was 80,555.
The gap in WI was 20,682.
The gap in GA was 11,779.
The gap in AZ was 10,457.

If sufficient fraud is identified to account for the 154,188-vote gap in Michigan, it should at least raise eyebrows regarding the election results in other states.

As we review the evidence, you can decide for yourself if

a. America was the victim of a coup
b. the facts presented merit further investigation in the form of a forensic audit of statewide election results
c. we should stop questioning the integrity of our election system and move on

Recall, our theory is that an election would likely be stolen in four distinct phases:

- Preparation Phase: Create or expand weaknesses in our election system
- Main Attack Phase: Exploit single greatest weakness, mail-in ballots, to stuff the ballot box with fraudulent votes
- Backup Attack Phase: Leverage networked electronic voting systems to modify the vote tally directly in order to ensure victory
- Defense Phase: Make sure that no one discovers the fraud, communicates the fraud or overturns the fraudulent election results.

Let's see if there is any evidence to support this theory.

PREPARATION

We start with an examination of the preparation phase. The purpose of this phase is to create or expand weaknesses in our election system. Just as we proposed in our theory, we will look for evidence in the following tactical groups: Process Anomalies, Record Anomalies, and Influence Operations.

Process Anomalies

During the 2018 election cycle, there were sweeping changes to election law in Michigan promoted and funded by leftist organizations such as the ACLU, labor unions, ACORN, and the Sierra Club.

Among the changes proposed in Ballot Proposal 2018-3 were the following:[2]

- No reason absentee voting
- Same day voter registration
- Automatic voter registration

Michigan Proposal 3 was passed into law by an overwhelming 66% majority of Michigan voters. Opponents of the adopted provisions cite the proposal's adverse impacts upon election integrity as reason for their dissent. Proponents of the provisions promoted them as a remedy to voter suppression. The changes adopted appear to have been part of a national campaign. The assertion that this proposal was part of a national, not state-based, campaign is supported by the fact that most of the funds behind supporting Michigan's Proposal 3 can be tracked to organizations and individuals outside of Michigan.[3]

Prior to the passage of the 2018 ballot initiatives, elections in Michigan were largely decentralized. Elections were effectively a bottoms-up affair driven by local clerks. The 2020 election was a predominantly top-down affair driven by the policies established by the MI Secretary of State.

The Michigan secretary of state was at the center of a textbook example of lawfare being used to subvert election processes. In 2018, the citizens of Michigan elected Democrat governor Gretchen Whitmer, Democrat attorney general Dana Nessel, and Democrat secretary of state Jocelyn Benson. Both the senate and the house, however, were controlled by Republican majorities. With a divided executive and legislative branch, it was unlikely any partisan legislation would be passed. So, progressives intent upon weakening the integrity of our election system chose to change policies via the judicial branch instead.

On December 30, 2019, the progressive advocacy group, Priorities USA filed a federal lawsuit against Jocelyn Benson in her official capacity as the Michigan secretary of state claiming that Michigan's signature matching laws" were arbitrary and standardless."[4] Mind you, Jocelyn Benson was and is sympathetic to the progressive mission of Priorities USA. Priorities USA was and is sympathetic to the efforts of Jocelyn Benson. So, why did they file a lawsuit against Jocelyn Benson? From a tactical perspective, such legal action provides them with a mechanism to circumvent the legislative process and leverage the judiciary to change election law. From a strategic perspective, it appears to be a key element of a nationally orchestrated strategy to relax signature verification for mail-in ballots. Michigan was not the only state victimized by the relaxation of signature verification requirements as will be shown later. I'm sure it is purely a coincidence, but one of the board members at Priorities USA is Hillary Clinton lawyer Marc Elias. You may recall that Marc Elias also funded the fake Steele Dossier which was used to create the discredited Russian collusion narrative against President Trump.[5]

How did Jocelyn Benson respond to the lawsuit filed by Priorities USA? In April 2020, she issued revised guidance to election officials regarding signature verification. Her new guidance relaxed signature verification requirements and directed clerks to "presume that the signature is valid."[6] To most people interested in election integrity, this new signature verification policy didn't resolve the stated "arbitrary and standardless" issue. It simply expanded the existing weakness in Michigan's mail-in voting process.

In response to her guidance, Republicans filed a lawsuit after the November 3rd election on December 14, 2020. In March of 2021, Michigan Court of Claims judge Christopher Murray ruled that her revised signature guidance violated the state Administrative Procedures Act and that the "presumption is found nowhere in state law."[7] This legal action occurred well after it would have been useful to ensure that it was a real voter that cast a given ballot during the 2020 election. The Michigan secretary of state is now pursuing her revised signature guidance through the rule-making process authorized under the Administrative Procedures Act.

Jocelyn Benson didn't stop with the relaxation of the absentee ballot signature verification requirements. She took advantage of the weaknesses in the absentee ballot process to mail out absentee voter applications to every Michigan resident not already flagged as being permanent absentee voters.[8] She spent $4.5 million in funds from the U.S. Coronavirus Aid, Relief, and Economic Security Act to finance her mass mailing. The purpose of the mailing was ostensibly to ensure that all 7.7 million voters registered in Michigan's Qualified Voter File knew they could vote absentee… as if this was a big secret. At least 500,000 request forms were returned to the SoS PO Box as undeliverable. Only the Michigan secretary of state was privy to this information. This means that the Michigan secretary of state knew which of the voters in the QVF were real and which were fake. Local clerks were simply fed the data provided by the state. The state's list of fake voters would be very useful information to anyone seeking to match them to ballots in a ballot factory.

In response to the MI SoS actions, former Michigan secretary of state and current Michigan state senator Ruth Johnson publicly asserted that Jocelyn Benson's "changes and attempts to centralize certain election functions ... are really truly alarming" and illegal.[9] Once again, legal action was taken against the secretary of state. In a 2-1 ruling, the Michigan Court of Appeals asserted that her actions were lawful. In his dissenting opinion, Judge Patrick Peter stated that the law explicitly only gives local clerks the power to distribute absentee ballot applications, not the secretary of state. The ruling of the majority of judges on the Michigan Court of Appeals, however, held sway. As a result, the management of Michigan elections was further centralized.

Additional process-related issues pertain directly to the integrity of the ballots used in the November 3, 2020, election. Michigan required two last-minute ballot changes on September 2 and 3 of 2020. These changes invalidated all ballots that were already printed, and delayed delivery of all ballots across the state. A decision was made to print absentee ballots prior to test decks. This means public accuracy testing would not occur prior to sending out absentee ballots in many municipalities.

What were the changes?

On September 2, Michigan Department of State notified everyone there had been an error in the party order. They had mistakenly placed Libertarian in the fifth slot on the ballot instead of the third.[10]

The political party order had initially been changed by the secretary of state in March 2019. On September 3, 2020, the ballots needed to be updated to reflect a change to the Republican candidate for the Wayne State University Board of Governors. Diane Dunaskiss was replaced with Terri Lynn Land due to failure to pay 2018 campaign fees.[11] Any ballots that had been re-created the day before had to be updated.

Why are last-minute ballot changes important? They were at the heart of the official explanation for how 7,060 votes in Antrim County were flipped in favor of Joe Biden. This explanation surfaced after Antrim County resident Bill Bailey filed a lawsuit in the wake of initial reports from the Antrim County clerk that Joe Biden had won by a landslide over President Trump in his traditionally Republican county. On September 18, ballot changes due to issues with local races were finally approved in Antrim County. The Michigan Constitution requires that forty days prior to an election, absentee ballots must be available to those who have requested them. In order to meet this requirement for the November 3, 2020, election, absentee ballots would have needed to be available by September 24, 2020. On September 29, 2020, there were communications between a vendor for Dominion Voting System (the electronic voting hardware and software company that provided voting machines in Michigan and many other states), Election Source, and Echo Lake election officials in Antrim County regarding replacement ballots. The Echo Lake officials are advised to "be careful about that" and "pack up the wrong ballots and carefully mark them Do Not Use."

On October 6, 2020, Election Source notified election officials in Antrim County that they needed to "roll the election back and add in a new contest with new candidates" due to a missing contest for Warner Township.[12] On October 7, 2020, Mancelona Village in Antrim County needed to update their ballots because a trustee was missing on the ballot. At the time of these communications, it is unknown how many ballots had already been printed, whether any had been shipped to municipalities, or how the invalid ballots were handled. If uncorrected ballots were submitted by voters, it would explain the extremely high tabulation error rate experienced in Antrim County. Furthermore, without an accounting for the location of all ballots including earlier versions of the ballots, we have no idea if any of these ballots were cast fraudulently or not.

Was Antrim County the only county out of 83 counties in Michigan that may have experienced vote anomalies due to late ballot changes? Both our elected and election officials displayed a concerning lack of interest in this question. And that's just one possible explanation for the vote switch. Bill Bailey's attorney Matt DePerno identified additional vote switch explanations that merit more in-depth investigation. Ballot formatting, modems, internet connectivity and software configuration anomalies were among his findings.

The only way to know for sure to what extent these anomalies impacted statewide election results would be to conduct a forensic audit of the statewide election results. Despite being a right guaranteed to the citizens of Michigan under Article II Section 4 of the Michigan Constitution, no such audit has yet been conducted.

To make matters worse, the preparation phase saw to it that even if an audit were executed in accordance with the state's lax audit guidelines, it would be of insufficient rigor to detect any of the fraud that was perpetrated. The audit guidelines captured in Michigan's Post-Election Audit Manual were almost exclusively dedicated to ballot evaluations making it almost impossible to differentiate from a simple recount. In particular, there are no provisions for auditing any electronic records—such as the qualified voter file, Pollbook, ballot images, or election night reporting logs—in the chain of custody. Furthermore, the manual instructs election officials to violate federal law by deleting electronic pollbook data "seven days post canvass."[13] Under federal law, such records must be preserved for twenty-two months after the election.

The bottom line is that any audits performed in accordance with the post-election manual would have been of limited value and actually encourage election officials to violate the law. It should be noted, however, that the audit guidelines were useful to give the majority of citizens the false impression that a real audit may have been conducted.

Election process integrity was further degraded as a result of the COVID pandemic. The COVID pandemic provided a convenient incentive to discourage in-person voting and encourage less secure mail-in voting. It also interfered with pre-election attempts by poll challengers to meet with election officials in order to gather information on the election processes to be executed during the election. The Michigan Bureau of Elections even implemented a six-foot rule in response to COVID that effectively limited the ability of poll challengers and poll watchers to oversee election activities.

Evidence of interference with poll challenger oversight was not limited to COVID rules. In fact, one of the most effective ways to interfere with election oversight pre-dates COVID by a few years. In 2017,

Michigan issued contracts for three electronic voting systems for county clerks to choose from: Dominion Voting Systems, Election Systems & Software (ES&S), and Hart Systems. These systems featured vote scanners, tabulator workstations, adjudication workstations and centralized election management servers. Electronic voting systems effectively digitized what had previously been a physically observable process. Since the advent of electronic voting systems, poll challengers have been unable to monitor the chain of custody for key election records, including voter registration, pollbook entries, ballot images, and election night reporting. Data modifications and transfers in the physical world featuring paper transactions can be readily observed by poll challengers. Data modifications and transfers in electronic voting systems cannot typically be observed at all by poll challengers on election day. One can only evaluate these modifications and transfers after an election and only after a forensic audit has been authorized and initiated.

The one opportunity that Poll Challengers had to ensure some measure of integrity in the configuration of the electronic voting systems prior to the election was the Public Accuracy Test. Under MCL 168.798, clerks are required to provide at least 48 hours of public notice via newspaper regarding when and where the board of election commissioners would be testing electronic tabulating equipment. Rather than provide public notification, the City of Detroit notification was limited to specific parties which did not include independent non-profit organizations such as the Election Integrity Fund.

So, are there any features of the electronic voting systems selected that could be used to modify election data in a fraudulent manner? Yes. The Dominion Voting System's ImageCast Precinct (ICP) system, as well as similar systems from other vendors, are susceptible to subversion of vote tally integrity through the modification of a single file. This file resides within each tabulator. This file is part of a package of files that are deployed on the compact flash cards that are used in each tabulator in each individual precinct. There are multiple files stored on these cards.

One could modify either the file containing the instructions on how the tabulator maps ballot marks to votes or skip this intermediary step and modify the results file directly. For Dominion Voting Systems, the file name for tabulator instructions is a *.DVD file found on a removable memory card.[14] The file is a binary file that contains the instructions on how the tabulator will process ballots, how vote totals are assigned to each candidate, and ultimately how the paper tapes and results files are generated. Being able to edit this file and modify the mapping of the bullets on the ballots (vote selections) to the candidates allows for manipulation of the vote results. This editing could be performed at time of installation or later via remote network connections. The results file is also a *.DVD format. According to analysis provided by expert witness in the Bailey v Antrim County lawsuit, Jeff Lenberg, a "malicious actor can swap internal Machine IDs within the same Contest for any candidate so long as the index remains in the correct range for that same contest".[15] These files are simply one means of compromising election integrity using the voting systems deployed on November 3, 2020.

Any malware resident in the file or on any electronic equipment connected to the tabulator featuring the installation of the flash card containing either of these files would be impossible for any poll challenger to detect. But malware doesn't need to be some hidden script on a compact flash card. What if it was part of the "trusted build" software configuration?

As it turns out, during the Antrim County investigations, non-certified software was found to be installed in Dominion voting systems as part of their trusted build. The software discovered is Microsoft SQL Server Management Studio.[16] SQL Server Management Studio is a powerful software tool that not only enables direct modification of the election results database, it also allows custom programs or "scripts" to be run on databases. The presence of non-certified software able to change election outcomes provides grounds for de-certification of an election, but this did not happen.

To date, a full forensic audit of the entire election record chain of custody for electronic voting systems has yet to be conducted anywhere in America. Why is this concerning? Electronic voting systems are designed to enable data transfers with other electronic systems. These capabilities are found throughout their operating manuals, contracts and technical specifications. In other words, our nation's electronic voting systems are designed to be networked together. When these electronic voting machines are networked together, we effectively centralize the management of our election processes. By centralizing the management of our election processes, we effectively reduce the number of bad actors necessary to hijack an election.

There are many different types of network connections. When it comes to elections, the most concerning of these connections are internet connections. Whenever you see the term IP address, remember, the IP stands for "internet protocol." In the case of internet connections, if any single node in a cluster of networked electronic voting systems has been compromised, the entire network of systems is at risk. If these centralized networks feature internet connections at any node in the network, the system is vulnerable to a single bad actor being able to manipulate election outcomes. In this scenario, all it takes to control the elections is a single bad actor with an IV drip of a highly caffeinated energy drink working out of their parent's basement to determine who the leader of the free world would be.

So, do we have evidence of internet connections? Yes.

Each of the voting systems contracted with by the state of Michigan have the ability not only to network with components within the system, they also all have the ability to connect to the internet. Their contracts explicitly reference these connections. Devices could be connected to the internet via external USB cellular modems, hardwired ethernet connections, or via internal wireless data modems.

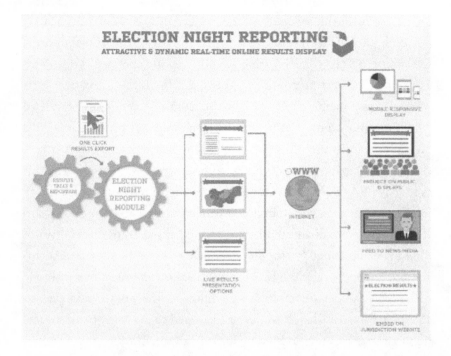

In fact, we have evidence of quotes for modems being supplied to election officials including those in Antrim County prior to the 2020 election. We also have evidence that election officials were aware that their voting equipment was connected to the internet.[17]

Internet connectivity was not limited to Dominion Voting Systems. Wireless modems were discovered embedded upon the motherboards of ES&S systems.[18] These systems are connected to the internet as soon as a voting machine is turned on. These wireless modem chips are not visible to any election worker unless the computer chassis is opened. How many clerks do you know that would think about opening up the voting equipment chassis to look for a wireless data modem chipset on the motherboard of their election equipment? How many would even know what a wireless data modem chipset looks like? Even Hart System equipment had wireless modems installed in their voting equipment.[19]

Despite all this evidence, election officials and their complicit reporters in the media continue to deny that these systems were connected to the internet. Anyone asserting anything to the contrary is dismissed as a tinfoil hat wearing conspiracy theorist. Why is this a concern? Networked components enable centralized communications. Centralized communications provide the ability to manipulate election data across multiple jurisdictions. Election equipment was connected across precincts, municipalities, counties, state, and across the nation. There is even evidence of election records being shared internationally. During forensic examination of Dominion Voting Systems ICX computers, two IP addresses were discovered in unallocated space on the hard drive of the Linux operating system. The existence of these IP addresses in unallocated space implies the ICS had previous communications with one or both of the devices at these IP addresses. The first IP address was 120.125.201.101. This IP address is registered to the Ministry of Education Computer Center located in Taipei, Taiwan. The second IP address was 62.146.7.95. This IP address is registered to EDV-BV GmbH QSC Subkunde located in Nuremberg, Germany. The ICX machine appears to have been manufactured in Taiwan and shipped to the United States via China Airlines.[20] If any single device on this network were compromised anytime between the certification of the voting equipment (assuming of course that the certification was the result of a truly substantive evaluation of its integrity) and the certification of the election, the integrity of the entire election would be at risk, particularly if this device is connected to the internet.

Was there evidence that the security of networked election systems was breached? Yes.

On December 13, 2020, FireEye announced the discovery of a highly sophisticated cyber intrusion that leveraged a commercial software application made by SolarWinds. It was determined that the advanced persistent threat (APT) actors infiltrated the supply chain of SolarWinds, inserting a backdoor into the product. As customers downloaded the Trojan Horse installation packages from SolarWinds, attackers were able to access the systems running the SolarWinds product(s).[21]

The 2020 SolarWinds hack was executed via downloads of software updates to its Orion platform between March and June of 2020. The malware planted in these updates compromised the security of eighteen thousand of its customers including the Cybersecurity and Infrastructure Security Agency (CISA) itself. The CISA acting director Brandon Wales said, "The compromise of SolarWinds' Orion Network Management Products poses unacceptable risks to the security of federal network."[22] Another one of its customers is Dominion Voting Systems. The *Epoch Times* issued a report that clearly showed evidence of a Dominion login page hosted on the SolarWinds SERV-U platform. The SolarWinds SERV-U platform acts as an FTP server. FTP stands for File Transfer Protocol. FTP servers are used to transfer files over the internet. It is unclear whether or not the breach of the SolarWinds Orion Platform also compromised the ServU platform. The SolarWinds security breach targeted the software update components of the Orion Platform. The SERV-U platform likely has common software components with the Orion platform including the software update components. This indicates that the security of Dominion's voting systems across twenty-eight states, including battleground states such as Michigan, Georgia, Pennsylvania, and Arizona, was likely compromised. This merits further investigation especially for election systems which have been designated as "Critical Infrastructure Components".

It should be noted that Dominion is not the only voting system manufacturer which uses FTP servers. Voting system manufacturer ES&S uses the Cerberus FTP Server platform which has been flagged as having significant critical security vulnerabilities.[23] Which begs the question, where are Dominion and other voting system manufacturers transferring their files if their voting systems are "not connected to the internet"?

Given that it is virtually impossible for poll challengers to monitor the integrity of election processes managed by electronic voting systems, there is a significant reliance upon third parties to certify that the hardware and software configurations for the "trusted builds" of these systems can actually be trusted. "Trusted build" is software industry lingo for a configuration controlled, certified version of a given piece of software.

Before we trust these builds, however, it is first necessary to trust the organizations which certify these trusted builds. This is especially important since every attempt by third parties to evaluate the integrity of these trusted builds is met with resistance as lawyers insist that any such inspection be performed by one of these "trusted organizations."

As it turns out, there are only two such organizations recognized by the federal Election Assistance Commission: Pro V&V, which was accredited by the Election Assistance Commission (EAC) on February 24, 2015, and SLI, which was accredited on February 28, 2007.[24]

Which begs the question, how were these organizations approved? According to the Voting System Test Laboratory Program Manual,[25] there are two methods:

1. National Institute of Standards and Testing (NIST) Recommendation
2. Emergency EAC Accreditation without NIST Recommendation

It is clearly a "who you know" not "what you know" accreditation process. It is worth noting that the NIST is the same organization which is responsible for "leaving the key under the mat" for hackers interested in subverting our election systems. They post a list of all of the key files and file attributes needed by hackers on their website.[26]

The accreditation of these "trusted" vendors features another concerning twist. It turns out that one of the EAC officials responsible for the certification of voting systems is Jessica Bowers, a former senior vice president with Dominion Voting Systems.[27] In other words, the only vendors entrusted by election officials all across America to ensure the integrity of our election system were accredited on the basis of knowing someone at an organization that continues to compromise the security of our voting systems and one featuring a former executive at one of the voting system manufacturers. What could go wrong with that?

The concerns with the certification process don't stop there. The certification responsibility for Michigan is about as murky as it gets. While Pro V&V and SLI are cited as authorized investigators for voting equipment nationally, according to the Election Assistance Commission, Michigan's certification standards are as follows:

An electronic voting system shall not be used in an election unless it is approved by the board of state canvassers ... and unless it meets 1 of the following conditions: (a) Is certified by an independent testing authority accredited by the national association of state election directors and by the board of state canvassers. (b) In the absence of an accredited independent testing authority, is certified by the manufacturer of the voting system as meeting or exceeding the performance and test standards referenced in subdivision (a) in a manner prescribed by the board of state canvassers."[28]

It is worth noting that one of the founders of the National Association of State Elections Directors is former Michigan elections director, Chris Thomas, who served as a consultant to the Detroit City Clerk during the November 2020 election. His duty station was the Detroit Absentee Vote (AV) Counting Board at the TCF Center in Detroit where he was named in multiple poll challenger affidavits related to interference with poll challenger duties.

The contracts between the electronic voting system vendors and the State of Michigan, however, seem to point back to the EAC not the NASED or State Board of Canvassers. There is a provision in the voting systems contracts with the state of Michigan which says that the contractor's system shall have been tested and successfully completed all EAC certification steps, however, there are some substantive differences between the EAC testing and certification program requirements and the contract requirements stipulated by the state of Michigan. Most notably, under the EAC certification requirements, "wireless systems are disallowed."[29] Yet, under Michigan contract requirements, "a cellular or analog modem is required" to support communications.[30] Remarkably, Chris Thomas was the State Elections Director at the time Michigan entered into the current voting system contracts. In media stories and court exhibits, he has repeatedly denied that these systems were connected to the internet even though he is responsible for the state requirement for them to be able to do so. Regardless of the EAC requirement that wireless systems be disallowed and the fact that the voting systems in Michigan all support wireless communications, Dominion, ES&S, and Hart Intercivic systems all received their EAC certifications. How did they receive certifications if "wireless systems are disallowed"? This deficiency in our certification procedures for a critical infrastructure component is a national issue not simply a Michigan issue.

The bottom line is that certification of the hardware and software configurations in use in Michigan on November 3rd is as clear as mud at best and meaningless from an election integrity perspective. In this environment, it is no wonder that non-certified software such as SQL Server Management Studio software was found installed as part of the trusted build throughout Michigan and other states. Not a satisfactory state of affairs, especially for what has been designated a critical infrastructure component of our nation.

This begs the question whether our electronic voting systems can truly be trusted to manage our election hidden from the oversight of poll challengers or not.

Unfortunately, evidence of misplaced trust does not end with certification or internet connectivity concerns. Trust in our electronic voting systems was also compromised because of poor credential management. In Antrim County, there were multiple examples of poor account credential management practices leading to heightened security risks. Rather than tie user credentials to specific individuals, generic accounts with administrative credentials were utilized. The admin credentials give the user the ability to make changes to the system, including to the votes. Credentials for the Election Management System were stored in the system database using a well-known hashing algorithm subject to decoding without significant difficulty.[31] Worse yet, admin credentials were stored in plain text without any encryption allowing anyone with access to a network connected to the database to manipulate the data within the database.

Thus far, we have focused on evidence of security vulnerabilities, but do we have any evidence of anyone exploiting these vulnerabilities to effect election results? We do, but first we need to share a bit more information on how these vulnerabilities could be be exploited so we know exactly what to look for.

A whitepaper on the use of PID controllers to "optimize" Election Campaign results was presented by faculty at the Guangdong University of Technology at 2010 IEEE Conference in Wuhan, China. Their effort was financed by the Provincial Science Foundation of Guangdong which has significant ties to the Chinese Communist Party.[32] As an engineer, the use of the term "optimize" indicates that PID controllers had been used in the past, but users were not satisfied with their performance. This whitepaper was clearly an effort to perfect the application of PID controllers in the management of election outcomes.

While the fact that there was a paper presented in 2010 in Wuhan, China on how to control the outcome of an election is indeed suspect, it does not by itself indicate that a digital controller was used to subvert the integrity of the 2020 election. It does, however, encourage us to look specifically for any evidence of a PID controller in relation to our elections.

A PID controller is commonly used in industry to regulate the output of a system to achieve a desired setpoint. PID controllers use these output values to adjust future input values in what is known as a feedback control system. PID controllers are a specific example of a digital controller that we referenced earlier. These controllers are used to regulate the temperature of our homes and the cruising speed of our cars. PID controllers represent one of many practical applications of the calculus many of us grew to love or hate during high school or college. You may recall formulas featuring integrals and derivates. That's the stuff that PID controllers are made of. In fact, PID is short for common calculus terms:

P=Proportional

I=Integral

D=Derivative

PID control efforts would have unique "fingerprints" to look for in plots of the election night vote tally increments. For example, jumps in votes would denote increased proportional gain. Sudden drops in the number of votes would indicate that the cumulative or "integral" vote tally was being "reset" indicating what happens with a PID controller setpoint that has been changed. Derivative factors would likely not play a significant role in a PID controller for elections because of their tendency to result in system instability unless finely tuned. Derivative influence is typically adjusted to improve the speed of achieving a desired vote tally. Such manipulations would likely be too obvious for election fraud purposes. Early voting policy initiatives are a much stealthier alternative to derivative control efforts. The longer the time one has to count the votes, the more clandestine the manner in which fraudulent vote adjustments can be made by those intent on stealing an election.

Do PID controllers need internet connections to be effective? No. The 2010 Stuxnet cyberattack is a prime example of how a supposedly "air gapped" system could be compromised. "Air gapped" is a term used to denote that a given computer system has been completely isolated from outside networks thereby minimizing the risk of compromising the system via external sources. The Iranian uranium enrichment centrifuges were advertised as air gapped systems with zealous security measures befitting of a program of such strategic importance for the Iranian government. Despite these precautions, the Stuxnet virus managed to play havoc with their nuclear program. How did the virus breach these air gaps? The most likely method was via a USB flash drive similar to those used in electronic voting systems all across America.

The targets of the Stuxnet virus were the programmable line controllers in Iranian centrifuges used to enrich Uranium for nuclear weapons.[33] Programmable line controllers are effectively PID controllers. The virus would adjust the configuration settings in these controllers to induce catastrophic failures in the centrifuges. Guess what else has configuration settings that can be modified? Electronic vote tabulators. Our election system is designated as critical infrastructure for a reason.

Whether our systems are offline or online, programmable "bots" can be used to manipulate election results with minimal risk of detection. Vote tally changes could be affected at the precinct, county, or state level. They could proceed in a top down manner or bottom up. Once the vote tallies are changed, ballots aligned with the changes could be inserted after the fact if the chain of custody is not maintained. Then, one only needs to update the pollbooks to reflect the total number of ballots cast. When our election systems are networked together, all of this can be performed digitally.

It is worth noting that one of the organizations we will discuss later under Influence Operations called the Center for Tech and Civic Life lists the deployment of free election websites as one of their services. The mission of the Center for Tech and Civic Life per their website is "We connect Americans with the information they need to become and remain civically engaged, and ensure that our elections are more professional, inclusive, and secure."

The center is funded by Facebook founder Mark Zuckerberg and his wife Priscilla Chan. Their "free" election websites feature voter registration and election results links that amount to a convenient one-stop shopping center for election data for each municipality. The services provided by CTCL require digital access to sensitive election records such as the statewide voter registration database and even election results databases. Remember, nothing is truly free.

Record Anomalies

It is now time to see if there are any anomalies in our key election records that need to be addressed. Let's look at the first link in the election record chain of custody, the statewide voter registration database. In Michigan, this is referred to as the qualified voter file. Remember, this file determines who is eligible to vote in the state and provides information needed to validate the identity of these voters. If this record is corrupted, everything down the chain of custody is corrupted.

In October 2020, just days before the November 3, 2020, election, the Michigan Election Security Advisory Commission released a report that cited "If attackers were to gain access to Michigan's voter registration database or management software, they could cancel or alter voter registration records in an attempt to severely disrupt election administration processes."[34]

There is no evidence that this risk was mitigated in any way prior to the November 3, 2020, election. There is evidence, however, that

1,390,433 new voters registered for the 2020 election. That means that 17% of Michigan's registered voters for the 2020 election were new registrations.[35] It is likely that 1,390,433 of the 5,579,317 votes cast in the 2020 election were newly registered voters. That is a whopping 25% of the votes were newly registered. It may just be me, but that seems a bit hard to believe.

That is not the only reason to call into question the integrity of Michigan's QVF. According to the EAC, 207,229 confirmation notices for newly registered voters were sent out. Only 1,143 were confirmed. In other words, in an election reportedly decided by 154,188 votes, at least 206,086 registered voters were likely ineligible to vote.

An independent analysis of the number of registered voters in Michigan against the voting age population in Michigan further reveals that over 616,000 voters were likely ineligible to vote.[36]

In a lawsuit filed by the Public Interest Legal Foundation, they allege that Michigan voter rolls include 25,975 potentially deceased registrants including 334 who were registered after their death dates.[37]

In case this information is not sufficient to cause concern about the integrity of the QVF, former Michigan secretary of state and current state senator Ruth Johnson estimated in a letter to her fellow Senate colleagues that as many as 800,000 ineligible voters were seeded into Michigan's qualified voter file for the November 3, 2020, election.[38]

So, how were these ineligible voters seeded into the state qualified voter file? It is impossible to tell without a forensic audit. One thing we do know is that, prior to the election, the Michigan Secretary of State, Jocelyn Benson, entered into data sharing agreements with third party organizations, such as Rock the Vote, which gave them the ability to add voters to the qualified voter file.[39] If so inclined, Rock the Vote would not even need to add, change or delete election records to have some very useful data to share with anyone complicit with election fraud. Rock the Vote is part of a complex web of non-profits that are connected financially to progressive organizations bankrolled by Mark Zuckerberg and Priscilla Chan to the tune of $500 million. To what degree did organizations such as Rock the Vote influence the integrity of the data in the Qualified Voter File? Only a forensic investigation of the statewide voter registration file would tell us who updated which record and when. Ideally, this investigation would be supplemented by canvassing efforts that would examine the integrity of each record.

Let's shift gears to look at evidence of ballot anomalies evident during the preparation phase.

During his Antrim County investigations, Attorney Matt DePerno and his team discovered the following ballot anomalies. First, the ballots were printed on standard stock available at most office supply stores. The ballot images for every precinct and ballot type are also conveniently stored in PDF format on county Election Management System servers. When you store PDFs of ballot images in a central location, you allow anyone with access to the files, the ability to print blank ballots. Simply add a computer hooked to a printer capable of printing on standard stock 11 x 17 paper and you are well on your way to converting an election into a selection.

Another anomaly discovered by DePerno and his team pertains to variations in the ballot layout which could result in high error rates when scanning the ballot. High error rates when scanning absentee ballots would enable third parties to determine what the vote on the ballot should be without the actual voter being any the wiser. Such ballot errors are resolved by either a manual "spoil and duplicate" process, semi-manual adjudication process that updates the ballot image, or a batch adjudication process. Either way, the old ballot is replaced by a new ballot featuring the selections of a third party. These ballot anomalies alone highlight the fallacy that recounts are a significant measure of election integrity, but there is more evidence of concern regarding the integrity of ballots applicable to the preparation phase.

During the DefCon27 conference of 2019, two students of Professor J Alex Halderman from the University of Michigan in Ann Arbor—

Kartikeya Kandula and Jeremy Wink demonstrated how scanned ballot images could be modified in real-time as a means of subverting an election.[40] Tabulators read ballot images. If ballot images can be modified on the fly so that a vote for candidate A is replaced by a vote for candidate B on the ballot image, there is reason for concern when our elections are digitized. Suffice it to say, there is reason for concern.

Influence Operations

Now, let's see if there is evidence of any more subtle attempts to subvert our elections. Is there evidence of any influence operations? Yes. Quite a bit as it turns out.

While one hacker in a basement fed with an IV-drip of his favorite energy drink could indeed raise havoc with digitized election results, it would only cover the mechanics of changing votes. Any operation on the scale of a coup to overthrow the US Government requires a lot of money, a lot of manpower, and a lot of organization in order to be truly successful at convincing the American public that the fake election was actually real. As it turns out, there appears to be evidence that Big Media, Big Tech, Big Money, Big Labor, and Big Government all put significant effort into planning of not only the subversion of free and fair election processes but also the defense of the results of their subversion.

A prime example of influence operation collusion between Big Media, Big Tech and Big Government is evident in the media coverage of the Hunter Biden laptop. In the lead up to the 2020 election, the *New York Post* released a bombshell story with the headline "Smoking-gun email reveals how Hunter Biden introduced Ukrainian businessman to VP Dad."[41] The Big Tech response was highlighted by Twitter blocking the circulation of the story. Big Government intel officials came together to sign a letter asserting that the laptop appeared to be part of a Russian disinformation campaign.[42] Big Media outlets such as CNN, NBC, and MSNBC picked up this narrative. No less than fifteen major media personalities spewed allegations that the laptop and the information it contained was part of a Russian disinformation campaign.[43] In the wake of the election, MRC conducted a poll of actual Biden voters in Arizona, Georgia, Michigan, Nevada, North Carolina, Pennsylvania, and Wisconsin. The poll asked questions about what issues would have shifted their vote away from Joe Biden in the 2020 election.[44] The top response (9.4% of those polled) cited that the facts around Hunter Biden scandals revealed in his laptop would have shifted their vote away from Biden. It wasn't until the release of a March 16, 2022, story by the NY Times that Big Media admitted that the data in the laptop abandoned by Hunter Biden in a Delaware repair shop was "authenticated".[45] In the meantime, the election damage was done. Instead of truthful reporting as to the source and contents of the Hunter Biden laptop that would have shifted 9.4% of Biden voters away, Biden was awarded a 2.78% margin of victory in Michigan, 0.3% in Arizona, 0.2% in Georgia, 2.4% in Nevada, 1.2% in Pennsylvania, and 0.6% in Wisconsin. While this is a solid example of these "big" groups operating in collusion, they also operated independently of one another.

Big Government, in particular, was very active in preparing misinformation campaigns usually under the guise of preventing the dissemination of misinformation. Pre-election risk assessments at both the federal and state levels were invariably focused upon suppressing any discussion of election fraud in the public square. The rationale given for such suppression was to protect the public trust in our election system. But what prevents this censorship tactic from hiding real election fraud? Are we to assume that our election system integrity is beyond reproach? What happens when the state and media is weaponized to cover-up fraud under the guise of preserving the public trust in our election system? How would one go about exposing election fraud when even the mention of election fraud makes one a target of the media and law enforcement agencies?

It should be noted that the same Michigan Security Advisory Commission report that cited the vulnerability of our qualified voter file to cyberattacks chose to specifically call out "the Russian attacks" harkening back to the media narrative for the 2016 Presidential election.[46] It begs the question, is Russia the only nation with the capability to hack into the qualified voter file? If not, why wouldn't other nation-states with such capabilities be cited? Was this reference included in the report to invoke a connection in the minds of the public between 2020 election risks and the now thoroughly discredited "Russian collusion" narrative that served as the basis of the first impeachment trial of President Trump? Is it possible that the report was laying the foundation for a post-election narrative involving Russian hackers?

Yet another example of teeing up a one-sided post-election narrative relates to an October 14th Situational Awareness Bulletin issued by someone at the Michigan State Police. The bulletin warned that there was an "increased potential for malicious groups or individuals to attempt to intimidate voters, or otherwise disrupt the election process, under the guise of acting as poll watchers."[47] This security bulletin seems to promote the voter suppression narrative yet notably neglects the risk of intimidation tactics upon poll challengers executing their lawful oversight responsibilities.

Let's not forget the Cybersecurity and Infrastructure Security Agency. They released their report on election security risks at the end of July 2020. Just a few months before the election, the same organization behind the infamous quote that the 2020 election was "the most secure election in American history" cited numerous risks to key election components such as voter registration databases, pollbooks, ballot preparation equipment, tabulation equipment, and election websites.

This federal government report cited the following key findings:

- Compromises to the integrity of state-level voter registration systems, the preparation of election data (e.g., ballot programming), vote aggregation systems, and election websites present particular risk to the ability of jurisdictions to conduct elections.

- When proper mitigations and incident response plans are not in place, cyberattacks on the availability of state or local-level systems that support same day registration, vote center check-in, or provisional voting also have the potential to pose meaningful risk on the ability of jurisdictions to conduct elections.
- While compromises to voting machine systems present a high consequence target for threat actors, the low likelihood of successful attacks at scale on voting machine systems during use means that there is lower risk of such incidents when compared to other infrastructure components of the election process.
- U.S. election systems are comprised of diverse infrastructure and security controls, and many systems invest significantly in security. However, even jurisdictions that implement cybersecurity best practices are potentially vulnerable to cyberattack by sophisticated cyber actors, such as nation-state actors.
- Disinformation campaigns conducted in concert with cyberattacks on election infrastructure can amplify disruptions of electoral processes and public distrust of election results.

State government also joined the risk warning narrative. The Michigan election security commission released their report in October 2020. In their report, they made the following recommendations:

VOTER REGISTRATION AND IT SECURITY
- Prioritize implementation of multifactor authentication
- Evaluate user access to ensure appropriate number of users and levels of permissions
- Expand monitoring of suspicious activities

- Cultivate mature software engineering security practices
- Expand security training and requirements for election officials and other QVF users
- Ensure voter registration databases and systems are well secured
- Contain failures and maintain resilience through procedural fail-safes

POST-ELECTION AUDITS

- Implement risk-limiting audits as a cybersecurity defense
- Develop RLA procedures in close partnership with appropriate entities
- Determine parameters for full RLA implementation
- Consider statutory changes to further support RLAs
- Provide transparency and public education
- Continue use of other types of audits in addition to Risk Limiting Audits

COUNTERING MISINFORMATION AND DISINFORMATION

- Coordinate accurate information sharing among local officials
- Form bilateral partnerships to counter misinformation and instill confidence
- Develop a rapid-response strategy to counter misinformation at the State level
- Share information on data security best practices with campaigns

ELECTION NIGHT REPORTING

- Phase out the "modeming in" of election night results
- Build redundancies into electronic reporting
- Observe best practices when using removable drives

- Prioritize accuracy and prepare communication plans in the event election-night reports are late or inaccurate
- Conduct a county-by-county assessment of security practices in election night reporting, and address greatest deficiencies immediately

EMERGENCY/DISASTER PREPAREDNESS

- Conduct statewide, countywide, and local exercise
- Develop robust emergency response plans at the state and local level
- Prepare mitigation plans for election equipment and polling places

ADDITIONAL AREAS OF RECOMMENDATION

- Physical and Equipment Security
- Software Updates
- Vendor Accountability and Reporting
- Local Election Official Training and Resources
- Electronic ballot return for overseas voters

If the purpose of these reports was to mitigate the risks they highlight in the reports, the timing was less than optimal. If the purpose of these reports was to tee up post-election media narratives, the timing was more appropriate. If the media's preferred candidate had not been declared the winner, the findings in these reports would be featured prominently in media stories about how fraudulent the election was. That hasn't happened. As a matter of fact, the media continues to promote the narrative that 2020 was the most secure election in history even though there is plenty of evidence to the contrary.

The simple fact of the matter is that our election systems have always been vulnerable to subversion. Electronic voting systems simply make it easier than ever to do so. If our election systems were to be subverted, the impacts could be catastrophic to our system of government. This is the reasoning behind designating our election system as a critical infrastructure component.

Enemies of America are well aware of this vulnerability. They also have the resources needed to exploit this vulnerability. As the Wuhan technical paper mentioned at the beginning of this chapter implied, the Chinese government appears to be at least interested in controlling election outcomes. We have already cited evidence of conflicts of interest between the EAC and voting system manufacturers. One of the reasons for concern when it comes to these conflicts of interest is that there are significant ties between these voting system manufacturers and foreign interests. In October 2020, the Department of Homeland Security released a threat assessment that covered threats to our election integrity posed by China, Russia and Iran.[48] The report provided the following summary of these threats:

Ahead of the election, China likely will continue using overt and covert influence operations to denigrate the U.S. Presidential Administration and its policies and to shape the U.S. domestic information environment in favor of China. China will further use its traditional "soft power" influence toolkit— overt economic measures and lobbying—to promote U.S. policies more aligned with China's interests. Iran will continue to promote messages supporting its foreign policy objectives and to use online influence operations to increase societal tensions in the United States. Tehran most likely considers the current U.S. Administration a threat to the regime's stability. Iran's critical messaging of the U.S. President almost certainly will continue throughout 2020. Russian influence actors see divisive issues regarding the 2020 Census, such as the consideration of adding a citizenship question, as an opportunity to target a fundamental democratic process. In addition to potential cyber operations, Russia might use social media messaging—much like it does in the context of US elections—to attempt to discourage public participation in the census, to promote a loss of confidence in census results, or to undermine trust in public institutions.

The Iranian threat is also highlighted by CISA Alert AA20-304A, released on October 30, 2020. The alert cited awareness of an Iranian advanced persistent threat (APT) actor targeting U.S. state websites – including election websites. In the wake of the damage done by the Stuxnet virus to the Iranian centrifuge program, the Iranians were likely very motivated to interfere with US elections. Their centrifuge program is a key component of their nuclear weapon program. The United States has been implicated by the Iranians as the source of the Stuxnet virus.

The Russian threat is further highlighted by a Report of the Select Committee on Intelligence of the United States Senate regarding the 2016 election. They concluded that "the Russian government directed extensive activity, beginning in at least 2014 and carrying into at least 2017, against US election infrastructure at the state and local level."[49]

In addition to the DHS threat assessment, an affidavit from a former intelligence analyst with the 305th Military Intelligence Battalion cited significant connections between DominionVotingSystems.com and China.[50] The affidavit includes evidence of China accessing Dominion servers and Nameserver configuration settings pointing to an IP address connected to Guangdong Mobile Communications. In what I am sure is a matter of pure coincidence, the *New York Post* has identified $31 million in contributions to the Biden family from individuals with direct ties to Chinese Intelligence.[51]

Big Governments were not the only ones engaged in misinformation campaigns. Another example of a disinformation campaign alluded to earlier is when Democrats and sympathetic groups such as the Brennan Center,[52] ACLU,[53] and League of Women Voters[54] promoted the narrative that Republicans and their sympathetic groups seek to suppress the votes of minorities. This voter suppression narrative has been used to promote legislation and election practices which compromise election integrity by relaxing voter identification requirements.

One of the organizations formed in the lead up to the 2020 election was the Transition Integrity Project. Their stated mission per their website is: "The Transition Integrity Project (TIP) was founded to identify and mitigate risks in the period between Election Day and Inauguration." Their name says it all. Their focus was upon transition not election integrity. They are known for their report that analyzed what they referred to as "2020 election crisis scenario planning exercises." The recommendations cited in their report were as follows:

- Plan for a contested election. If there is a crisis, events will unfold quickly, and sleep-deprived leaders will be asked to make consequential decisions quickly. Thinking through options now will help to ensure better decisions. Approach this as a political battle, not just a legal battle. In the event of electoral contestation, sustained political mobilization will likely be crucial for ensuring transition integrity. Dedicated staff and resources need to be in place at least through the end of January.

- Focus on readiness in the states, providing political support for a complete and accurate count. Governors, secretaries of state, attorneys general, and legislatures can communicate and rein-force laws and norms and be ready to confront irregularities. Election officials will need political and public support to see the process through to completion. (NOTE: The details regarding this recommendation cite how they need to use the media to influence public perceptions so as to not execute recounts or audits to ensure the accuracy of the results.)

- Address the two biggest threats head on: lies about "voter fraud" and escalating violence. Voting fraud is virtually non-existent, but Trump lies about it to create a narrative designed to politically mobilize his base and to create the basis for contesting the results should he lose. The potential for violent conflict is high, particularly since Trump encourages his supporters to take up arms.

- Anticipate a rocky administrative transition. Transition teams will likely need to do two things simultaneously: defend against Trump's reckless actions on his way out of office; and find creative solutions to ensure landing teams are able to access the information and resources they need to begin to prepare for governing.

Their website has since been taken down, but one can still view its content via the Wayback Machine (http://web.archive.org/web/).

The AFL-CIO appears to have provided the organization structure and planning skills needed by those opposed to President Trump.[55] Their plans were so precise that they predicted that "The Trump vote relative to Biden's will never be better than it will be at 10:59 when the polls close on the West Coast". This precision is not necessarily an indication of fraud, as there was empirical data available at the time that would support such a conclusion, but it was strange for them to highlight nonetheless. Among their initiatives was one called Power the Polls which mobilizes workers to staff the polls as poll workers.[56]

On July 29, 2020, a group calling themselves the Sunrise Movement announced the beginning of what they referred to as the 100 Day Siege leading up to the November 3, 2020, election.[57] They claim to be finishing the work of Reconstruction purposely seeking to reignite our Civil War. In video footage obtained by Millie Weaver, they outline a plan for revolution encouraging youth to take to the streets.

Aracely Jimenez, the Deputy Communications Director of the Sunrise Movement is on record saying,

"This is really the moment that this broken system can all come crumbling down but it is up to us to take action and make it happen. We have to bring the crisis to their doorsteps...No justice, no sleep. This is a daily haunting to make it clear that our generation is a force to be reckoned with when it comes to the revolution in the streets and at the ballot box."

She is followed by Sunrise Movement Organizer, Nikayla Jefferson, a UCSB PhD Student, who states,

"My dream is that we bring these failed and corrupt institutions to their g** d**n knees and build something new.... We are not taking this bu***sh*t anymore. They will see us. They will feel us and they will hear us until they are deaf with our demands......Every single day from now until the election is a day we are preparing for ballot con battle and the post-election eruption of our pent up anger"

Is this what passes for "higher learning" at our universities nowadays?

This campaign of harassment, violence, and intimidation was launched by an alliance of the Sunrise Movement, March for Our Lives, United We Dream and Black Lives Matter. Collectively, these groups and others like them enforced a national chill on the conservative side of political discussion. Very few individuals had the courage to call out the fallacies of these groups' narratives. Anyone doing so would instantly be accused by the media of inciting a riot. Even after evidence of significant election fraud began surfacing in the wake of the election, most of the nation, including the vast majority of legislators, chose silence rather than action in large part due to fear of riots by these groups and their supporters. The rule of law in America was effectively held hostage by a group of violent thugs.

On September 19, 2020, a leftist organization called Shutdown DC held what they referred to as an Election Simulation. It is clear to anyone who has seen the video recording of this meeting shared by Millie Weaver (MillenialMillie.com) that there was significant effort expended towards the planning of what certainly appeared to be a coup in the lead up to the election. The meeting features Nadine Bloch who is the Training Director for an organization called Beautiful Trouble. They proceeded to divide themselves into five role-based teams to execute a simulation of the election.

1. KeepGoing.org – A national nonprofit that invests heavily in campaigning and get-out-the-vote for Democratic candidates. Has a base in every state that can be mobilized for actions, but the legal team insists that all actions be legal and that participants sign a waiver saying they will not break the law.

2. Wisconsin United – A Wisconsin state-wide community organization that organizes around racial and economic justice issues. Maintains strong relationships with local labor unions and some progressive officials. Wisconsin United has endorsed Biden in the upcoming election but the organization's base is much more engaged in supporting local progressive candidates.

3. United Grocery and Bakery Workers – A labor union representing 130,000 grocery store workers, mostly in major cities around the US. A new progressive leadership slate was swept into power in the most recent union election but there is still a significant old guard that wants to take a more conservative approach. The union is bound by no-strike/no-lockout clauses in all of its contracts.

4. Liberty City Antifa – Militant Anti-fascist network in Philadelphia, Pennsylvania. Has about 25 active participants but can turn out around 200 people for big actions. Very few existing relationships with local community organizations.

5. Capitol Disruption – DC-based network of organizations and individuals that's been around for about a year, organizing direct action events around climate justice and other issues.

These organization profiles provide a very interesting window into what occupies the thoughts of leftist organizations.

1. They have internal party struggles between pro-revolution agitators and traditional, pro-America activists
2. It highlights the importance of an agitator organization not bound by the rule of law such as Antifa
3. It highlights the importance of organized labor
4. It highlights that they have created a networked federation of leftist groups
5. It highlights the centrality of race, climate change, and social justice narrative as a mechanism for unifying leftist groups
6. It highlights the importance of non-profit organizations as funding mechanisms for communications and legal counsel

Shutdown DC's planning efforts didn't stop there. Millie Weaver has additional recordings[58] of their meetings to discuss strategy and tactics prior to the November 3, 2020, election.[59] These meetings were attended by representatives of progressive organizations such as BLM DC and United for Peace and Justice along with quite a few federal employees and contractors, including those embedded within organizations responsible for national security. They are very clear in their desire to label Trump supporters as the perpetrators of a coup when it is obvious from their discussion that it is they who were planning an insurrection. In fact, they express their concern about the invocation of the Insurrection Act during the meeting. Why? The Insurrection Act enables the President of the United States to use the military to suppress civil disorder. They were planning how to shutdown DC and take over government buildings well before the election and well before the events of January 6.

The progressive organizations involved in this planning were not limited to the usual suspects strongly aligned with the Democratic Party. Sympathetic Republican organizations inspired by the Lincoln Project were also involved in the simulation. One of the attendees, Stuart Karaffa (he/him), shared the following strategy in his fictitious role as the head of the "Nixon Project".

"Our strategic point of intervention because we are prominent Republicans. We are first going to approach the mainstream media and to also lean into our networks that we will use our positions of corporate prominence to lock out all Republicans including those on the Trump Team from future corporate jobs, media interviews, etc."

It seems like he is teeing up the media lockout and threats to livelihood that have been experienced by many prominent election investigators in the defense phase.

One of the featured speakers on the video conference call was Lisa Fithian, she/her, Tutelo Land. According to Wikipedia, Ms. Fithian is a member of the Extinction Revolution and serves on the National Steering Committee for the United Peace and Justice coalition of 1,300 international and domestic leftist organizations. During the meeting, she made the following startling assertions,

"We don't have a lot of experience taking over government buildings. We might need to think about that…we may find ourselves in the streets with people with different tactics than ours. There may be some people that are willing to break the windows to get into the government buildings. Like if that's what we need to do, we shouldn't fight about that. Let's do that."

"Chaos is the suit by which change emerges. Let's get cooking."

She then proceeded to show excerpts from what appears to be a strategic planning document for the Egyptian "Freedom and Justice" Party. The Freedom and Justice Party has strong ties to the terrorist organization known as the Muslim Brotherhood. The presentation she shared in Arabic and English featured the warning: "Please distribute through email printing and photocopies only. Twitter and Facebook are being monitored." This would seem to indicate that she was working with some of the same foreign agents who orchestrated the anti-government Arab Spring protests of the early 2010s under President Obama's watch. As a minimum, it indicates that she was sympathetic to such anti-government activities.

The goal of the Freedom and Justice Party was to remove Egyptian President Hosni Mubarek from office. Their Egyptian Revolution of 2011 was successful in this pursuit behind their slogan of "freedom, social justice, equality."[60] Sound familiar? Fithian's apparent use of the same anti-government playbook that was successfully employed in Egypt to force the resignation of a sitting president sure seems to indicate she was planning a coup in the United States. She now appeared to be using this playbook to guide meeting attendees as to how they could force the removal of President Donald Trump from office.

In the presentation, Fithian shared a slide entitled "Strategic Goals of Civil Disobedience". The slide featured the following goals:

1. To take over important government buildings
2. To attempt to win over members of the policy (police) and army to the side of the people
3. To protect our brothers and sisters in revolution

It might just be me, but she seems to be promoting revolution. Another word for revolution is *insurrection*.

In case this point has not yet been made clear enough, Fithian went on to state that "If Biden overwhelmingly wins and Trump doesn't concede… and he's calling out the white… the Proud Boys, etc., will we be able to get our Tunisian moment? Our Arab Spring? It is in that place of chaos and crisis when there is uncertainty that is that place of emergence where something new is going to come through."[61]

This is a clear call to her fellow activists for chaos and crisis so that something "new" can come through. Another word for what she is planning is a *coup*.

On October 28, 2020, just days before the November 3 election, an online event referred to as Democracy Defense was organized by the progressive organizations Feds for Democracy and Democracy Kitchen.[62] Attendees were predominantly federal employees and contractors. For reference purposes, there are approximately 2.93 million federal employees. The stated objectives of the event were to explore options for defending the federal workplace in the event that Trump were to win the election and provide them with action plans to prepare for various post-election scenarios. They openly discussed how to avoid Hatch Act violations, how to leak information, how to push back against President

Trump's executive orders, and how to slow down the wheels of government to suit their objectives.

The organizers of the event referred attendees to the website ProtecttheResults.com, which popped up on the web during the June 2020 timeframe and went quiet on January 22, 2021, two days after the presidential inauguration.[63] The website was formed by the progressive organizations Stand Up America and Indivisible Action. The site listed 148 partner organizations including Black Lives Matter, SEIU, the National LGBTQ Taskforce, and Indivisible (See Appendix A for full list). They developed a forty-four-page toolkit for organizing protest events. Do you find it interesting that a group formed five months before the election was named Protect the Results? They could have called themselves Protect the Vote or Protect the Election, but they didn't. Did they know something we didn't know? Would they have "protected the results" if Donald Trump was declared the winner? It sure seems to indicate that there was some electioneering in the works.

There were many other organizations that appear to have been working on electioneering. An organization founded in 2012 called the Center for Tech and Civic Life (CTCL) received very special attention during the run up to the 2020 election. In addition to funding from leftist organizations such as the Rockefeller Brothers Fund and the Democracy Fund, Big Money also came from progressive billionaire Mark Zuckerberg and his wife Priscilla Chan. They donated $350 million to CTCL, yielding significantly more operating revenue than the previous year's tally of only $2.8 million. CTCL became a slush fund that funded other electioneering efforts including $7.4 million to towns and cities that were historic strongholds of Democratic Party machines.[64]

Funding continues to be the strength of the progressive movement. While conservative groups struggle to find $6,424 in support of FOIA requests in the wake of the 2020 election, progressive organizations are fueled by a seemingly endless stream of funding.

Zuckerberg and Chan also donated $50 million to the Center for Election Innovation and Research which also became a slush fund for electioneering efforts.[65] The Michigan Center for Election Law and Administration (MCELA) received 100% of its 2020 funding from a CEIR grant of $12 million.[66] The MCELA was founded by Michigan secretary of state Jocelyn Benson. Funds from this grant reportedly went towards TV and radio ads encouraging citizens to vote as well as text messages sent directly to voters who had not voted yet.

Zuckerberg was not alone in his Big Money efforts. Bill Gates chipped in with another $319.4 million towards media projects to influence the public narrative.[67] One of the groups financially supported by Bill Gates to the tune of $250 million is the New Venture Fund. The New Venture Fund runs The Hub Project which was formed to shape media coverage and help Democratic causes. The Hub Project is jointly funded by the 1630 Fund and the New Venture Fund. In 2017 the Hub Project organized protests to demand that President Trump release his tax returns. The Hub Project controls a super PAC called Change Now. In 2020, the New Venture Fund was the largest donor to the 1630 Fund contributing more than $86 million. New Venture Fund contributions to the 1630 Fund were supplemented by $135 million over the course of five years from the Berger Action Fund controlled by Swiss billionaire Hansjorg Wyss. It should be pointed out that foreign nationals are prohibited under federal law from contributing directly or *indirectly* to PACs. The 1630 Fund donated more than $63 million to super PACs backing Democrats or opposing Republicans in 2020, including the pro-Biden group Priorities USA and the "bipartisan" Lincoln Project. The 1630 Fund "spent $410 million (more than the DNC) to help the Democrats defeat President Donald Trump and win back control of the Senate with attack advertisements and get-out-the-vote campaigns. The group "operates under dozens of trade names and projects so that they can appear to be separate grassroots organizations."[68]

One thing that becomes abundantly clear when looking at the web of organizations financed by progressive billionaires, the deep state is very deep. It even reaches down into local units of government.

Prior to the 2020 general election, Detroit received a $7.4 million grant from the Center for Tech and Civic Life (CTCL), nearly doubling the city's Department of Elections budget. Remember, CTCL, in turn, receives the bulk of its financial support from Facebook founder, Mark Zuckerberg. These funds nicknamed Zuck Bucks were allocated as follows: $200,000 went toward "planning and operationalizing" the administration of the election; $3.5 million to "expand voter education and outreach efforts" and to assist with processing mailed ballots. Another $3.7 million went to dramatically increase pay for poll workers and "election staff working at the Receiving/Verification Boards." In addition, $350,000 went to the purchase of ten high-speed Dominion Voting Systems tabulators for the TCF Center.

This wasn't the only financial anomaly identified during the preparation for the 2020 election. On September 22, 2020, the Detroit City Council approved a poll worker staffing contract for over $1 million for PIE Management, a staffing firm owned and operated by William A. Phillips, the personal lawyer of former Detroit Mayor Kwami Kilpatrick who was convicted of twenty-four federal felony counts pertaining to fraud.

Against this backdrop, many Republicans submitted affidavits that their applications to serve as poll workers were rejected. Additional affidavits cite little or no Republican poll workers at many election stations in Detroit in violation of state election law. The net result was that there were only a handful of Republican poll workers executing election processes for 503 precincts including 134 absentee voter counting boards in Detroit.

In the lead up to the 2020 election, progressive organizations were unified toward an aggressive campaign to promote the idea that Republicans were pursuing laws aimed at suppressing the votes of minorities. This narrative was intended to invoke memories of the racially motivated Jim Crow laws after a year of racial unrest in America. This narrative conveniently neglects to mention the Democratic Party origins of such laws. The voter suppression narrative was pushed by prominent progressive organizations such as the Brennan Center, the ACLU, and the League of Women Voters. The net impact of such a narrative was to encourage election officials and poll workers to exert less rigor when attempting to determine that a given voter is who they say they are whether they seek to vote in-person or via the mail. The voter suppression narrative provided convenient cover to Jocelyn Benson when she relaxed the signature verification requirements for absentee voters.

Big Tech played a prominent role in Preparation Phase influence operations. In addition to providing progressive organizations with an effective vehicle for communicating false narratives such as the voter suppression narrative, they had more subtle ways of influencing the results of the election. Prior to the election, researcher Robert Epstein[69] published an article in the *Epoch Times* called "10 Ways Big Tech Can Shift Millions of Votes in the November Elections Without Anyone Knowing."[70] His list included the following mechanisms:

1. Search Engine Manipulation Effect
2. Search Suggestion Effect
3. Targeted Messaging Effect
4. Opinion Matching Effect
5. Answer Bot Effect
6. Shadowbanning
7. Programmed Virality and the Digital Bandwagon Effect
8. The Facebook Effect
9. Censorship
10. The Digital Customization Effect

In conclusion, he estimated that "upwards of 12 million votes" could be shifted "without anyone knowing". Remember, the margin of victory in Michigan was 154,188, 10,457 in Arizona, 12,670 in Georgia, 33,596 in Nevada, 81,660 in Pennsylvania, and 20,682 in Wisconsin.

Another tactic employed by Big Tech to influence the public narrative was their "Ministry of Truth" inspired "fact checkers." Thanks to a lawsuit brought by John Stossel,[71] Facebook was forced to admit a year after the election that their "fact checks" are merely opinion. The damage to the truth particularly regarding election fraud, however, had already been done.

Influence operations were not limited to Big Tech, Big Money, Big Government and Big Media. They also applied to contract stipulations. There were contract anomalies between the state of Michigan and vendors like Dominion Voting Systems. The contract it had with the state included a clause that restricted the state from making copies of the software except for purposes of backup and prevented it from analyzing the software in whole or in part.[72]

Shouldn't clerks be allowed to make copies of the software to protect election record chain of custody? Shouldn't investigators be allowed to analyze the software used in an election?

The clause in the Dominion contract restricts investigations of electronic voting systems to only those vendors approved by the EAC. This clause has been used as the basis of a court-ordered redaction of evidence. It has also been used extensively to prohibit clerks from conducting independent investigations of their voting system configurations. Remember, the EAC features a former electronic voting system executive as their voting system certification authority. There seems to be a concerted effort to limit oversight to a select group of insiders rather than duly elected clerks responsible for the integrity of the election records for their jurisdiction.

Not only were state officials and our clerks restricted from investigating its own voting system, but poll challengers were also prevented from investigating how the election would be conducted before the election. Of particular note, poll challengers were prevented access to the third floor of the Detroit Elections Bureau which has been implicated in several affidavits related to suspicious election activities. This obstruction rationale seemed to persistently revolve around COVID-related excuses.[73]

In fact, COVID was used consistently as the basis for subverting election integrity. The Michigan Secretary of State, Jocelyn Benson, set the tone with statements such as the following from her June 3, 2020, press release, "As we collectively endure this moment of great uncertainty, caused by a global pandemic that has taken the lives of 100,000 Americans and many more worldwide, it is within both my authority and my responsibility as Michigan's chief election officer to ensure every voter knows that they do not need to risk their health to cast a ballot." Less than a month before the election, October 16, 2020, the Michigan Bureau of Elections under her authority updated the Michigan Elections Manual to implement a six-foot rule enforcing separation between poll workers and poll challengers attempting to oversee election processes.

On October 23, 2020, a lawsuit was filed in the State of Michigan Court of Claims by Bob Cushman and Rep Steve Carra requesting an injunction upon this new rule implemented unilaterally by the MI Secretary of State.[74] The court-issued an injunction, however, it was not well-communicated by election officials to poll workers prior to the election. This failure to publicize the injunction, be it deliberate or innocent, resulted in significant conflict between poll workers and poll challengers at tabulation centers such as the TCF Center in Detroit. There is evidence that the six-foot rule was intended as a mechanism to interfere with poll challenger oversight of election processes. During a training session for Detroit poll workers, the following recording was made:

TRAINER: (Challengers and poll workers) "They have to wear masks. That's important because they can come behind your table. But if you don't have six feet they can't come back there."
TRAINEE: "So six feet back. Unless they have really good vision, they can't actually see."

TRAINER: "EXACTLY. Unless they got really good vision, or they brought their binoculars (laughter). Six feet. That's the rule, right? And you are entitled to your six feet."[75]

Rather than conduct an investigation into this obvious example of poll challenger interference, the Michigan Attorney General demanded that BigLeaguePolitics.com remove this incriminating evidence from the public square.

Summary

In summary, we have shown evidence in Michigan of the following preparation phase tactics being employed successfully:

- Voter registration file was stuffed with as few as 206,086 and as many as 800,000 ineligible voters (Both greater than the 154,188 presidential vote margin)
- Ballot initiatives implemented to weaken election integrity
- Identity verification standards for mail-in voters were compromised
- Election operations were centralized via use of networked electronic voting systems which exposed the entire election record chain of custody to internet-based intrusions
- Foreign agents demonstrated both capabilities and interest in managing election outcomes via electronic voting systems
- Poor credential management practices in place that not only posed a serious security risk but also aided in concealing who was responsible for any security breaches
- Significant critical infrastructure risks to our voting systems were identified weeks before the general election
- Post-election audit standards were insufficient to address electronic voting system risks

- COVID used as premise to interfere with election oversight and compromise election integrity
- Key election management responsibilities were outsourced to private companies protected from oversight by illusory contract clauses
- Big Tech, Big Money, Big Government and Big Media colluded to shape the pre-election public narrative
- Significantly more effort was expended shaping the post-election narrative regarding election fraud than mitigating the technology risks that open the door to such fraud
- There was evidence of a well-funded, well-organized, bi-partisan deep state seditious conspiracy of at least 148 organizations across the country committed to protecting the election *results*—over four months before any results would be tallied.

MAIN ATTACK

Just because we have evidence of preparations to subvert a
does not mean that the election was actually subverted. Do we
evidence that any weaknesses established prior to the election wer
ally exploited? Let's see if there is any evidence that supports our th
that the Main Attack phase would seek to exploit our single grea
weakness, mail-in ballots, to stuff the ballot box with fraudulent votes.

Process Anomalies

Our main attack theory features the exploitation of process execution anomalies centered around the mail-in voting process. Is there
evidence of an increased emphasis upon mail-in voting?

As it turns out, the 2020 election featured a significant increase in
mail-in voting. Nationwide, we saw a 220% increase in mail-in voting
over 2016. In Michigan 3,318,609 absentee ballots were requested and
2,841,696 absentee ballots were returned.[76] The total number of ballots
cast was 5,579,317.[77]

For the first time in American history, more people voted by mail
than in-person.[78]

Was the mail-in voting process secure?

Prior to the 2020 election, the absentee voter process was a bottoms-up process initiated by the voter and featuring data provided by
local clerks. During the 2020 election, the absentee voter process was
shifted to a top-down process initiated by the Michigan secretary of state
and featured data provided by the secretary of state (SoS).[79]

1. SoS registers people to vote automatically when they get a
    driver's license (motor voter law put into statute as a result of
    Ballot Proposal 2018-3).
2. SoS uploads driver's license information and signature to
    QVF.
3. Clerks use the QVF as voter information database.

4. SoS *sometimes* mails a voter's signature to the clerk to tape onto the master card; SoS sometimes does not. Master cards are used by poll workers during elections to verify the identity of a voter.
5. If the voter's signature is not provided, the clerk prints the driver's license signature from the QVF onto the master card *or* the master card is left blank.

In theory, the signatures on the absentee voter application, driver's license, and voter registration master card should all match. In practice, they often don't. What happens if a clerk's office receives two absentee ballot request forms for the same person that feature two different signatures? The clerk would check it against the QVF.

What happens when the QVF doesn't match the signature on the absentee ballot request form? The clerk checks it against the signature on file with the master card. What happens when the master card is blank or simply has the QVF signature printed on it? Clearly, further investigation is warranted. Such investigations were often not possible during the 2020 election due to the record number of mail-in votes.

By centralizing the key information flows in the absentee voting process, the preparation phase was successful in weakening the integrity of the state mail-in voting processes. Voting by mail is not an indicator of fraud in and of itself, though.

What else was observed that would indicate election fraud?

Despite the assurance of election officials and the Dominion CEO repeatedly denying that our electronic voting systems were connected to the internet, there is a significant body of evidence to suggest that the voting equipment in Michigan was indeed connected to the internet— even during the tabulation of votes.

At the TCF Center in Detroit, while serving as a poll challenger, I noted in sworn testimony that the tabulator workstations, adjudicator workstations, and central control computers were all networked together *and* connected to the internet as indicated by the internet connectivity icon on each monitor. This observation was later confirmed when video of the pre-election walkthrough of the Detroit Absentee Vote (AV) Counting Board was discovered.

On election night, when I asked senior Detroit election official and former Democrat Michigan State Representative David Nathan to prove my assertions of internet connectivity wrong by floating the mouse cursor over the internet connectivity icon, he refused to do so. When pressed, he responded that I should simply "trust [him]."[80] I didn't and don't to this day. I do trust my eyes, though. The AV Counting Board computers were indeed connected to the internet. Detroit election officials continue to deny any internet connectivity despite evidence to the contrary.

Even if these computers were not connected to the internet, they were still connected to each other and controlled by a single workstation in the center of the AV Counting Board. The Detroit AV Counting Board computers were responsible for processing over 174,384 votes.[81]

Our vote tallies were not the only records under the control of a networked computer system at the TCF Center in Detroit—so were our pollbooks. During the January 28, 2021 testimony of the Chair of the Wayne County Board of Canvassers Monica Palmer before the Michigan Senate Oversight Committee, she shared a conversation between her and Michigan Bureau of Elections Director Jonathan Brater regarding election night operations at the TCF Center. Brater acknowledged in her call that "that system bogged down and they switched to the Qualified Voter File."[82] *That system* referred to the electronic pollbooks at the TCF Center. The only way to access the state hosted Qualified Voter File is via an internet connection. Such a connection of our election systems to the internet would provide bad actors with valuable intelligence related to voter turnout, who has not yet voted, and vote tallies that could be used to trigger contingency plans. This data could be used to "order" new mail-in ballots with which they could stuff the ballot box in order to obtain the desired results.

Why would so many election officials deny internet connectivity?

Either they don't know they are connected to the internet, or they do know but don't want others to know.

In fairness, voting system vendors consistently tell their customers that their equipment is not connected to the internet. Now mind you, their product manuals feature countless diagrams depicting how their devices connect to the internet. They offer modems in their quotes. The interface panels on their equipment have connectors for ethernet cables or USB-based modems. Some voting equipment even has wireless data modems installed on their motherboard, but they still say their equipment does not connect to the internet. How do they make that claim with a straight face? Word games.

Here's a sample of vendor jargon to be on the watch for:

"Your data is transferred over a cellular network"

"The system is not connected to the internet… during tabulation"

"We have a firewall"

"Your data is encrypted"

"We use secure VPN technology"

"Your system is air gapped"

Such vendor claims often result in reflexive claims by election officials that they are "not connected to the internet."

But is that true? In general, no. Why? Every one of those responses imply that the voting system IS connected to the internet. They simply attempt to hide that fact with security jargon. While there is a measure of protection afforded by firewalls, VPN's, encryption, and cellular networks, they all feature internet protocol-based interactions vulnerable to hacking. Vendors give their customers a false sense of security when they assert that their systems are "air gapped" and not connected to the internet.

During the August 2021 CyberSymposium hosted by Mike Lindell in Sioux Falls, South Dakota, an election voting system network was setup to conduct mock elections. The mock election system featured the same components used in many of our elections. Within five minutes of issuing a challenge to attendees to hack into this network, the network was compromised by an elected official who hacked into the system using his smartphone while watching the main presentation.

Firewalls can be hacked.

Encryption can be hacked.

VPN's can be hacked.

I guess there is a reason that I was never in sales.

Now, what happens when these elected officials know their systems are connected to the internet, but refuse to admit it? As a minimum, they are complicit with hiding critical security vulnerabilities. At worst, they are depending upon these vulnerabilities to steal the election.

Record Anomalies

We just saw how the process anomalies could have been used in a main attack. Now let's look at specific record anomalies related to pollbooks. For starters, Michigan voter records reveal that 171-year-old Jason Lemoyne Daniel of Flint, Michigan voted on October 7, 2020.[83] Either this is a sign of amazing dedication to civic duty by Jason or this should never have happened. While this is but one example, it is important to know exactly how this happened during the most "secure election in history." Why didn't the pollbook record prevent this from happening? It may reveal a more systemic problem.

During the preparation phase, we cited significant evidence that Michigan's Qualified Voter File had been seeded with ineligible voters prior to the election. Just because there are hundreds of thousands of ineligible voters in the voter registration database doesn't mean that they were able to follow Jason's lead and vote.

Was there any evidence that Jason's amazing accomplishment was repeated on a scale significant enough to overcome a 154,188 vote margin? Yes.

Dr. Doug Frank produced an analysis of voters against 2010 census data for counties across America.[84] He found that he could predict voter turnout during the 2020 election by demographic group in any county based upon 2010 census data. What does this indicate? It appears that someone was allocating ballots to voters using a machine-based algorithm. The formula driving the algorithm was consistent for each county within a given state but varied state to state.

Michigan was no exception. Dr. Frank analyzed voter data in the following counties to determine if the voter turnout aligned with his predictions:

- Wayne
- Oakland
- Macomb
- Kent
- Livingston
- Grand Traverse
- Barry
- Charlevoix
- Antrim

Every single county had a better than 99.3% correlation to his model. In the words of Dr. Frank, "That ain't natural buddy." In fact, the bellwether community of Macomb County featured a remarkable 100% correlation. This indicates that it was likely used to define the coefficients for Michigan's version of an algorithm to match voters to ballots (See Appendix A for more information).

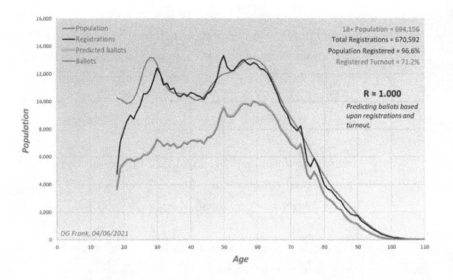

Figure 1 – Macomb County Correlation
Between Predicted and Actual Ballot Allocations

This further indicates that someone or some group of people had access to the voter rolls prior to the election and was systematically allocating ballots to voters listed in the qualified voter file. This activity is the defining characteristic of a ballot factory.

In fairness, just because it appears that ballots were allocated to voters based upon community demographics with highly improbable, machine-based precision, doesn't mean that the community didn't actually vote that way. How could we determine that Dr. Frank's analysis indicates widespread election fraud?

Canvassing.

Canvassing is essentially a field audit of the pollbooks. Canvassing simply answers the fundamental question: Do the pollbook records match what actually happened during the election? If a registered voter is said to have voted in the 2020 election, did they actually vote? Does the registered voter actually exist? In order to perform a canvass, citizens simply must obtain a transcript of who voted in the 2020 election complete with their address and whether or not they voted absentee or in person. This is all publicly available information. With this transcript in hand, they can knock on the doors of those who election officials said voted and simply ask them if they actually voted. Not very complicated. No need to ask them who they voted for. All they need to do is verify the publicly available information captured in the voter registration database.

Canvassing reveals if any of the following anomalies occurred:
- Someone voted who says they did not vote.
- Whether or not a voter actually lives at the specified address.
- Whether or not the address is really an address rather than an open field or sports arena.

In summary, canvassing lets us know if the pollbooks were effective in ensuring that only eligible voters are allowed to cast a ballot. In Maricopa County, Arizona, the canvassing effort was led by Liz Harris. In a state decided by only 10,457 votes, Liz and her team discovered evidence of 173,104 lost votes and 96,389 phantom votes. Lost votes pertain to registered voters who cast a vote (usually by mail) yet there is no record of their vote having been counted. Phantom votes pertain to votes being cast without a registered voter's knowledge, on behalf of a fictitious voter, or by a voter who moved away prior to the election.

Back in Michigan, there are also significant anomalies. Jacky Eubanks is a former elections worker at the Chesterfield Township Clerk Office in Macomb County where she specialized in the processing of absentee ballots. She quit her job as a congressional staffer in the wake of the 2020 election as a result of disgust with the lack of investigative action by state legislators. She formed a group of fellow citizens called the Concerned Citizens Initiative. Through their canvassing efforts, the group found that 17.6% of the people contacted resulted in voter file anomalies. In other words, 17.6% of the 494,219 votes cast for President in Macomb County were likely fraudulent. That translates to as many as 87,489 fraudulent votes in only one out of Michigan's eighty-three counties. If this 17.6% anomaly rate were to be found in other counties, as many as 974,917 votes may have been cast fraudulently in Michigan against a reported margin of victory for Joe Biden of 154,188. Remember, this vote gap corresponds to 2.78% vote margin. In other words, any anomaly rate greater than 2.78% qualifies as *significant* evidence.

The most common anomaly was when someone stated they had voted in person and not by mail as indicated in the statewide voter file. The second most common anomaly was when the person who voted did not live at the address indicated in the voter file. The third most common anomaly was an invalid address, which begs the question how did they get the ballot mailed to them? This last anomaly seems to indicate that the list of fake voters, known only to the Michigan secretary of state, found its way to some people who cast ballots in their name.

In addition to these anomalies, canvassers noted that there was greater than 100% voter registration in the majority of cities in Macomb County. Voter turnout was 10% higher than the historic average which was greater than 3 standard deviations from the mean variations. Furthermore, six out of ten of the most conservative cities in Macomb County saw *zero* change in the Trump percentage of vote from 2016 to 2020, but Biden received a greater percentage of votes in those cities than Hillary. For those of you keeping score, that adds up to more than 100% of the vote. Clearly, there was some massaging of the numbers in Macomb County that strain credulity.

So, what has been observed in other counties?

In Muskegon County, citizens investigating the 2020 election obtained a list of people who voted in the 2020 election but had not voted previously for twenty years. According to the National Voting Rights Act, these people should not have been listed in the qualified voter file at all, but they were. Furthermore, when contacted, seven out of the first ten people on this list asserted that they did not vote in the 2020 election.

A common theme across all of the canvassing efforts is that nursing homes and apartment complexes seem to be hotbeds for anomalies. Residents with cognitive disabilities were being registered to vote without their approval. In particular, there are significant anomalies among individuals who are 65 or older who registered to vote for the first time in 2020.

Canvassing of other counties in Michigan are ongoing at the time of this writing,[85] but early indications continue the theme of significant pollbook discrepancies… significant enough to account for a 154,188-vote margin.

There certainly seem to be significant issues with the integrity of voter information in the State of Michigan. Is there evidence that these integrity gaps were leveraged to cast fraudulent ballots? Yes.

Ballot harvesting activities were at the center of these subversion activities in Michigan.

For example, there is an affidavit which asserts that a woman was observed arriving in front of the Detroit Election Headquarters with three Tupperware containers filled with ballots taken from her SUV and dumped into an open postal collecting tray being carried by a postal worker. There is another affidavit from a worker swearing to have seen a gentleman dropping off boxes of ballots in a similar fashion in front of the Detroit Election Headquarters.[86] Investigators have also submitted an affidavit of witnessing a young woman visiting multiple nursing homes dropping off and picking up ballots from residents. Furthermore, I have been advised that the same evidence of ballot harvesting captured by True the Vote in Georgia is also evident in Michigan.[87]

Under Michigan law, ballot harvesting is only legal if an individual has been designated as an authorized assistant by an election official prior to engaging in ballot harvesting. In order to be an official authorized assistant, such harvesters should be able to answer the following questions per Michigan Public Act 116 of 1954, Section 168.764b (MCL 168.764b):

1. Were they asked by the clerk for the city of Detroit to be an assistant to accept delivery of absent voter ballots?
2. If so, when did they receive this designation for the 2020 general election?
3. Do they have any written communications to that effect which they could share?
4. Did they take an oath of office?
5. Did any of them have immediate family members who were candidates during the 2020 general election? Were they themselves candidates?

Prime targets for ballot harvesting are nursing homes and apartment complexes. Coincidentally, these locations are also sites of the highest anomaly rates for canvassing activities. Where else could ballot harvesters obtain ballots?

Let's look at ballot factories.

Remember, ballot factories are where low-propensity or phantom voters in the state voter registration file are matched with ballots. The fake voter data obtained by Jocelyn Benson when she sent out AV applications to many of the voters in Michigan's QVF would come in very handy for this exercise. Once low propensity or fake voters have been matched to ballots, these ballots are then stuffed into ballot envelopes and distributed en masse to tabulation centers or parsed out to ballot harvesting "mules" for them to place into the appropriate drop boxes. Evidence of ballot factories would supplement canvass-based evidence in the validation of Dr. Frank's assertion that voters were matched to ballots via a machine-based algorithm.

Was there evidence of a ballot factory in Michigan? Yes. Although further investigation is indeed warranted.

The third floor of the Detroit Elections Bureau is suspected to be a ballot factory. What leads one to suspect that this was the site of a ballot factory? Suspicions start with the observation that access to this location by poll challengers prior to the election was expressly forbidden ostensibly due to COVID-based rationale. It was then learned that the city of Detroit was in possession of a Relia-Vote solution that was deployed at this location. The Relia-Vote provides a turnkey solution for anyone interested in deploying a ballot factory. It is a machine that links with the state registered voter database, prints ballots, and even packs ballots in ballot envelopes. In the days before the election, the Detroit Elections Bureau was evasive in its response to inquiries about exactly how their Relia-Vote system would be used in the 2020 election. Poll challengers were denied the ability to observe this ballot processing system in action.[88]

There was another handy tool available to any aspiring ballot factory foreman courtesy of Dominion. The Dominion contract with the state of Michigan features what they refer to as the Mobile Ballot Printing Module. The module has the tag line, "Ballots when and where you want them." Using this tool, ballots could be printed at "vote centers," precincts, or the central office—you know, like the Detroit Elections Bureau. This module would indeed be a handy tool for anyone seeking to deploy a ballot factory.

Does a ballot factory need to be located in Michigan to impact Michigan elections? No.

Elections featuring mail-in ballots could be subverted by a ballot factory located anywhere in the world. Shipments of completed ballots could be packed in boxes and shipped to local operatives in Michigan who could discretely drop bundles of boxes off at election offices, drop boxes, or satellite voting centers.

Was there evidence of a ballot factory that could have supplied Michigan? Yes.

An alert security official discovered a possible ballot factory at the Wigwam Conference Center in Lynchfield Park, Arizona.[89] Upon walking into a conference center ballroom, he discovered that the room was filled with boxes of ballots sitting on tables throughout the ballroom. The ballots were organized into stacks and appeared to be readied for shipment. Potentially related to this discovery was the discovery of clandestine air shipments of ballots at the nearby Phoenix Airport. The ballots were reportedly secured by members of the Arizona National Guard.[90]

While none of these observations provide conclusive evidence of the existence of ballot factories, they certainly warrant further investigation by law enforcement along those lines.

What else was suspect during the main attack phase?

At the TCF Center in Detroit, Dominion Contractor Mellissa Carone observed batches of fifty ballots being recounted as many as eight times without resetting the counter at the tabulator.[91] She was not alone. Other poll challengers observed similar process infractions. Then there were the high error rates associated with tabulators in some jurisdictions. The Federal Election Commission VVSG 1.0 standard requires that voting systems exhibit no more than 1 error in 500,000 scans yet investigations of tabulator logs in Antrim County, Michigan, revealed an error rate of 68%.[92] In Central Lake Township alone, 1,222 out of 1,491 ballots cast were reversed, producing an 81.96% rejection rate. Why is there such a high error rate? Why is a high error rate a concern? High error rates are merely a nuisance in the case of poll-based voters. If the scanner fails to read a voter's ballot, the voter can correct their ballot on the spot and resubmit their ballot. High error rates for mail-in ballots, however, can be much more serious in jurisdictions where there is not a balanced party representation by those who are adjudicating the errors. At the Detroit AV Counting Board, there were high adjudication rates that sent thousands of ballots from tabulators to adjudication stations often manned by pairs of Democrats with GOP challengers straining to look past "walls" of Democrat operatives deliberately blocking their views.[93] To make matters even more concerning, the city of Detroit neglected to hire a balanced number of Republican and Democrat poll workers to staff the AV Counting Board. That means that the adjudication of ballot scanning errors was typically left in the hands of Democrat poll workers in violation of state law.

Under Michigan law, all counting centers are subject to public supervision.

Was there any evidence of ballots being counted at centers not open to the public?

Yes. The first example of such a center has been referred to as the Chicago warehouse. Despite the name, it was located in Detroit. Why would there be a location called the Chicago warehouse in Detroit?

IT contractor Mellissa Carone was trained to maintain tabulation and adjudication equipment for Dominion Voting Systems in Detroit. Her original assignment location on election night was the Detroit Elections Bureau. It was an odd assignment since the Detroit Elections Bureau is not a recognized precinct or counting board and therefore should not have any tabulator or adjudication equipment.

Miss Carone had safety concerns with this assignment due to the designated parking location. She requested reassignment and was subsequently moved to the Detroit Absentee Vote Counting Board at the TCF Center in Detroit. During her shift at the TCF Center, she noted that one of the election workers split time between the TCF Center and what this worker referred to as the "Chicago Warehouse."[94] Later inquiries appear to indicate that the Chicago Warehouse referred to the third floor of the Detroit Elections Bureau.

Remember, Poll Challengers had previously been denied access to the third floor of the Detroit Elections Bureau by Detroit Elections officials.

The same worker who split time between the TCF Center and the Chicago Warehouse was also one of two individuals responsible for entering in the final vote tallies into the election management system at the TCF Center. Why these vote tallies required manual entries when all the tabulator and adjudicator workstations were networked to the election management system remains unknown. A forensic audit would likely shed significant light on the answer to this question.

Another suspected counting center that was closed to the public was also in Detroit at the Northwest Activities center. Poll challengers observed a team of approximately one dozen young men unloading voting equipment and other supplies. Upon questioning, the youths indicated that they were planning to count votes at the facility. Furthermore, a young lady was observed at the facility collecting ballots from voters in their cars with a ballot collection cannister on wheels.[95]

Additional support of the assertion that ballot factories were active in Detroit is another interesting observation. At 9:57 p.m. on election night, the *Detroit Free Press* published an online story entitled "Detroit election officials project Voter turnout highest in 20 to 30 years." The story features an interview with Detroit City Clerk Janice Winfrey. The clerk is quoted as having said that "80,000 absentee ballots have been counted as of 7:30 p.m. out of a total of roughly 120,000 absentee ballots that were received."[96] What is interesting about that statement is that, according to the official statement of votes, 174,384 ballots were cast.[97] Where did the extra 54,384 ballots come from between 9:57 p.m. on November 3 and the certification of the vote on November 17?

By themselves, these events are suspicious, but not clear evidence of fraud. When combined with other evidence, however, it starts to paint a pretty compelling case for systemic fraud. A forensic audit of the 2020 election would prove this case. Attempts to perform a forensic audit have been fought at every turn. If there is nothing to hide, why fight against such an audit?

Influence Operations

During the main attack phase, COVID rules were at the center of influence operation activities. It was clear that the court injunction against the Michigan Bureau of Elections six-foot rule was not shared with poll workers at the TCF Center in Detroit. When poll challengers provided evidence of the injunction to poll workers, they insisted on enforcing social distancing, effectively prohibiting poll challengers from observing their activities in violation of state law.

There were numerous examples of interference with poll challenger duties at the TCF Center in Detroit that went beyond the invalid six-foot rule. Most notably, many poll workers refused to insert challenges into pollbook journals. Without these journal entries, the Board of Canvassers would be unaware of pollbook or ballot issues as they deliberate on whether to certify the election or not.

Influence operations took on more subtle forms as well. For example, the central nerve center of the Detroit AV Counting Board controlling the operations of 134 AV counting boards, 25 tabulator workstations, and 12 adjudication workstations for 174,384 votes was designed to be inaccessible by poll challengers. This nerve center was surrounded by adjudication workstations so that it was not possible to access the nerve center without violating the invalid six-foot rule still being promoted by Detroit election officials. Poll challengers who attempted to access the nerve center were told to leave.

Poll challenger observation of operations at the nerve center were important. This oversight would help to ensure that the chain of custody regarding key election records such as the all-important vote tally was truly secured. The routing of ballot images from twenty-five tabulators to twelve adjudicators clearly had to be controlled from somewhere. There was no direct connection between a single tabulator and a single adjudicator. They were all cross connected via either a managed switch or router. Because of this arrangement, the data needed to be routed between devices by an election official or some automated algorithm. When election officials were asked by poll challengers how ballots and votes were routed among the various workstations, they responded that they didn't know. Poll challengers were only able to view terminal operations at the nerve center from a distance of fifteen feet or more. In spite of these challenges, I personally observed unexplained mass file transfers on nerve center computers. The data moved during these transfers could range from tabulator ballot images, pollbook entries, or vote tallies. Without a full forensic audit of the machines at the Detroit AV Counting Board, it is extremely difficult to discern whether or not the operations at this nerve center were lawful or not.

Summary

In summary, we have shown the following evidence of predicted main attack phase tactics being employed successfully in Michigan:

- For the first time in history, the number of mail-in ballots cast exceeded the number of poll-based ballots.
- The Michigan secretary of state changed the processing of mail-in ballots from a decentralized process implemented by local clerks to a centralized process driven by data provided by the state.
- There is evidence that voters were matched to ballots via machine-based algorithms.
- Ballot harvesting was observed despite being against the law.
- There is evidence of suspicious access prohibitions and equipment that would enable ballot factories in the city of Detroit.
- COVID was leveraged to obstruct oversight of election processes.
- Post-election canvassing indicates that as many as 974,917 fraudulent votes may have been cast in Michigan during the 2020 general election.

Is it possible to know exactly how many votes may have been fraudulently inserted in the main attack phase as a result of ballot stuffing? No, because once a ballot is cast, we have no way to connect a specific ballot to a voter. We cast secret ballots in America. Secret ballots are a very good thing—except when it comes to auditing. Once a ballot is submitted into a tabulator, we have no way of identifying which voter cast which ballot. So, we don't know if the votes cast on a given ballot were cast fraudulently or not. Which means we don't know how many of the votes cast for a given candidate were fraudulent. Thanks to the canvassing efforts of "meddling kids" in the wake of the election, we do now have a pretty good idea of how many fraudulent ballots were cast, but the scale of this fraud was virtually undetectable on election night.

The main attack phase had one critical flaw, though. A stealthy, mail-in ballot stuffing campaign depends upon an accurate prediction of voter turnout. An accurate prediction of voter turnout enables one to calculate how many ballots would be needed to be manufactured and stuffed into drop boxes in order to sway the results of an election.

As late as August 14, 2020, progressive think tanks, such as the Brookings Institution, predicted a record nationwide voter turnout of 145 million voters during the November 3, 2020, election.[98]

The actual nationwide voter turnout? Almost 160 million people.

While they did accurately predict a record turnout, they undershot the total number of ballots cast by almost 15 million votes. A 15 million-vote shortfall translates to a potential 10% vote margin shortfall in races within battleground states such as Michigan which were often decided by less than 5% margins.

Shortly after midnight on November 4, this shortfall revealed the first sign of trouble for the main attack phase. The Associated Press called the race for Trump in Florida at 12:34 a.m. At that time, Trump led Biden by over 375,000 votes in Florida with 96% of the precincts reporting.

Florida was a critical state. Trump's opponents needed a backup plan if they were to avoid a repeat of the disappointing 2016 election with Hillary Clinton.

Not long after Florida was called for Trump, ballot counts slowed to a trickle in large municipalities such as Detroit. Despite having bins full of military ballots available to count, poll workers at most of the counting boards at the TCF Center were not counting, processing, or doing anything related to election work.

It was quiet. Too quiet.

BACKUP ATTACK

You've now seen evidence of preparations to steal the election by creating weaknesses in our election system. You've seen evidence of a mail-in ballot main attack designed to stuff the ballot box with fraudulent votes. You've also seen that this main attack phase was at risk of not being successful due to a record-breaking voter turnout that exceeded pre-election predictions by more than 10%.

Was there evidence of a backup attack being executed? Yes. Remember, the goal of the backup attack phase would be to leverage networked electronic voting systems to modify the vote tally directly in order to ensure a fraudulent victory.

Process Anomalies

As November 4 progressed, GOP affiant Matt Mikolajczak noticed a change in tone from Election Day at the TCF Center in Detroit. In contrast to the passive-aggressive posture of Democrat poll workers towards Republican poll challengers on November 3, Democrat poll workers were now overtly hostile, causing some Republican challengers to leave the hall and go home. Accusations of taking videos and pictures were levied against many poll challengers. When Jennifer asked one of the accusers if he was referring to her, the worker yelled, "you people ain't allowed to talk to us! Shut your mother*cking mouth, racist!" Another poll worker called her a mother f*cking co****cker and a racist.[99]

It was rapidly becoming an unbearably hostile work environment for many poll challengers, but not all poll workers exhibited hostility. Some were simply attempting to process election returns with integrity. Jessy Jacob was notably one of these poll workers with integrity.

GOP challenger and affiant Polly McNichol watched as a supervisor named Mrs. C brought an estimated five hundred ballots down from the raised platform in the center of the absentee vote counting board. She distributed them to three poll workers located next to the platform. Each ballot had a yellow sticky note on it. The workers began entering the ballots into the Qualified Voter File system. Polly and GOP challenger attorney Jessica Connarn asked a Department of Elections (DOE) official in a gray polo shirt, who was standing on the platform, what the three poll workers are doing. Per her affidavit, the official "was instantly combative and refused to tell our attorney anything, including his name."[100] The man not only watched the poll workers intently, but even used his phone, even though they are strictly prohibited, to record challengers and poll workers from the raised platform. McNichol continued to observe ballot processing with a fellow GOP challenger.

Shortly after the confrontation with the Detroit election official, Ms. Connarn spotted Jessy Jacob, one of the poll workers, attempting to pass her a yellow sticky note. Connarn retrieved the note after Jacob intentionally dropped it on the floor. It read: "Entered receive date as 11/2/20 on 11/4/20. JJ."

Minutes later, Jessy Jacob walked very close to McNichol and quietly murmured something that sounds like bathroom. Seeing the combative DOE official watching her and Jacob like a hawk, McNichol decided not to follow Jacob. Instead, McNichol quietly asked another GOP challenger, Julie Maday, to run and meet Jacob in the bathroom. Following a restroom rendezvous, Maday returned with another sticky note from Jacob with a more explicit description: "Received into QVF on 11/4/20 was asked to enter the ballot received date as 11/2/20."

The DOE official then yelled at the three poll workers not to talk to the GOP challengers or to show them anything. A while later, Jessy Jacob turned her laptop so McNichol could see the screen. McNichol testified that she saw "a large signature that consisted of a bunch of circular shapes. [She] looked at the signature on the secrecy sleeve for that ballot and it was a very small signature consisting of a bunch of little vertical lines. No part of either signature looked anything like the other."[101]

Mrs. Jacob did her best to highlight clear violations of the law to poll challengers in the presence of an overtly hostile Detroit election official. It is the responsibility of law enforcement officials to protect citizens such as Jessy. That didn't happen.

Against the backdrop of DOE officials mercilessly enforcing fake laws and fake rules, law enforcement officials failed to enforce any actual laws and rules. This is perhaps the single greatest process anomaly of the 2020 election. During the backup attack phase alone, there is evidence of numerous Michigan election laws being violated many times over.[102] Law enforcement was simply not enforcing the law especially in cities like Detroit. What good is it to have election laws if these laws are not enforced?

Michigan Public Act 116 of 1954 Section 168.735 states:

(1) At each primary and election, election inspectors shall keep 1 pollbook and 1 poll list. An election inspector shall enter in the pollbook, in the order in which electors are given ballots, the name of each elector who is given a ballot and immediately after the name, on the same line, shall enter the number of the ballot given to the elector. For an absent voter ballot, when an election inspector removes the ballot from the sealed absent voter envelope, the election inspector shall enter in the pollbook the name of the absent voter and the number of the ballot.

(2) If an elector is issued a provisional ballot, an election inspector shall enter a proper designation in the pollbook, including whether the provisional ballot was tabulated in the precinct or was secured for verification after the election.

(3) At the completion of the precinct canvass, an election inspector shall record on the certificate provided in the pollbook the number of each metal seal used to seal voting equipment and ballot containers. Each member of the board of election inspectors shall sign the certificate.

Despite this law, in Detroit, four not one unique instance of pollbooks were being used. These unique instances were (1) the initial e-pollbook downloaded onto counting board laptops, (2) the supplemental paper pollbooks included with ballots delivered to the AV Counting Board during the middle of night, (3) a "virtual" pollbook in which voters not in either of the previously mentioned pollbooks were added manually to the electronic pollbooks by poll workers on election night, and (4) some poll workers with internet access also added voters directly to the state QVF. One could also add a fifth pollbook to the equation if one were to add the pollbook instance used to screen in-person voters at the voting precincts. This is a real problem. That is illegal and it is exactly what one expects to see in the case of any attempt to steal an election.

To make matters worse, all challenged ballots were counted right along with the non-challenged ballots. This should be concerning in light of the large number of challenges which were not captured by poll workers in the pollbooks. The fake "voter suppression" narrative appears to have been used to incentivize a reckless bias towards counting any ballot regardless of verification status.

Under Michigan Public Act 116 of 1954, Section 168.734, interference with poll challenger duties is subject to fines and/or imprisonment.

> Any officer or election board who shall prevent the presence of any such challenger as above provided, or shall refuse or fail to provide such challenger with conveniences for the performance of the duties expected of him, shall, upon conviction, be punished by a fine not exceeding $1,000.00, or by imprisonment in the state prison not exceeding 2 years, or by both such fine and imprisonment in the discretion of the court.

Poll challengers were routinely prohibited from executing their duties by election officials at the Detroit AV Counting Board.

Under Michigan Public Act 116 of 1954, Section 168.727, challenges made by poll challengers must immediately be entered by election inspectors into the pollbooks.

(1) An election inspector shall challenge an applicant applying for a ballot if the inspector knows or has good reason to suspect that the applicant is not a qualified and registered elector of the precinct, or if a challenge appears in connection with the applicant's name in the registration book. A registered elector of the precinct present in the polling place may challenge the right of anyone attempting to vote if the elector knows or has good reason to suspect that individual is not a registered elector in that precinct. An election inspector or other qualified challenger may challenge the right of an individual attempting to vote who has previously applied for an absent voter ballot and who on election day is claiming to have never received the absent voter ballot or to have lost or destroyed the absent voter ballot.

(2) Upon a challenge being made under subsection (1), an election inspector shall immediately do all of the following:

(a) Identify as provided in sections 745 and 746 a ballot voted by the challenged individual, if any.

(b) Make a written report including all of the following information:

(i) All election disparities or infractions complained of or believed to have occurred.

(ii) The name of the individual making the challenge.

(iii) The time of the challenge.

(iv) The name, telephone number, and address of the challenged individual.

(v) Other information considered appropriate by the election inspector.

(c) Retain the written report created under subdivision

(b) and make it a part of the election record.

(d) Inform a challenged elector of his or her rights under section 729.

(3) A challenger shall not make a challenge indiscriminately and without good cause. A challenger shall not handle the pollbooks while observing election procedures or the ballots during the counting of the ballots. A challenger shall not interfere with or unduly delay the work of the election inspectors. An individual who challenges a qualified and registered elector of a voting precinct for the purpose of annoying or delaying voters is guilty of a misdemeanor.

Despite this provision in law, challenges by poll challengers were routinely denied by poll inspectors. Failure to incorporate these challenges into the pollbook meant that county canvassers would not have access to this information when considering whether or not to certify the election. Poll challenges would not therefore be subject to inquiry until lawsuits are filed and tried.

There were significant violations of the spirit if not the letter of MCL 168 .765 which among other stipulations requires at least 1 election inspector from each major political party to be present at a location. As previously mentioned, the city of Detroit did not have balanced representation at their AV Counting Board. Bi-partisan poll inspectors were not present to oversee execution of many of the AV Counting Board procedures.

The violations of election continued. There is evidence that there were numerous provisions of MCL 168.765a, which were not adhered to.[103] Absentee ballots were not stored in approved containers nor were they sealed properly. Plus, approximately 50% of the poll workers on duty left the AVCB at 7:30 p.m. which is before polls closed at 8:00 p.m. Furthermore, AVCB instructions were not made available to the public as required.

Finally, there are numerous affidavits citing violations of MCL 168.931 including one attesting to seeing City of Detroit election workers coaching voters to vote for Joe Biden.[104]

Election laws are often implemented to prevent the recurrence of fraudulent behavior from previous elections. Failure to enforce such laws merely encourages election fraud.

Record Anomalies

Let's move beyond general process observations and look at some concerning anomalies with election records.

One peculiar observation regarding the election night reporting of vote tallies pertains to the formatting of the election results data stream. According to testimony provided in the Antrim County court case, vote tally data is tabulated by race and candidate. Election results tables in the precincts feature integer-based whole numbers. There are no decimal places. Yet somewhere between the precinct tabulators and the Edison Research vote tally reports there was a switch in vote tally format from integers to decimals. [105] Instead of tracking the cumulative vote tallies for each candidate in integer format, only the vote tally was represented as an integer in the Edison Research data stream sent to media outlets. The votes for a given candidate were now reflected as a decimal percentage of that total vote—out to only three significant figures.

Why is this significant?

For one thing, in each state millions of votes are cast. In Michigan, 5,579,317. votes were reportedly cast. When a candidate's votes are presented as a product of the total vote and the candidate vote percentage, the actual vote tally reported could be off by thousands of votes due to rounding errors. Why would someone convert from a 100% accurate reporting format to one subject to a rounding error? An audit of the vote tally reporting would help to answer this question—starting with exactly who that "someone" might be.

Another pertinent observation is that tracking election results by the percent of total votes received by a given candidate is an ideal variable for a digital PID controller setpoint. Using cumulative vote tallies as a setpoint would not guarantee victory for a given candidate. Using the percentage of total votes as your setpoint would.

Mike Lindell's *Absolute Proof* documentary series shared evidence of cyber-based attacks shifting votes across all fifty states including a reported shift of 202,657 votes from Trump to Biden in Michigan.

Remember the SolarWinds cyberattack? A professional cyber investigation in the wake of this attack not only revealed that the security of eighteen thousand SolarWinds customers was compromised prior to the 2020 election, it also revealed that Dominion was a customer of Solar-Winds.[106] Other voting system manufacturers may have been customers of SolarWinds as well, but we only have evidence that Dominion was one of their customers at this time. SolarWinds provides rather expensive IT network monitoring services. SolarWinds platforms would come in very handy, if you were seeking to remotely update or monitor thousands of electronic voting system components across the twenty-eight states that used Dominion machines in the 2020 election. Could the SolarWinds hack have opened the door to the attacks revealed in Mike Lindell's documentary?

In Lindell's documentary series, he showed the IP address of the source of the main attack and destination of the main attack along with a summary of the votes changed during the main attack. It would be very illuminating to see if any of the IP addresses revealed in the Lindell documentaries correlate at all with any of the devices connected to the Dominion SolarWinds platform.

It would also be useful to examine whether or not there were any mechanisms available in the electronic voting systems that could be used to convert this compromised security into changed votes. If we understand the mechanisms by which votes could be switched, we could investigate to see if there is any evidence of such mechanisms.

As it turns out, we do have evidence of mechanisms that could be used to change votes.

Remember the VIF _CHOICE_INSTANCE.DVD file? It controls the allocation of votes for each ballot. If installed on a networked device, this file could be modified in much the same way as the Stuxnet virus modified the settings for the Iranian centrifuge controllers.[107]

Remember the installation of SQL Server Management Studio software? It allows someone to manipulate records in a database such as a qualified voter file, electronic pollbook, tabulator database, or election management server database. If installed on a device connected to the internet, SQL scripts could be installed and executed remotely in response to changing election conditions.

You may ask yourself, but what about the ballot images? Wouldn't an examination of ballot images indicate a discrepancy with the vote tallies? Remember, ballot images are electronic files. PDFs of the ballots are available months before an election. Plenty of time to create fake ballot images that can be inserted as needed. Plus, at the 2019 DefCon, hackers showed how to create fake ballot images on the fly.[108]

Wait a second, though. A hand recount is all that is needed to expose any ballot image manipulation. Not really. First, there is no way to guarantee a given ballot was cast by an eligible voter once the stub that connects the ballot to a given voter is torn off in preparation for tabulator processing. Second, in a high profile recount, bad actors would likely take the risk of swapping out physical ballots. This is why chain of custody around ballot containers is extremely important.

Bottom line? Digital voting systems make it easier than ever to steal an election. Change the vote tallies, then change the ballot images, then change the pollbooks, which then change the statewide voter registration file once synchronized. When your election system is digital, all these adjustments can be made without anyone noticing. Poll challengers are effectively rendered useless when it comes to monitoring the digital execution of what used to be manual election processes.

So, is this scenario too much of a stretch? Surely such subversion would be readily recognized if executed for real, right?

In August of 2021, Mike Lindell hosted a cybersecurity symposium in Sioux Falls, South Dakota. Skeptics from all over the world were in attendance. Once again, one of the exhibits at the symposium was a mock-up of an election using software and equipment that was used in the 2020 election. More than sixteen demonstrations of the theft of an election were provided to observers less than six feet away from all election equipment which was in full view. Nothing was hidden. Paper ballots were reviewed. No one discovered how the election was stolen during any of the demonstrations—and they were at the conference to find evidence of election fraud.

In this light, what are the odds that such subversion could be executed under the guise of COVID restrictions designed to obstruct observation of election records? What are the odds that such subversion could be executed when there is not 24/7 monitoring of election records?

The only way to rule out such a scenario is to demonstrate that the chain of custody regarding key election records such as the qualified voter file, pollbooks, ballots, and vote tallies had been maintained. Forensic audits of these records are the only way to examine the chain of custody. That is why recounts are insufficient to determine the integrity of an election. Forensic audits of all election records are the only way to truly prove the integrity of an election.

Another record anomaly that needs to be addressed is the suspicion from vote tally observation that suggests as many as 289,866 ballots were cast fraudulently in Michigan.

When one looks at the number of ballots tabulated across specific locations within select time periods and cross references that data with the tabulation capacity of the tabulators in those locations, we find that impossible vote tally results were found. In about two and a half hours, the Michigan counties of Kent, Macomb, Oakland, and Wayne reported that they had processed 384,733 ballots. This is an extraordinary achievement when one considers that these counties only had the tabulator capacity to process 94,867 ballots in that amount of time. That means that 289,866 more ballots were processed than the counties had the capacity to process.[109] Either (1) these counties had additional tabulators not known to the public, which would be a serious oversight issue, (2) vote tallies were being accumulated for large vote tally dumps in contrast to consistent reporting intervals aligned with capabilities of voting systems, or (3) someone was entering vote tally data directly into election result databases without the use of tabulators processing ballots.

One of the most interesting vote tally reporting anomalies was first brought to my attention by Draza Smith. This anomaly appears to provide compelling evidence of the existence of a digital controller manipulating election results. During the early hours of the day after the election, President Trump had a comfortable lead in all the battleground states. He led in Pennsylvania (56-43, a lead of just under 700,000 votes), Georgia (51-48, a lead of nearly 120,000 votes), Michigan (53-45, a lead of nearly 295,000 votes), Wisconsin (51-47, a lead of more than 116,000 votes), and North Carolina (50-49, a lead of nearly 77,000 votes).[110]

That all changed after Florida was called in favor of President Trump at 12:34 a.m.

Prior to this event, there was a consistent ratio of Trump to Biden votes being reported. The trendline for this ratio would have ensured Trump victories in multiple battleground states. After Florida was called, the frequency of the reporting intervals slowed. While Trump votes continued on the same basic trajectory, the Biden votes started narrowing the gap with a series of step changes that brought the Trump to Biden vote ratio to near 50:50 in multiple states.

Then we saw a series of "resets" across all fifty states that some refer to as the "Edison Reset" because the election night reports are aggregated and streamed by a company called Edison Research. During the wee hours of November 4, 2020, the cumulative vote tally for each state was reset to zero. In Michigan, the timestamp for the reset was 2020-11-04T10:00:04Z or 5:00:04 a.m. Eastern Standard Time. This is exactly what one would expect to see if the setpoint on a PID controller was adjusted. After the Edison Reset, all precincts begin reporting the same vote split between Democrats and Republicans. From that point forward, if you know the Democrat voter turnout, you can predict the Republican voter turnout with 98% certainty.

It certainly appears that there was some sort of digital controller manipulating the results to achieve a specific objective. A forensic audit of election night reporting records would provide significant insights into the presence of a digital controller. It would be very interesting to trace the complete chain of vote tally handoffs starting with the precinct tabulators through county vote aggregators all the way to the results portrayed on your favorite cable news network.

Performing such an audit of the vote tally would also likely help us get to the bottom of how negative vote increments occur.[111] The Edison Reset was an extreme negative vote increment all the way to zero, but we also have multiple accounts of less dramatic negative vote increments occurring on live TV in the wake of the election. Drop 1 shows a loss of 113,870 votes for Trump in Pennsylvania on CNN between 9:16 p.m. and 9:17 p.m. on election night. Drop 2 shows a loss of 11,490 Trump votes and 17,170 Biden votes in Georgia results between 1:12 and 1:13 a.m. the day after the election. Drop 3 occurs between 9:53 and 9:54 p.m. on 11/4/20 in Georgia as well. It features a drop of 700 votes for Trump and 652 votes for Biden. Drop 4 occurred on CNBC between 9:16 and 9:24 p.m. on election night. Trump lost 66,085 votes and Biden dropped by 25,771 votes in Pennsylvania. Drop 5 occurred between 11:09 and 11:10 p.m. on CNN. Trump lost 19,958 votes while Biden gained 19,958 votes. Drop 6 occurred on CNN between 2:04 and 2:05 p.m. on 11/4/20. Trump dropped 666 votes and Biden dropped 312 votes in Pennsylvania. Drop 7 was another Pennsylvania vote drop on CNN. This time the vote drop occurred between 2:42 and 2:43 p.m. on 11/4/20. Trump dropped 149 votes and Biden dropped 85 votes. Drop 8 occurred on Fox. Between 11:44 and 11:45 p.m. on election night, Trump lost 121,090 votes and Biden lost 426,921 votes in Virginia. Drop 9 also pertained to Virginia. On Telemundo between 11:41 and 11:47 p.m. on election night, Trump dropped 121,090 votes while

Biden lost 426,921 votes. The subject of drop 10 was the Minnesota presidential vote count. On ABC between 10:37 and 10:40 p.m. ET on election night, Trump lost 104,312 votes while Biden dropped 80,916 votes. Drop 11 occurred on CNN and pertained to Florida. Between 7:57 and 7:58 p.m. on election night, Trump lost 12,650 votes. Regardless of the vote tally impacts of these results, there is no legitimate reason why the CUMULATIVE vote tallies would show negative vote increments. Vote tallies should only be increasing in a normal election.

We also need to get to the bottom of how total precincts reporting can be posted as 96% one moment and 94% minutes later. Data was being manipulated in an unnatural manner somewhere along the way. We need to know who exactly in the vote tally chain of custody was performing this manipulation. Do you think it is mere coincidence that attempts by investigators to examine electronic election records such as transaction logs, pollbooks, software configurations, router configurations, and IP addresses are routinely obstructed by election officials and vendors?

In Antrim County, a traditionally red county, the initial election results revealed that Joe Biden had defeated Donald Trump. Biden received 7,769 votes to only 4,509 for Trump. Subsequent recounts revealed that Trump, not Biden, was the appropriate victor, but the initial vote tally would likely have been certified if Antrim County citizen Bill Bailey had not questioned the results.

The official explanation for the 7,060-vote switch is that the errant tally was a result of human error. We are told that the clerk failed to update the ballot configurations on the tabulator Compact Flash (CF) Cards to reflect late ballot changes. These CF Cards are simply removable storage devices similar to USB flash drives that contain instructions for the tabulators. Court exhibits provided by Attorney Matt DePerno and affiant Jeff Lenberg bring the official version of what happened into question. Jeff Lenberg demonstrated how security vulnerabilities in the Dominion voting equipment could be exploited to shift the votes in the manner observed.[112]

There are at least two ways to detect whether or not such a shift occurred. One is a hand recount of the actual ballots counted on Election Day, which presumes that the ballot chain of custody has been maintained and that the ballots were submitted by eligible voters. The other way to detect the shift is to review the VIF _CHOICE_INSTANCE. DVD file or equivalent for any vote shifting algorithms. This information would only be discovered in a thorough forensic audit of election equipment and removable storage devices. Transaction logs would be needed for such an audit. These transaction logs were deleted. This deletion of election records is against federal law.

Now let's see if we have any ballot anomalies. Election fraud investigators are told to look at the ballots. We are repeatedly told that the ballots are the ultimate indicators of election integrity. So, was there anything unusual about ballots that should be noted?

In Grand Rapids poll workers returned from a short break only to find that the stacks of ballots they intended to process after their break had disappeared. When inquiries were made as to where the ballots went, the poll workers were told that they were sent to Detroit for processing. Detroit is a two-and-a-half-hour drive from Grand Rapids. This would seem to be an indication of how "lost votes" such as those cataloged in the Maricopa County, Arizona audit become "lost." Lost votes are when a voter swears that they cast a vote, but voting records reveal that their ballot was never counted. It should be noted that the Grand Rapids area of Michigan is significantly more Republican than most other areas of Michigan. Anyone seeking to assist Joe Biden's vote tally illegally would likely have the destruction of Republican ballots in their bag of tricks.

Another ballot anomaly involved haphazard ballot markings. One of the poll challengers in Detroit made the following observation:

The thing that bothered me most was that almost every ballot was for Biden with a few exceptions for Trump. Many of these ballots had just X's in the boxes as if filled in haphazardly. I questioned whether they would be counted because the boxes weren't shaded and I was told they would go through fine.[113]

How would an X "go through fine"? An X would be sufficient for a recount but would likely result in a scanning error during machine tabulation. That raises some questions: What if the vote tally was already pre-determined? What if all that was needed was a certain number of ballots in the ballot box that, if tallied by hand, would agree with the pre-determined vote tally?

There were more ballot anomalies including late night ballot drops at the rear entrance of the TCF Center well after the polls had been closed. Perhaps these ballot drops explain the 54,384-ballot difference between the absentee ballot count provided by Detroit City Clerk at 9:57 p.m. on election night and the final count certified by county canvassers? I witnessed these drops in the wee hours of the morning of November 4 firsthand, but you can witness them as well in video footage obtained via FOIA by the Gateway Pundit.[114] Here is a timeline account of what happened on November 4, the day after the election:[115]

At 3:11 a.m. a black sports car arrives outside the sally port directly adjacent to the AVCB [Absentee Vote Counting Board] room and a man walks out of the AVCB, approaches the car and appears to exchange something with the driver at 3:17 am. The car then turns around and drives off at 3:18 am.

At 3:25 a.m. a white van arrives at the same port. Men get out and unload an estimated 50-60 boxes of what appear to be thousands of ballots and bring them inside the TCF room on a dolly. Multiple GOP challengers on scene would later report them as being positively identified as ballots. Former State Elections Director Chris Thomas, who was assigned to the TCF center as Senior Advisor to City Clerk Janice Winfrey, will later state in a deposition: "No absentee ballots received after the deadline of 8:00 p.m. on November 3, 2020, were received by or processed at the TCF Center."

At approximately 4:00 a.m. GOP affiant William Carzon notices the white City of Detroit van, which is marked "Vote Mobile," arriving at the AVCB's rear entrance sally port. He watches an estimated 60 postal boxes with cardboard sleeves being unloaded and taken to the receiving tables. When the sleeves are removed, he identifies the manila envelopes containing absentee ballots.

At 6:30 a.m. challenger and affiant Ulrike Sherer returns and, throughout the morning, observes numerous ballots being "verified" despite their not being present in the e-pollbook or the absentee voter lists. She describes these ballots as "sequential, highly suggestive of fraud." This disturbing observation would later be echoed in detail at the House Oversight Committee testimony by GOP challenger Hima Kolanagireddy, who also observed sequential absentee ballots being processed.

Under MCL 168.765, absentee ballots received after the close of the polls shall be plainly marked with the time and date of receipt and filed in the clerk's office. They are not to be counted. At the TCF Center in Detroit, however, there is evidence to suggest that these ballots were counted. While the exact number of mail bins asserted by poll challengers and election officials vary, there is no denying that a significant number of mail bins were delivered in this manner. In fact, as many as 68 mail bins may have handled in this manner. Each bin has the capacity to hold 350 ballots in envelopes. Using these figures, as many as 23,800 fraudulent votes may have been counted at the Detroit AV Counting Board during the 2020 general election.

If a digital controller was used to modify the vote tallies directly, someone would have had to make sure there were a sufficient number of ballots stuffed into ballot boxes to cover their tracks. These late-night deliveries of thousands of absentee ballots almost eight hours after the polls were closed would seem to indicate that last-minute ballot stuffing of some sort occurred.

In case you are inclined to think this scenario is merely partisan conjecture, please consider the claims made by Democrat Mayoral Candidate for Detroit, Tom Barrow, in his recount petition.[116] Mr. Barrow cited the following factual claims in his petition:

1. Prior to August 3, 2021, the city of Detroit entered into a contract with Accuform Printing and Graphics (and or other unknown vendors) hereinafter "the printer" to supply ballots to be used by the city in its August 3, 2021, primary election.

2. The ballots ordered, among others, included "precinct" and "AVCB" ballots and pre-oval filled "test" ballots. The "test" ballot ovals being perfectly shaded in and pre-marked using lithographic printer ink with candidate names.

3. The test ballots are identical in appearance to regular "precinct" and "AVCB" ballots but are never accounted for.

4. As set forth in its contract, the printer is required to print the precinct number on each ballot, and sequentially number ballots beginning with the number one up to the number of ballots ordered for each precinct. All ballots are required to be bundled and delivered in cellophane packs of 100.

5. Prior to the election, the printer delivered the ballots as ordered but to the same malfeasant city actors and officials believed to have engaged in this and prior fraudulent acts described previously.

6. At the time of delivery, the printer also prepared and delivered its manifest, bill of lading and/or packing slip and

invoice for their services. The documents, along with the printer's contract, explicitly depict the number of "ballots" and "test ballots" ordered and the number delivered in fulfillment of the contract.

7. The identical official looking "test ballots" are in numbers substantially beyond that necessary for the accuracy test procedure or for training.

8. At the time of delivery, and without knowledge of the printer, malfeasant city actors removed an unknown number of the packs of 100 ballots from varying precincts and AVCBs and secreted those for later insertion into the precincts and counting boards once the polls have closed.

9. The number of each style and type ballot, both printed and delivered, is readily determined by a subpoena of the printer's contract, invoices, bills of lading, change orders and corresponding manifest and packing slips.

10. This petitioner is prepared to testify that during the August 3, 2021, day he received dozens of telephone calls from absentee electors complaining that after timely submitting the applications, they never received their ballots.

11. Sometime around 10:45 p.m. and thereafter on August 3, 2021, a van, with the words "Mobile Voting" on the side, was observed repeatedly entering and leaving the TCF Center Absentee Voter Counting Board area from which thousands of believed false ballots were unloaded.

12. Around 1 a.m., a black luxury SUV vehicle also arrived and was observed entering the TCF center from which additional absentee ballots were observed to be unloaded.

13. Malfeasant actors or contractors, then caused the insertion of the fraudulent "test" and previously secreted regular ballots into the absentee cases which were observed to still be open and unsealed.

14. That this Petitioner is reliably informed that the facts in paragraph 11 and 12 was observed by multiple election challengers and city employees.

Much as what was reported during the early morning hours of November 4, 2020, Mr. Barrow cited late night drops of ballots. Mr. Barrow lost in his primary election bid to Mayor Mike Duggan who won his initial election to this position via a write-in campaign.

How did the media respond to such evidence of late-night ballot drops? The *Detroit Free Press* published a story on the Gateway Pundit video footage entitled "Video does not provide evidence of election fraud in Detroit."[117] The story maintains that the ballots in question were collected up until 8 p.m. and processed by the clerk's office. Credible chain of custody documentation for the ballots dropped off in the middle of the night has yet to be presented. Additionally, the story failed to mention the applicable statute wherein ballots delivered after the polls were closed were to be filed in the clerk's office not counted. Interestingly, the story has since been removed from their website Freep.com. It appears that it served its purpose.

So far, we have identified significant vote tally and ballot anomalies. What about pollbooks? Pollbooks anomalies were very prominent during the Backup Attack Phase. First of all, the pollbooks were now clearly connected to the internet. Remember, the chairwoman of the Wayne County Board of Canvassers, Monica Palmer, testified before the Michigan Senate that she "was told that at some point during processing the electronic pollbook [in the] TCF Center—that system bogged down, and they switched to the Qualified Voter File." *The qualified voter file is only accessible through an internet connection.*[118]

Then there was the issue of non-registered voters being allowed to vote as observed by poll challenger Bob Cushman and others. Mr. Cushman noticed that none of the voters on the ballots he observed were found in the electronic pollbook. All the names were being located on supplemental sheets provided with the ballots. He was curious, so he began writing down the names of the voters. A supervisor then told him to view the monitor instead of looking over the poll worker's shoulder. He tried, but since the ballots appeared on the screen for only a fraction of a second, he could not accurately record the information. When he resumed his original position behind the poll workers, they started turning the ballots face down, preventing him from seeing anything. He complained to Supervisor Browner who stated that the ballots are "just fine the way they were" and then left the area.[119]

His observations were later supported by Hima Kolanagireddy in her House testimony. She observed a large stack of ballots that were accompanied by a note saying, "Not in EPB/S' which means "not in electronic pollbook."[120]

GOP poll challenger and affiant Robert S. Brown witnessed ballots being rejected with this message: "no voter by that name is registered in this precinct". The poll worker he observed then typed in a different name read off a piece of paper containing a long list of names. The paper appeared to be a computer printout with all the pages connected "like an accordion." Those names were rejected as well. He entered more from the list of names. All were rejected. The worker then entered the ballot with the original name but with the now infamous birthdate of 01/01/1900. The ballot is again rejected. The worker then entered the other names from the list and again entered 1900 as the birthdate. They were all rejected too. Brown asked the poll worker how the list was generated and where it came from. The man said he didn't know. The supervisor was called for a huddle, but Brown was unable to hear their conversation. Brown then asked the supervisor about the origin of the computer list. She refused to answer him and soon became "huffy." He informed them that he was challenging the ballot, but the supervisor refused to enter it into the pollbook (necessary to make a valid challenge). Brown again asked the supervisor where the computerized list of names came from, but she again refused to answer. She then grabbed both the ballot and the computer printout list of names and left. Later, Brown observed a similar computer-generated list being used in the same manner at another table.[121]

While challenging at the absentee vote counting board in Detroit, affiant Francis Cizmar observed provisional ballots being placed by poll workers into a box labeled "to be tabulated," in apparent violation of Michigan election law. Provisional ballots need to be flagged accordingly in the pollbook. Cizmar then viewed a poll worker scanning an envelope and finding no record of that voter in the electronic pollbook. The worker then typed the voter's name directly into the electronic pollbook. The date of birth field was blank, but as did so many other poll workers at TCF, she typed in the infamous date 01/01/1900, indicating that the voter was 120 years old. As had been reported all morning, hundreds, or more likely thousands, of supposed voters appeared with the same birthdate.

The official explanation for the use of this deliberately implausible birthdate is to flag the late-registering voter in order to update in the system later. Sounds perfectly reasonable. This does not, however, explain why the poll workers were processing ballots for these voters prior to verifying that they were indeed eligible to vote. Another, more plausible explanation is that the bizarre birthdate could have been used to serve as a tool for flagging fake voters introduced into the system to be removed later from the voter rolls to prevent any discovery during an audit.

On November 5th, ballots and pollbooks were transferred from the absentee counting board at the TCF Center in Detroit to the Wayne County Canvassing Board on Jefferson Avenue in Detroit. Poll challengers and canvassers noted that precincts were coming back out of balance by as many as six hundred votes. An out of balance precinct is when the number of votes cast per the pollbook does not agree with the number of ballots counted.

Then, on November 16, a mysterious black box was delivered to the Wayne County Canvassing Board at 12:30 p.m. via a Vote Mobile delivery van. An alert poll challenger inquired about the unusual delivery and discovered that the box was filled with new voter lists. The updated pollbooks, submitted nearly two weeks *after* the election, resulted in a maximum vote discrepancy of 29. Down significantly from 600. In spite of this update, 71% of the absentee ballot counting boards were still out of balance and not subject to recount without explanation.

The canvassers were never given access to the electronic pollbooks in Detroit for review.

Influence Operations

We've identified both process and record anomalies that support our theory of the backup attack phase. Is there any evidence of influence operations during the backup attack phase? Yes.

Intimidation tactics were the primary indicator of influence operations during the backup attack phase. While there were examples of intimidation tactics during the main attack phase, these tactics were much more aggressive during the backup attack phase as mentioned earlier.

Poll challenger affidavits noted that Democrat and groups sympathetic to Democrats were standing around counting board tables blocking the view of Republicans during ballot duplications. Numerous GOP poll challengers were removed from the floor of the absentee vote counting board on the basis of accusations of masks not covering the nose. A Republican lawyer was removed by police amidst shouts of "Get the f*** out!" "That's what you get, racist!" "Take them all out!"

City clerk senior advisor, Chris Thomas, responded to allegations that Republican challengers were hindered in their duties by telling the *Detroit Free Press* that "nobody was mistreated" and ultimately concluded that the chaos and disruption at the TCF Center "was caused by the attitudes of the challengers."[122]

Media reports echoed Thomas' stance, implying that the challengers were there at the pleasure of the election staff, but Detroit polling site assessor, Ted Dickens, disagrees:

One point seems to be consistently overlooked when challengers are discussed: They are as entitled to be there as any
election inspector— or any DOE employee. All of us are participating as a result of state laws. . ... This is one area where
I hope there is broad agreement: It was unconscionable for
DOE to encourage inspectors to try to prevent challengers
from doing their jobs – and it was worse for the Clerk to ignore a court order on the subject.[123]

Poll challenger obstruction was rampant. One possible explanation
for the "change in tone" may be the flyers observed by GOP observers
entitled "Tactics to distract GOP challengers" on the floor of the absentee vote counting board.

One of the most obvious examples of poll challenger obstruction
happened during the afternoon of November 4. Republican poll challengers were prohibited from entry or re-entry by law enforcement. Officials said it was because the approved capacity of the facility had been
reduced due to COVID. That left roughly a dozen Republican poll challengers to cover 134 counting boards, 25 tabulator workstations, and 12
adjudicator workstations. There were significantly more Democrat poll
challengers in the AV Counting Board at that time.

Soon afterwards, cardboard boxes were used to block people locked
outside the counting board from observing what happened inside. During this lockout, military ballots were finally counted. They had been
available to count by idle poll workers since roughly midnight, yet the
election officials saw fit to count these ballots when the vast majority of
Republican poll challengers were prohibited from doing their job. Not
only was the obstruction of the windows a blatant example of interference with observation of ballot processing, but the timing of this interference also corresponded with the selected time for military ballot processing which has elevated risk of fraud due to the ballot transcription
process. Military ballots are unique in that they are received in a format

not compatible with the tabulation scanners. As a result, these ballots need to be spoiled and duplicated onto blank ballots in a compatible format. This duplication process must be witnessed by representatives from both major political parties. It was not.

Media reports on the events at the TCF Center and the election as a whole were decidedly one-sided. There were no attempts to highlight election law violations. There were no attempts to investigate the allegations made by poll challengers except to interview the same election officials alleged to have violated election laws.

Here is a sample of the headlines for the most egregious examples of influence operations by media operatives:

"Get to TCF': What really happened inside Detroit's ballot counting center", Tresa Baldas, Kristen Jordan Shamus, Niraj Warikoo, M.L. Elrick, Joe Guillen, and Evan Petzold, *Detroit Free Press*

"New videos falsely claim fraud in Detroit on 2020 election night", Grant Hermes WDIV

"Fact check: Videos showing crowd locked out of Detroit TCF Center with windows obstructed are missing context", Devon Link and Ashley Nerbovig, *USA Today*

Remember, I was at the TCF Center for more than twenty-four hours straight. I personally observed the van delivering ballots at 3:30 a.m. I was personally prevented from re-entering the AV Counting Board during the counting of military ballots. I personally observed the internet connections for tabulator and adjudicator workstations. The reporters who submitted the stories above obviously were not present or were seeking to hide the truth about what actually happened.

Here's a few samples of the fallacious assertions made by reporters in their stories.

Let's start with the Free Press story:

The Detroit vote had everyone on edge.

One group wanted to challenge it, while the other wanted to protect it. . . .

Republican attorney Tim Griffin found himself pacing in the wee hours of the night, frantically calling for volunteers to head to Detroit to challenge the ballots, suspicious that something nefarious was happening.

Poll volunteer Jeffrey Nolish ditched his dinner and rushed to the scene, where he would monitor the counting process at the request of the American Civil Liberties Union (ACLU) to ensure that every vote was counted. . . .

On Monday, Republican challengers were standing by. So were police, who within 15 minutes of the process starting removed a man wearing a white horror movie mask from the center. [124]

This unknown "Republican" man became the centerpiece of the news story. The man in the mask that the writers highlighted was just as likely to be a Democrat as a Republican. In fact, he looks a lot like a notorious Democrat who has run previously as a Republican from the Detroit area. One facet of the story was inadvertently correct. It exposed the arbitrary nature of COVID rules. Republican poll challengers were removed for too much of a mask and too little of a mask.

The story went on to assert, "Some saw the battle at the TCF Center as an example of some conservatives, trying to restrict the voting rights of African Americans."

What leftist propaganda news story would be complete without ad hominem race-baiting? They neglected to mention that the "conservatives" who were present as poll challengers included African Americans, Indian Americans, Chinese Americans, and Caucasian Americans.

I prefer the simple term Americans but that wouldn't fit most media narratives. As testimonials before the Michigan senate and house would later indicate, it was the Democrats, not Republicans, who were guilty of racial profiling while executing our election processes.

Then there was the explicit bias given to the testimony of election officials over that of certified poll challengers who submitted notarized affidavits. One example of this bias is evident in the following report:[125]

"Chris Thomas, a former longtime director of elections for the Michigan secretary of state, addressed the concerns of Republican challengers and debunked rumors of foul play that circulated on social media.

Thomas, who has worked for both Democratic and Republican secretaries of state, and who has offered constructive criticism of the Detroit clerk's performance in previous elections, said he was "extremely confident" that Detroit's final vote tally will be right. "They're in a good position to come through with a nice clean report," Thomas said. "I don't have any questions about it." Thomas also debunked rumors that every Republican challenger had been removed from the counting room"

The media goes out of their way to push the bonafides of Chris Thomas as the basis for dismissing the legitimate claims of Republican poll challengers. The ACLU representative, Nolish, also received significant buildup of his bonafides. It was almost as if the media reporters knew Chris Thomas and Jeffrey Nolish much better than they knew any of the Republicans they chose to quote. Also, no one ever claimed that "all Republicans had been removed from the counting room" yet that became the line pushed by the reporters. By my count, there were roughly a dozen Republican poll challengers remaining to cover 134 counting boards, 25 tabulators, and 12 adjudicators at the time of the lockout by Detroit officials under some phony, arbitrary COVID rule "coincidentally" at the time chosen to count military ballots.

The "news" report goes on to quote Chris Thomas as saying. "Challengers are usually confused when they first arrive. A lot of them don't know the intricacies of the process."

Interestingly enough, Chris Thomas, state elections director under multiple administrations, was the one who appeared to be confused on election night. As the former Vice Chair of the Michigan Senate Elections and Government Reform Committee, I was a poll challenger who was well-versed in election statute. My mission at the TCF Center was to ensure that the chain of custody regarding vote tallies was maintained. In this light, I asked Chris Thomas to walk me through the chain of custody for vote tallies from each of the 25 tabulators to the 12 adjudicators and to the central election management server. He said, "I don't know." This may just be me, but it seems that Mr. Thomas was confused and unable to answer what should have been a very easy question for someone of his experience. You see, the intent of most jurisdictions is to preserve the vote tally integrity by enforcing a 1:1 relationship between tabulators and adjudicators. Tabulator and adjudicator workstations are typically only networked with each other to ease the transfer of ballot images from the tabulator to its paired adjudicator workstation. Not so in Detroit. There were 25 tabulators and 12 adjudicators. How would I or any other poll challenger know which ballots scanned at the tabulator workstations were routed to which adjudicator workstation? Was the routing of ballots automated or was someone at the center stage manually routing the ballots? My concern about the vote tally chain of custody was legitimate. It remains a legitimate concern to this day.

Now, let's address the propaganda piece put forward by Grant Hermes of WDIV. In his story, he makes the following assertions:

> Over the weekend, a video from a far-right site known for spreading false information allegedly shows a van dropping off ballots in the early morning hours of November 4, 2020, at the TCF Center. The video claims that the ballots came eight

hours past the deadline. The deadline, however, was when ballots needed to be turned into the clerk and not when they
needed to be delivered.[126]

What does Michigan law actually say? Under MCL 168.765, "If a
marked absent voter ballot is received by the clerk after the close of the
polls, the clerk shall plainly mark the envelope with the time and date
of receipt and shall file the envelope in his or her office."[127] The ballots
received by the clerk after the polls are closed are not to be delivered to
the counting board. They are *filed* in the clerk's office not counted at the
counting board. Hermes went on to take pot shots at Mike Lindell while
promoting Jocelyn Benson's "human error" talking points about Antrim
County and push the term "conspiracy theories" multiple times. The
piece was successful at blunting what at the time was picking up steam
as the smoking gun of election fraud in Detroit.

The last story was by Devon Link and Ashley Nerbovig of *USA Today*. The headline for the story was "Fact check: Videos showing crowd
locked out of Detroit TCF Center with windows obstructed are *missing
context.*" The use of the term "fact check" by the media is always a red
flag for me since it typically indicates a propaganda piece designed to
deflect investigation of a significant event. This story did not lead me to
reconsider such rushes to judgment.

"We were well over the 134 maximum," said the city of Detroit's
lead attorney Lawrence Garcia." This assertion was later clarified to assert a maximum of 134 for each party.[128]

Talk about missing context. The number 134 was *never* communicated as a maximum number of poll challengers. Coincidentally, there
were 134 counting boards. That "maximum" for each party would effectively preclude non-partisan oversight of each of the 134 counting
boards not to mention prohibit oversight of the tabulator and adjudicator workstations.

Once again, Jeffrey Nolish was the go-to guy for the media. He was quoted as saying, "But we saw them not respecting the six-feet rule and then asking questions and interfering with the process."

Talk about missing context. First of all, a Michigan court had issued an injunction on the so-called six-foot rule prior to the election. Second of all, poll challengers asking questions is a right protected under Michigan law. Failure to honor that right can result in fines and imprisonment.

Once again, Chris Thomas was quoted as saying that he was "extremely confident Detroit would come through with a nice clean report."[129]

I'm not sure what Mr. Thomas definition of "nice clean report" is but I would not classify the fact that 71% of Detroit's counting boards were out of balance as nice and clean. But maybe that's just me.

Reporters consistently reported the perspective of election officials overseeing the election as fact and the perspective of certified poll challengers as unfounded allegations. This is a pattern that continues to this day.

Summary

The fall of Florida appears to have triggered a backup plan. In support of this assertion, we have shown evidence in Michigan of the following backup attack phase tactics being employed successfully:

- Record voter turnout exceeded projections by 10%
- Election night reporting anomalies revealed the presence of a digital controller
- Internet connections during vote tallies enabled direct manipulation of vote tallies
- As many as 289,866 ballots were cast fraudulently

- Thousands of ballots needed to cover up vote tally adjustments were injected as late mail-in ballot drops
- Pollbooks were updated to cover up ballot drops
- Poll challengers were subjected to aggressive obstruction by election officials impeding collection of further evidence of election fraud

Is it possible to know exactly how many votes were shifted in the backup attack phase? Maybe. Unlike the main attack featuring mail-in ballot stuffing, the backup attack evidence reveals a focus upon digital manipulation of the vote tallies. Digital manipulation of vote tallies will leave digital breadcrumbs. While we do have some evidence of these breadcrumbs, many consider this evidence to be inconclusive. A forensic audit of election night reporting is necessary to provide conclusive evidence.

DEFENSE

Now we've shown evidence of preparation tactics, evidence of a main attack featuring mail-in ballot stuffing and evidence of a backup attack featuring digital control of vote tallies.

For those of you who may find this evidence compelling, it begs the question "why haven't the election results been overturned?"

Good question. Let's examine evidence of what we have referred to as the defense phase that might provide answers to that question for your consideration.

Process Anomalies

Fraudulent vote tallies would be meaningless without a certification of the election. Certification of election results is supposed to be an indicator that all election processes were followed in a satisfactory manner.

The process of certification begins with precinct election inspectors signing off on the results for their respective precinct. These results are handed off to the city and township boards of canvassers which certify the election results. Then, the results are handed off to the county boards of canvassers for certification and finally to the state board of canvassers. Canvasser is simply another term for auditor.

All the county boards of canvassers in Michigan proceeded to certify their 2020 election results without any issues except for Wayne County. In Wayne County, Monica Palmer, the chairperson of the Wayne County Board of Canvassers, and the late William Hartman both voted no on certification of the election results due to lack of process integrity. For example, the *official* vote results for the largest county in the state, Wayne County, shows zero registered voters associated with 174,384 votes. The official story is that those registered voters "were already counted earlier in the report under each Detroit precinct. However, their votes were not." Under MCL 168.765a election inspectors are required to format the accumulation report to clearly indicate both precinct and absentee voter returns as well as compare the totals for each, but we've already established that "laws" were simply suggestions to Detroit election officials. To date, there has not been an accurate mapping of votes to voters as exemplified by the fact that a whopping 71% of Detroit AV Counting Board precincts were out of balance.[130] Furthermore, the Wayne County Board of Canvassers have not been shown all the pollbook data for Detroit regarding the November 3, 2020, election. The board's initial no vote was later changed to a conditional yes vote followed by another no vote the next day. More about this when we discuss influence operations in the defense phase.

The State Board of Canvassers certified the 2020 general election results on November 23, 2020, via a 3-0 vote. One of the Republican members of the state board abstained in the wake of the testimony provided. The election was certified over his objection in spite of the presentation of evidence that election records were not in order.

In the wake of the certification of the statewide election, the Michigan secretary of state committed to performing post-election audits. On April 21, 2021, she released a memo claiming that post-election audits of the 2020 general election were the most extensive in Michigan history. In her release, she claimed that more than two hundred *in-person* voting precincts were subject to procedural audits. She also claimed that absentee vote counting board audits were conducted that focused upon how many absentee voter counting boards were out of balance. She claimed that 18,000 out of the 5,579,317 ballots cast were compared with the statewide tabulated total—whatever that means. She also claimed that the Bureau of Elections conducted a full hand-count audit of all presidential election ballots in Antrim County. Another term for a full hand-count "audit" is a "recount". The use of the term "*audit*" in her release was clearly intended to satisfy a December 4 court order for an "audit." It was clear to those who participated in the "audit" that it was indeed simply a "recount." Workers who identified sets of ballots with identical signatures were told to simply count the ballots.

On June 25, 2021, Judge Elsenheimer dismissed the Antrim County lawsuit filed by Bill Bailey requesting a full audit on the basis that the requested remedy had already been executed—but is that true? Not according to Assistant MI Attorney General, Erik Grill. During his oral testimony on behalf of the defense in the *Bailey v. Antrim County* election fraud case, Mr. Grill, is on record regarding the December 17 "audit" ordered by Judge Kevin Elsenheimer as saying, "There's something of a misconception there, that I think probably needs to be addressed. That wasn't an audit, per se. That was a hand count that the secretary did to try to reassure the public that the results were accurate."

Even if it were true that an audit had been conducted, the value of any post-election audit conducted using the standards defined by the Michigan secretary of state prior to the election is in doubt since, among other deficiencies, it failed to address any security concerns associated with the use of electronic voting systems.

Judge Elsenheimer's ruling is on appeal, but the clock continues to tick for the preservation of the election records needed to conduct a true audit of the election.

Record Anomalies

Is there any evidence of election record anomalies during the defense phase?

Let's start by looking at the official vote tally records posted by the Michigan secretary of state on her website.[131]

REPORTING LEVEL	TOTAL BIDEN VOTE	TOTAL TRUMP VOTE	TOTAL NUMBER OF VOTES	VOTE MARGIN (BIDEN – TRUMP)
State	2,804,040	2,649,852	5,539,302	154,188
County	2,804,040	2,649,852	5,539,302	154,188
Precincts	2,801,470	2,649,234	5,536,017	152,236

If you tally the total number of votes cast according to the counties and compare it to the total number of votes cast per the precincts, there is a difference of 3,285 votes. The primary differences between precinct and county vote tallies occurred in Eaton and Clinton Counties. These differences are explained to be the result of "statistical adjustments" without further explanation. Eaton and Clinton Counties are coincidentally next-door neighbors of the home county of the Michigan Capitol, Ingham County. Quite a few state officials call these neighboring communities home. The 2016 margin of victory for President Trump was only 10,704 votes.

To compound matters, the list of people whom the state says voted during the 2020 general election does not match the number of votes cast. In other words, the statewide voter registration file does not provide an accurate list of who voted. How bad is the discrepancy? The official number of votes cast in Michigan during the 2020 election was 5,579,317. Of these votes, 5,539,302 were cast for President.[132] Yet, the

December 1, 2020, instance of the qualified voter file showed that only 5,475,179 voted in the 2020 general election. That means that the official state voter registration database entries for the November 3, 2020, election has 104,138 fewer voters than ballots cast in the election. The official explanation for this discrepancy from the Michigan secretary of state? These voters were "cancelled," or the voting history had not yet been updated by some jurisdictions—almost a month after the election. Bottom line? The Michigan secretary of state appears to be presiding over at least 104,138 counts of violations of federal law regarding election record retention. Where are these records?

Federal law requires the preservation of *all* election records for twenty-two months after an election. It turns out that there has been a concerted effort to destroy these records prior to the end of the twenty-two months. Vote tally gaps and voter deletions are not the only concerns. Voting record changes are perhaps even more concerning. An analysis of changes to the qualified voter file reveals that as many as half a million voting history records were deleted as of January 1, 2021.[133] Toggling a voter record from having voted in 2020 to having not voted is one way to hide voting anomalies that would otherwise be discovered during a forensic audit or canvassing activities. Voter records are not only subject to the federal twenty-two-month record protection, but they are also subject to protection for five years under Michigan law.[134]

On February 12, 2021, the Bureau of Elections, under Michigan secretary of state Jocelyn Benson, issued a directive to clerks that appears to take exception with federal law. She told clerks there were election records which "must be deleted." The directive from the Michigan Bureau of Elections stated that "ballots, programs and related materials are released" from security requirements. In a departure from the all-inclusive nature of the federal law, the same letter, however, only specified that a subset of the ballot information should be secured for twenty-two months.[135] There are no such caveats in the federal law. They literally made-up assertions about the law that simply were not true, which is exactly what one would expect during a cover up. Federal law stipulates that "all records and papers" shall be retained and preserved for twenty-two months. Under US Code 52, Section 20702 these violations are subject to fines and imprisonment.

The Election Bureau's directive went on to state that the electronic pollbook software and associated files must be deleted, which also is a clear departure from the "all records and papers" must be secured provision of the federal law.

In addition to directives from the Michigan secretary of state, clerks were also issued directives by vendors that would result in the destruction of election records. Electronic voting system vendor Election Source issued letters to the clerk of Oceana County informing them that they would be visiting her office to perform "preventative" maintenance on her voting machines. The preventative maintenance featured in their letter to the clerk pertained to the removal of batteries from the machines. This is odd because the preventative maintenance checklist submitted as part of the contract between the state of Michigan and Election Source did not specify removal of the batteries as a maintenance item.[136]

Why would someone need to remove the batteries? What happens to these voting machines when the battery is removed? According to operations manuals, they reset their configuration settings to factory settings. Among the settings that would be erased by such a procedure would be the server connection settings. These connection settings would be important data in any forensic analysis of the election.

The directive from Election Source also raises an important question for consideration. Who really runs our elections? Our elected officials or the vendors which are supposed to serve them?

Sometimes the destruction of records is a bit more explosive than what happens when a battery is removed from electronic equipment. On Christmas day 2020, there was an explosion in downtown Nashville. Turns out that the explosion impacted a data facility that had been owned by a company called SunGard. SunGard is the former parent company of SolarWinds. Is this merely a coincidence or does it indicate that somebody was very serious about destroying configuration data and communication logs? This information may have provided some very valuable breadcrumbs leading to who exactly was responsible for modifying election records during the election held less than two months earlier.

For an examination of the importance of retaining election records in the wake of an election, let's return to Antrim County. The events in Antrim County revealed how our vote tally records were truly vulnerable to manipulation.

On November 3, the Antrim County clerk released startling election results. As mentioned previously, she reported that Joe Biden had won the presidential election in the traditionally red county of Antrim with an official vote count of 7,769 for Biden and 4,509 for Trump.[137] Antrim County resident Bill Bailey responded in disbelief and contacted county officials to share his concerns.

On November 5, the Antrim County board of canvassers certified the election with 7,289 votes for Biden and 9,783 votes for Trump.

On November 21, the Antrim County board of canvassers released an updated certified vote tally that showed 5,960 for Biden and 9,748 for Trump.

On November 23, attorney Matt DePerno filed a lawsuit on behalf of Antrim County resident Bill Bailey citing the following counts:

1. Constitutional right to accuracy and integrity of elections
2. Violation of purity of elections clause
3. Election fraud as a result of violations of MCL 600.4545(2) and MCL 158.861
4. Common law election fraud
5. Equal protection violation
6. Statutory election law violations

The remediation sought by the suit included a call for an independent and non-partisan audit to determine the accuracy and integrity of the November 3, 2020, election. This is a right guaranteed to the citizens of Michigan under Article II Section 4 of the Michigan Constitution.

On December 4, the Court ordered an audit of Antrim County's election results.

On December 17, a hand recount was conducted that was advertised as an audit. The vote tally from this recount was 5,959 for Biden and 9,759 for Trump.

A total of four vote tallies were performed in Antrim County. Each with a different result. Examination of the difference between the original vote tally on November 3 and the final vote tally on December 17 showed a whopping 7,060 votes had been shifted from Trump to Biden in a county where a total of 15,660 votes were reported to have been cast. The official explanation for the vote tally discrepancies was clerical error resulting from last-minute ballot updates. During his testimony before the Michigan Senate on December 15, 2020,[138] the CEO of Dominion, John Poulos explained the clerical error as follows:

- When a new election project is created, every tabulator needed to be updated with the new election project not simply the tabulators in the effected precinct.
- Error #1: Election officials did not update all tabulator memory cards.
- Error #2: Election officials forgot to conduct public accuracy test on new election project. This is also a violation of Michigan election law.
- Mr. Poulos goes on to assert that if all of the tabulators had been updated as per procedure, there wouldn't have been any error. If public logic and accuracy test would have been run, he asserts that the error would have been caught.

It is unclear to this day how a precinct tabulator public accuracy test that doesn't involve the county EMS server would have corrected an error that was only recognized when the county attempted to import the precinct results. The only way that the public accuracy test of a precinct tabulator could be used to correct a county server error would be if those machines were connected to the internet. Election officials and John Poulos himself have asserted repeatedly that there was no internet connection.

The evidence of election fraud in Antrim County culminated on March 4, 2021, during an Antrim County Commissioners meeting. During the meeting, Antrim County clerk Sheryl Guy publicly admitted to ordering the destruction of election records.[139]

> **Clerk Sheryl Guy:** "I did it. My office staff did it. Under my authority to get those numbers right. It wasn't fraud. It was doing my job. Getting my numbers certified as the canvassers certified."
>
> "I trust Dominion"
>
> "It's the programming in the cards. So, if you want to call it fraud, it's me. But… it's not fraud. It's getting the job done right…. Weren't just replacing. We had to delete. That's why our numbers were inflated. We double published."
>
> **Commissioner Christian Marcus:** "Sounds like you just admitted to 1) breaking the law by making changes to a thing within a 30 day period 2) admitting that you deleted files and destroyed the integrity of the election in Antrim County. You admitted to directing your employees to do so. So… basically Antrim County's vote was completely skewed by your office and you're admitting it."

She could have made an effort to retain a copy of the records for use later in support of audits, but she didn't. While some have called her actions "human error," others would more accurately join Commissioner Marcus in calling it a violation of the law. In spite of this evidence, there have been no charges pressed by authorities to date. If this was the most secure election in history, why is there such an unapologetic push to destroy election records that would ostensibly support such a bold claim?

Influence Operations

Influence operations took center stage during the defense phase. Let's start by examining an assessment of the impact of foreign threats in the wake of the 2020 election.

On March 15, 2021, the National Intelligence Council under newly installed DNI Haines released a declassified report on Foreign Threats to the 2020 US Federal Elections.[140] The report featured the following assertions:

Key Judgment 1: We have no indications that any foreign actor attempted to alter any technical aspect of the voting process in the 2020 US elections, including voter registration, casting ballots, vote tabulation, or reporting results.

Key Judgment 2: We assess that Russian President Putin authorized, and a range of Russian government organizations conducted, influence operations aimed at denigrating President Biden's candidacy and the Democratic Party, supporting former President Trump, undermining public confidence in the electoral process, and exacerbating sociopolitical divisions in the US. Unlike in 2016, we did not see persistent Russian cyber efforts to gain access to election infrastructure.

Key Judgment 3: We assess that Iran carried out a multi-pronged covert influence campaign intended to undercut former President Trump's reelection prospects-though without directly promoting his rivals-undermine public confidence in the electoral process and US institutions, and sow division and exacerbate societal tensions in the US.

Key Judgment 4: We assess that China did not deploy interference efforts and considered but did not deploy influence efforts intended to change the outcome of the US Presidential election.

Key Judgment 5: We assess that a range of additional foreign actors-including Lebanese Hizballah, Cuba, and Venezuela-took some steps to attempt to influence the election.

Clearly, these intelligence officials would have you believe that China was playing nice during the 2020 election while their favorite Russia bogeyman was pushing Pro-Trump and anti-Biden propaganda. You may recall that it was a group of fifty-one intelligence officials included nine current intelligence officials who signed a now-debunked letter asserting that the Hunter Biden laptop appeared to be part of a Russian disinformation campaign. What role did these intelligence officers play in the development of these important judgments? What was the influence of the $31 million[141] provided by individuals connected to the Chinese Communist Party intelligence community to the Biden family?

On January 7, 2021, the DNI under President Trump, John Ratcliffe, issued a damning indictment of what was still a classified report on Foreign Threats in the 2020 US Federal Election.[142] His statements received little attention at the time due to events of January 6. In his memo entitled "Views on Intelligence Community Election Security Analysis", he made the following observations:

"China analysts were hesitant to assess Chinese actions as undue influence or interference. These analysts appeared reluctant to have their analysis on China brought forward because they tend to disagree with the administration's policies, saying in effect, I don't want our intelligence used to support those policies. This behavior would constitute a violation of Analytic Standard B: Independence of Political Considerations (IRTPA Section 1019).

Furthermore, alternative viewpoints on China's election influence efforts have not been appropriately tolerated, much less encouraged. In fact, the Ombudsman found that:

'There were strong efforts to suppress analysis of alternatives (AOA) in the August [National intelligence Council Assessment on foreign election influence], and associated IC products, which is a violation of Tradecraft Standard 4 and IRTPA Section 1017. NIC officials reported that Central Intelligence Agency (CIA) officials rejected NIC coordination comments and tried to downplay alternative analyses in their own production during the drafting of the NICA.'

Additionally, the Ombudsman found that CIA Management took actions "pressuring [analysts] to withdraw their support' from the alternative viewpoint on China 'in an attempt to suppress it. This was seen by National Intelligence Officers (NIO) as politicization,' and I agree. For example, this ICA gives the false impression that the NIO Cyber is the only analyst who holds the minority view on China. He is not, a fact that the Ombudsman found during his research and interviews with stakeholders. Placing the NIO Cyber on a metaphorical island by attaching his name alone to the minority view is a testament to both his courage and to the effectiveness of the institutional pressures that have been brought to bear on others who agree with him.

....

As a result, similar actions by Russian and China are assessed and communicated to policymakers differently, potentially leading to the false impression that Russia sought to influence the election but China did not."

As a minimum, it is clear from DNI Ratcliffe's memo that there was division in the intelligence community on whether the efforts of China indicated an attempt to influence the US Federal Election. As a worst-case scenario, intelligence operatives were pressured by conspirators in the intelligence community to downplay the role actually played by China during the election. Notably, it was the NIC Cyber that was singled out for their dissenting opinion. This indicates that NIC Cyber likely had significant evidence of China attempting to influence the election via cyberspace tools and methods. This "minority" assessment would be consistent with the Wuhan paper on PID Controllers, the financial relationships between voting system manufacturers and the CCP, the risks to our election infrastructure highlighted by national security experts as late as July 2020, and the fact that, in contrast to Biden's pro-China policies, President Trump's China policies were demonstrably anti-China.

Could it be that the same national intelligence apparatus that promoted the false Russian collusion narrative during the first failed Trump impeachment trial and the false assertion that Hunter Biden's laptop appeared to be part of a Russian disinformation campaign right before the 2020 election may not be serving the best interests of America? Is it mere coincidence that analysts felt "pressured" to promote a pro-China perspective in a report on foreign influence in the 2020 election? Could it be that those who pressured analysts into silence on China's role in the election are guilty of treason? Don't forget that Biden is connected to over $31 million in funds provided by individuals connected to the Chinese Communist Party intelligence community.

Influence operations take on many forms. Not all of them take place in the complex arena of our national intelligence community grappling with foreign threats. Sometimes they are a relatively simple campaign of distraction. Like a magician who tries to keep you focused upon what the right hand is doing while the left hand executes a switch, there is significant evidence to suggest that citizens are being conditioned to focus on the ballots to hide the main thrusts to undermine our qualified voter file, pollbooks and vote tallies.

The media stories on the Arizona audit report were perhaps the most glaring example of this narrative. Despite an avalanche of evidence of election fraud being presented, the lead stories were all about the ballot recount.

This narrative was evident in Michigan as well. It was featured in the December 15, 2020, testimony by Dominion CEO John Poulos.[143] "In the states that do use rank choice voting it is a separately installed module with separate 'trading' and the telltale sign of whether or not it's on is you *look at the ballots.*"

It was also featured in communications from legislative bodies responsible for overseeing the conduct of our elections. On June 23, 2021, the Michigan Senate Oversight Committee released its long-awaited report on the November 2020 election in Michigan. Among the assertions by Senator Ed McBroom featured in the report was a continued emphasis upon recounts of the ballots being the deciding factor for determining the integrity of a given election. "This incredibly conclusive fact, along with the hand recount of the ballots, serve as the irrefutable bulwarks against all allegations.... "There is no evidence to suggest the original, official results reflected anything but what was marked on the ballots.... "Rectifying precincts where this mistake happened is usually not difficult to do and involves taking the ballots out of the box, counting the total number to see if it matches the pollbook, and processing all the ballots through the tabulator again."[144]

The report concluded that the committee "found no evidence of widespread or systemic fraud in Michigan's prosecution of the 2020 election." Even though the report was released under the auspices of an investigation having been performed, it is unclear if any such investigation had truly been conducted and, if so, whether the investigation was performed with the professionalism required of any pursuit that would help decide the leader of the free world. Remarkably, investigations into committee expenditures revealed that they had hired legal firms to assist them with the preparation of the report not trained investigators. The report was promoted by media outlets as the definitive voice on 2020 election malfeasance. The report was derided as incredulous and lacking in scholarly pursuit by those who had submitted affidavits asserting election fraud under penalty of perjury.

President Obama sang praises for the report's authors in a July 5, 2021, tweet that included a link to a story in the *Atlantic* entitled "The Senator Who Decided to Tell the Truth."

In the wake of the SCOTUS ruling further weakening the Voting Rights Act, take a look at how one Republican in Michigan was subjected to harsh attacks from within his own party for simply acknowledging the validity of the election results in his state.

While no longer able to tweet due to censorship, President Trump was still able to share significantly less flattering prose for those behind the report in his statement on June 24, 2021.

Michigan State Senators Mike Shirkey and Ed McBroom are doing everything possible to stop Voter Audits in order to hide the truth about November 3. The Senate 'investigation' of the election is a cover and a method of getting out of a Forensic Audit for the examination of the Presidential count.

Corrupt (?) politicians falsely claim there was no Voter Fraud in Michigan (has anyone looked at what is considered the most corrupt election city in the U.S. DETROIT?), however, they admit to 'problems with the numbers' that rigged 7,048 votes to illegally give a very conservative county to Joe Biden, which raised big signals, only to then find out that it was actually President Trump that won the county by 3,788 votes not Biden.

The focus on the ballots narrative also supports a common corollary narrative: *Count every vote.* While this phrase sounds proper, it deliberately ignores the importance of the chain of custody. In fact, the Michigan Senate Oversight Committee demonstrated their lack of appreciation for the importance of the chain of custody in the following statement:

Frequent demands to decertify all or a portion of the vote are accompanied by high sounding language regarding the "chain of custody." This verbiage evokes images of evidence utilized in trials, such as sealed envelopes and locked evidence rooms with sign-out sheets. However, investigating the claims regarding problems with the chain of custody usually finds highlights about the handling and transmission of the unofficial vote counts and the computer systems used to handle them. While concerns about these systems may be justified, it is incredibly misleading and irresponsible to imply this holds any danger to the official vote counts, the tabulators, or the ballots themselves. Similarly, unfair allegations have been leveled against the secretary of state and county and local clerks regarding the instruction to, and deletion of, e-pollbook data. The letter instructing this and the action itself is a standard practice, ordered by the federal government and carried out shortly after every election. The law and the letter sent also provide specific instruction not to do so should there be an ongoing legal action regarding the data. All evidence the Committee found shows the law was followed. The Committee finds insisting this is evidence of a cover up, "Destruction of election artifacts prior to end of 22-month archival requirement," is incredibly misleading, demeaning, and irresponsible.[145]

So, the committee responsible for investigating the integrity of the 2020 election attempted to marginalize the importance of the chain of custody as "high sounding language" and chastised citizen investigators for expressing concerns about the destruction of election records that would be important in any real audit of the election. Instead, they repeat the narrative of the Dominion CEO and encourage citizens to focus upon a single link in the chain of custody...the ballots. This narrative is designed to suppress the push for a real audit and promote the pre-election narrative of voter suppression. This narrative stands in stark contrast to the supporters of election integrity who assert that we need to "count every *legal* vote."

How do you determine how many votes were cast illegally? Conduct an audit of the full election record chain of custody...not simply the ballots.

It is perhaps for this reason that many election officials consistently refer to recounts as audits. This confusion of terms provides a convenient cover for a consistent push to look at paper ballots in lieu of a full forensic audit. A full forensic audit would be a compelling means of validating any election fraud that has been detected.

Intimidation tactics also played an important role in the post-election influence operations.

The proceedings of the Wayne County Board of Canvassers meeting on November 17, 2020, provides one prominent example. The purpose of the November 17 meeting was to consider certification of the 2020 general election results for Wayne County. Upon review of the election records in their possession, two of the canvassers on the Wayne County Board of Canvassers, Chairperson Monica Palmer and the late William

Hartman, voted no on certification of the election. I was present during that vote. It was well-reasoned and on point. They cited concerns with the fact that 71% of the precincts at the Detroit absentee votes counting board were unbalanced. This was unacceptable.

A public comment period followed their no vote. What followed could only be characterized as intimidation. There was a litany of vile commentary, including racist accusations by public figures such as Wayne State University Vice President Ned Staebler:

> Just know that when you try to sleep tonight that millions of people around the world now on Twitter know the name Monica Palmer and William Hartman as two people completely racist and without an understanding of what integrity means or a shred of human decency. The law isn't on your side. History won't be on your side. Your conscience isn't on your side.

Democrat State Representative-Elect Abraham Aiyash also played the race card, plus he took the additional measure of doxing the daughter of Chairperson Palmer:

> Be very clear about this. The party that you are a part of had complete control of our state government for eight years. And they did not do a single thing. While you may show your caucasity today in refusing to certify the election and making it known that you are ok with certifying all of Wayne County except Detroit. Know that we see what is happening. Know that there is nothing other than Jim Crowing going on right now…. Know the facts. You as the board of canvassers do not decide who is to be elected, the voters do. Know the facts. You are standing here today telling folks that Black Detroit should not have their votes counted. Know the facts. You are certain-

ly showing that you are a racist. You may say that you are not. You may claim that you are not. But let's be very clear. Your words today and your actions today made it very clear. You are ok with silencing the votes of an 80% African American city. What that tells us is that you Monica Palmer from Grosse Pointe Woods which has a history of racism are deciding to enable and continue to perpetuate the racist history of this country. And I want you think about what this means for your kids who probably go to Grosse Pointe North.

On the topic of knowing the facts, during the hearing, Palmer and Hartman cited concerns with the records of two cities – Livonia and Detroit. Livonia is a predominantly white community. Furthermore, their No vote regarding certification pertained to all of Wayne County not simply Detroit as asserted. But that didn't fit the racist narrative they pursued as part of their intimidation tactics.

It should be noted that the comments by Aiyash and Stabler have been discretely deleted from the publicly available recording of the Board of Canvassers meeting's public comment period. What are they trying to cover up? There were no ramifications for the comments of a Vice President at a public university or an incoming public official. Does such inaction encourage or discourage such tactics in the future?

Upon the completion of the public commentary period including these vial diatribes, the two dissenters met with the other members of the board and received a commitment that an audit would be conducted by the state of Michigan if they were to certify the results. Canvassers Palmer and Hartman changed their certification vote to yes upon reaching this agreement. The Michigan Secretary of State was quick to assert in the wake of the vote that the agreement was not binding upon her.[146] The next day, Palmer and Hartman rescinded their conditional yes vote and reasserted their no vote. Democrats then asserted that they were unable to change their vote, which begs the question how the vote was ever changed from their initial no vote? There never was a vote on the reconsideration of their initial vote.

The threats didn't stop with the public comment period. A woman by the name of Katelyn Jones was arrested after law enforcement determined that she sent Monica Palmer threats, including pictures of naked, mutilated bodies along with pictures of Monica's daughter.

To make matters worse, in the wake of the hearing, local media stories featured investigations of canvassers Palmer and Hartman NOT the root cause of the 71% of precincts being out of balance. On November 19, 2020, NBC's local affiliate, WDIV, aired a story entitled "A closer look at Wayne County canvassers Monica Palmer and William Hartmann." The story featured profiles of each canvasser, discussed where they lived and even revealed footage of the home of William Hartmann who has since died from COVID.

WDIV reported, "Palmer has an ethics complaint against her claiming that because she ran what they called a dark money PAC in the local Grosse Pointe Woods school election this past cycle that was a conflict of interest. The county ethics board is taking that up. She refutes all the claims."[147]

The purpose of the story appears to have been to smear the two Republican canvassers. The reporters paid zero attention to the concerns cited by Palmer and Hartman in their initial "no" votes. The net impact was a shift in public focus from questioning the integrity of the vote to questioning the integrity of those responsible for evaluating the integrity of the vote.

More evidence of a cover up.

In the wake of the election results, it appeared that the narratives were predetermined.

A favorite local media narrative was that there was no election fraud because Donald Trump actually performed better in Detroit in 2020 than 2016.[148] He actually received five thousand more votes in 2020 than he got in 2016.[149] While this information is actually true, it was repeated often enough by election fraud detractors that it merits further investigation.

Why? If one were already picking the margin of victory overall, would it be inconceivable that they might seek to plant election result talking point nuggets pertaining to a city like Detroit which has been at the center of election controversies for decades? These talking points could then be leveraged to discourage investigations into their activities. Besides, there is reason to believe that Trump had more support in Detroit than the election results revealed.

Prior to the election, President Trump had earned growing support among minority communities as a result of his policies. In fact, polls show that he had the support of 24% of black voters and 32% of Hispanic voters. Yet Trump managed to receive only 5% of the vote in Detroit, which features a predominantly black and Hispanic population. But because he received five thousand more votes in Detroit in 2020 than in 2016, media outlets discouraged any attempts to highlight evidence of election fraud.

Another tactic employed as part of the defense phase influence operations was for the media and Big Tech to proclaim themselves "fact checkers." More often than not, what was portrayed as "fact checking" appears rather to have been a concerted effort to discredit anyone asserting election fraud who seems to be gaining traction in the public square. The rigor applied to their "fact checking" efforts was often limited to asking an election official how the election was supposed to be conducted as opposed to actually pursuing evidence as to how it actually was conducted. In fact, this investigation rigor, or lack thereof, continues to be a common theme in the testimony of those unwilling to address election fraud evidence. This "fact checking" deception was officially exposed as a farce as a result of a lawsuit brought by John Stossel. Facebook was forced to admit that their "fact checks" were merely opinion.[150]

The so-called fact checkers were only one facet of a larger campaign to discourage everyday citizens from doing independent research on a variety of topics not simply election fraud.

Pundits on media outlets such as CNN and even Forbes featured segments and articles quick to dismiss investigations by everyday citizens—even those with technical expertise in such matters.

CNN commentator Brian Stelter used clips from comedian Trevor Noah to ridicule citizens performing their own research in a story named "How 'do your own research' hurts America's Covid response." The story featured a guest named Renee DiResta who stated, "We need to teach people how to actually do research." Stelter even threw in a gratuitous dig at Qanon enthusiasts during the segment to amplify the propaganda value of the piece.[151]

Forbes featured a story by Ethan Siegel entitled "You must not do your own research when it comes to science." The story asserts, "Research both sides and make up your own mind." It's simple, straightforward, commonsense advice. And when it comes to issues like vaccinations, climate change, and the novel coronavirus SARS-CoV-2, it can be dangerous, destructive, and even deadly."[152]

Freedom of inquiry appears to be under attack right along with freedom of speech, freedom of assembly, freedom of religion and the freedom to seek redress for grievances.

What happens when we outsource our ability to do our own research? We become locked into the narratives of those to which the research task is delegated or has been assumed.

While you have been provided a significant amount of evidence of election fraud so far, I enthusiastically encourage you to perform your own research and draw your own conclusions.

Media outlets weren't the only ones discouraging independent investigations. The Michigan secretary of state was very aggressive on this matter too. In addition to the directive Benson issued ordering the destruction of election records, she was also responsible for directives to clerks prohibiting their access to electronic voting systems. In an August 4, 2021, memorandum from Michigan director of elections, Jonathan Brater, to all clerks in the state of Michigan, he stated:

"Clerks should never allow access to election equipment to entities other than election officials and staff, licensed vendors,
and accredited VSTLs. Granting access to election equipment
to unauthorized personnel may result in the decertification of
election equipment or require additional procedures be followed prior to the use of such equipment."

Most clerks do not have the technical expertise needed to evaluate
electronic voting systems. Subsequently, they often seek technology experts to evaluate systems for them. EAC-certified vendors were allowed
to tamper with equipment without oversight, yet clerks, duly elected by
the people of their respective jurisdiction, are prohibited from examining the equipment with technical experts of their own. Never mind that
the standards used by the EAC to approve these vendors are dubious at
best. We are simply supposed to accept their "seal of approval" without
question. And then when clerks seek to investigate concerns with the
voting systems, they are threatened with legal action or the decertification of their electronic voting systems resulting in significant cost to their
jurisdiction because they are then forced to purchase new equipment.

Clerks weren't the only ones subject to intimidation by the Michigan secretary of state and her staff. In Cheboygan County, the County Commissioners attempted to conduct a forensic audit of the voting
equipment. The secretary of state responded with a May 20, 2021, letter
from the director of the Michigan Bureau of Elections to the Cheboygan
County clerk, Karen Brewster, directing her *not* to provide access to the
electronic voting equipment citing statute not directly applicable to the
matter at hand.

Dear Clerk Brewster:

You are receiving this letter because the Bureau of Elections has
been informed that the Cheboygan County Board of Com-

missioners may attempt to allow an unqualified third party to gain access to voting equipment in Cheboygan County, purportedly to conduct a "forensic audit." The Board has no authority to require you or any municipal clerk to provide external access to voting equipment maintained by your offices, and neither you nor municipal clerks in Cheboygan County should provide this access.

[NOTE: Once again, there is a concerted effort to limit voting machine access to vendors chosen on the basis of who they know not what they know.]

The Michigan Election Law entrusts clerks with choosing and maintaining their voting systems and does not provide any authority for county commissions to take control of this equipment.

MCL 168.37a states that "a county clerk, in consultation with each city and township clerk in the county" will "determine which electronic voting system will be used in the county[.]" Custody, programming, and review and testing of election equipment is entrusted to qualified election officials, not county commissions.

Interest in granting access to unqualified third parties to conduct a "forensic audit" may stem from misplaced reliance on ongoing misinformation— which has been repeatedly, comprehensively, and definitively debunked—regarding both Dominion Voting Systems and the error that occurred in the initial reported unofficial results in Antrim County. As you know, the Bureau of Elections in cooperation with the Antrim County Clerk and a number of local election clerks conducted a public hand count of every paper ballot cast for President in Antrim County, which confirmed that the ballot tabulators counted ballots accurately.

[NOTE: The proceedings of the investigation conducted by Attorney Matt DePerno and his team reveal significant discrepancies with their assertion that concerns with Dominion voting equipment were "debunked". Furthermore, the hand recount was insufficient to demonstrate that the chain of custody for the ballots which were counted had been maintained with integrity.]

Statewide, more than 1,300 clerks of both parties participated in at least one election audit this year. A report on the results of the audits, which found no examples of intentional misconduct, is publicly available. Suggestions of tampering with election results are baseless.

[NOTE: The evidence presented in this book invalidates the claim that the "tampering with election results are baseless".]

The Department of Justice, FBI, Department of Homeland Security, and Cybersecurity and Infrastructure Security Agency "investigated multiple public claims that one or more foreign governments owned, directed, or controlled election infrastructure used in the 2020 federal elections; implemented a scheme to manipulate election infrastructure; or tallied, changed, or otherwise manipulated vote counts. The Departments found that those claims were not credible."

[NOTE: Before the election, federal agencies cited significant risks to the integrity of our election systems posed by foreign govern-

*ments and other actors due to vulnerabilities in our election struc-
ture. It would likely be very illuminating to be able to review any
report that may have been generated in support of the claim that
election fraud claims "were not credible". Instead, the letter hides
behind an assertion with a doubtful pedigree.]*

If you or municipal clerks choose to conduct additional re-
views of your voting systems, that is your prerogative. However, as we advised in the February 12, 2021 news update
and our April 20, 2021 email to county clerks and election
directors, only election officials, licensed vendors, or accredited voting system test laboratories should be granted access to
voting equipment. If you are interested in having any type of
physical review of your voting system, you should contact an
EAC-accredited voting systems test laboratory (VSTL).

Please let me know if you have any further questions.

Sincerely,

Jonathan Brater, Director
Michigan Bureau of Elections

Cheboygan County was not the only county in Michigan to step
up and attempt to investigate the electronic voting equipment. This en-
thusiasm, however, generally waned after consultation with municipal
legal counsel because the Michigan contract with voting equipment
manufacturers prohibited access to the equipment. The Dominion contract featured a prohibition against even an analysis of the software used
to manage our elections.

If this were the most secure election in history, what is there to
hide?

As the pressure to conduct audits mounted across the state, voting system vendors joined in the chorus of threatening letters to clerks advising them it would be a violation of their license agreement. Clerk intimidation was taken to new heights in Adams Township. The local clerk, Stephanie Scott, cited concerns about two aspects of one of her 2021 elections during a public meeting of the Adams Township Board. She was concerned that the public accuracy test deck she received had the same number of ballots as a previous election with a different number of ballot measures. If the public accuracy test were truly examining the ballot error permutations, one would expect a different number of ballots for each of these elections. Instead, she received the same number of test ballots. She thought that odd and expressed as much during her board meeting. She also cited her concerns about the election equipment being connected to the internet. In response to these comments, the Michigan Bureau of Elections submitted the following October 15, 2021, letter to Clerk Scott:

Dear Clerk Scott:

I write to advise and instruct you on your obligations under the Michigan Election Law, to correct numerous false statements you have made about the conduct of elections in Michigan, and to inform you of the consequences should you continue to fail to perform your statutory duties. If you continue to ignore correspondence from the Bureau of Elections, this will be the final letter you receive before legal action is taken.

[NOTE: Clerk Scott had not failed to perform a single one of her statutory duties. She simply questioned the integrity of the election process.]

The Bureau of Elections (Bureau) understands that you have continued to refuse to allow a technician from Hart Intercivic, Inc. (Hart) to perform preventative maintenance on your voting machines. Not only is preventative maintenance a service that Hart is contractually required to provide, it is also essential to ensure your tabulator and voter assist terminal (VAT) continue to be in good working condition and perform properly so that you can serve your voters on election day. For more information about the importance of the preventative maintenance, please see my letter of September 8, 2021, attached for your reference.

[NOTE: As a duly elected public official responsible for the integrity of records under her jurisdiction, she simply wanted their activities to be monitored by a technical specialist of her selection.]

The Bureau also understands that you have refused to perform the responsibilities required of you with regard to Public Accuracy Testing of your voting equipment. Under the Michigan Public Act 116 of 1954, MCL 168.798, and administrative rules promulgated by the Department of State, R 168.771, your election commission is required to conduct testing no later than October 28, 2021, following posting of public notice of the meeting. Upon completion of the testing, you are required to sign a certificate verifying that testing has been conducted.

[NOTE: Clerk Scott did not refuse to perform a public accuracy test. She merely asked for the basis of the number of test ballots she received.]

The Bureau understands that you intend to use certified Hart tabulators for the conduct of the November 2, 2021, election in Adams Township as required by law, but public statements indicate that you may refuse to use them for future elections. Neither you nor the township may conduct elections by counting ballots in any method other than the use of a certified electronic system in which tabulators count paper ballots. Decades ago, the Michigan state legislature enacted provisions of the Michigan Election Law that expressly require that ballots be counted by a certified electronic system. MCL 168.37, 795, 795a. The Michigan Election Law does not allow local, county or state officials to waive these requirements.

[NOTE: Clerks have statutory responsibilities for the maintenance of the integrity of records under their jurisdiction including election records. Electronic voting systems do not abrogate those responsibilities. They merely make them more difficult to execute due to attempts such as those by the MI Bureau of Elections to prevent clerks from investigating the integrity of her electronic records.]

For further information, see my September 8, 2021, letter:

Based on your public statements, I am concerned that your refusal to perform your legally mandated duties is connected to numerous false claims you have made about the conduct of elections in Michigan, which have been repeatedly debunked by election officials and experts of both political parties.

At a recent public meeting in your township, you made the following statements:

You claim that the test deck for the Logic and Accuracy Test (L&A Test) was "incomplete" for the March 2021 election, and you do not believe the tabulators were properly tested for the November 2020 election because in your estimation, in order to do so the test deck would have had to include over 200 million ballots. You also claim that the test decks were prepared by Election Source, which you found concerning.

[NOTE: Since when is questioning the methods used to perform the logic and accuracy test a violation of the law?]

Although Election Source is an accredited election contractor in Michigan, Hillsdale County does not contract with Election Source for any election-related services. The county uses Spectrum as their election service vendor. The test deck created by Spectrum for the March election (attached, along with invoices for the test decks for November 2020 and March 2021), did, indeed, meet the requirements of the Michigan Administrative Rules and the Michigan Election Law. You seem to mistakenly assume that a test deck must include every single possible combination of votes on a ballot in order to be sufficient, but that is not the case. Instead, for a special election, the test deck must test that the programming follows the applicable rules for undervotes, overvotes, and stray marks, and also correctly awards votes in properly marked races or questions.

[NOTE: What was the accreditation process for Election Source and Spectrum? Who accredited them?]

A review of your transcript in the Elections eLearning Center suggests you have never reviewed our instructional materials regarding the creation of test decks. The link to our module on L&A Testing for a Special Election can be found here and the manual can be found here.

[NOTE: Review of the instruction materials does not guarantee agreement with their content.]

You do not wish to participate in L&A Testing for the November 2021 election because you believe it could somehow destroy information that is on the tabulator now.

Michigan Administrative Rule 168.778 requires the election commission, of which you are a part, to conduct a public L&A Test prior to each election. You are also required to be present at the test and certify the accuracy of the test. The data from both the November 2020 election and March 2021 election are currently stored in the Election Management System (EMS) retained by Hillsdale County. No election information from those elections is retained on the tabulator following the election.

[NOTE: Where is the election information retained? Under federal law, it must be retained for 22 months after the election.]

Instead, information is sent to the county. The *unofficial* election night results are sent via secure modem transmission to the county after the election is completed and the tabulator tape has been printed, at which point the data is entered into the into the EMS. Additionally, it is the V-drive (what you refer to as the USB stick), not the tabulator, that contains the programming and results for the election. That drive is also returned to the county after each election. The Hillsdale

County Board of Canvassers then compares the electronic results to the paper tabulator tapes and pollbooks. There is no election information retained on the tabulator once the V-drive is removed.

[NOTE: "Secure modem transmission" is tech jargon for internet connection. The V-Drive configuration data needs to be retained in support of post-election audits.]

You do not want to allow preventative maintenance to be performed on your tabulator because you claim not to know who will be doing it and it might be Election Source. You are also concerned that, during preventative maintenance, data on the tabulator may somehow be erased.

You have already been repeatedly informed that preventative maintenance is mandatory and does not delete data. You were informed in a July 27, 2021 email from Abe Dane (attached) that Hart and a Hillsdale County employee would be performing the preventative maintenance. As I previously explained, preventative maintenance is routinely performed every two years and is a necessary security and maintenance process and does not destroy any records required to be maintained under federal or state law.

[NOTE: When batteries are removed from voting machines which are not plugged into a source of electricity, volatile memory is subject to being reset. Settings likely to be stored in volatile memory are internet connection settings which would prove helpful in any post-election audit. Mesa County clerk Tina Peters proved the fallacy of the assertion that servicing agents do "not delete data".[153] Not only did a forensics report of her equipment

indicate that information was systematically deleted, it also noted that her equipment was illegally certified and configured. She also found that her equipment was equipped with 36 wireless devices that enabled "any computer in the world" to connect with her EMS system.]

You claim you were instructed by the Bureau of Elections to destroy the electronic pollbook "data."

[NOTE: This is true.[154] Once again, these records are important when it comes to any substantive post-election audit. Affidavits assert that electronic pollbooks were connected directly to the state QVF at the TCF Center in Detroit. If this data was used as the basis for determining who should or should not receive a ballot, it needs to be made subject to evaluation during an audit.]

All electronic pollbook data is printed in paper form on election night. That information is then placed in the paper pollbook and retained for 22 months after the certification of the election. Clerks are instructed to delete the electronic version of the already-printed data to safeguard the personal information contained in the file.

You are concerned with using a Hart tabulator because of a 2007 report you found online regarding the Hart Intercivic Rally voting system. You further stated that you did not know if the software had been upgraded since then.

A 14-year-old report on a voting system that is no longer used has no bearing on the current voting system. The bipartisan U.S. Election Assistance Commission certified the most recent version of the Hart Verity voting system used in Michigan on

February 21, 2020, after it was tested by a Voting System Test Laboratory, and the bipartisan Board of State Canvassers approved it on April 20, 2020.

You are concerned that the modem is somehow turned on and the machine is somehow connected to the internet on election day.

While your tabulator has a modem physically attached, the modem is disabled while polls are open. Tabulator programming does not allow any modem communications to occur while voting is in progress; the secure transmission can occur only after the election is complete and the tabulator tape has been printed.

[NOTE: So goes the official narrative. Clerks and other concerned citizens should be allowed to verify that this is what actually happened. Peripheral settings can be toggled on or off remotely. They need to be able to examine configuration settings and event logs. Instead, clerks are forced to entrust the integrity of our elections to a private company not subject to FOIA requests.]

Additionally, data transmission is one-way. Data (unofficial results) is sent from the tabulator to the host, and no data is transferred from the host to the tabulator. The official results are compiled based on the tabulator tape that is printed, not the unofficial results. The actual paper ballots are also retained.

You claim the Bureau of Elections instructed clerks to destroy the chain of custody of ballots and said that ballots can be stored anywhere. Additionally, you claim you are reluctant to review the paper ballots from November 2020 so as not to "break" chain of custody of the ballots.

On February 12, 2021, the Bureau instructed clerks as follows:

> If the office of President, U.S. Senator or U.S. Represent-
> ative in Congress appears on the ballot (all appeared on
> the November 3, 2020 general election ballot), federal
> law requires that all documents relating to the election—
> including optical scan ballots and the programs used to
> tabulate optical scan ballots— be retained for 22 months
> from the date of the certification of the election. To com-
> ply with the requirement, the Bureau of Elections recom-
> mends that optical scan ballots and the programs relating
> to federal elections be stored in sealed ballot bags in a
> secure place during the 22-month retention period. The
> documents subject to the federal retention requirement
> must not be transferred to ballot bags for extended reten-
> tion until after they are released under Michigan election
> law as detailed in this memo (emphasis added).

> *[NOTE: Letters from the MI Bureau of Elections also in-
> cluded the following statements conveniently omitted from
> this letter:*

> *"Ballots, programs and related materials: The security of all
> optical scan ballots, programs, test decks, accuracy test results,
> edit listings and any other related materials are released.
> E-Pollbook laptops and flash drives: The EPB software and
> associated files must be deleted unless a post-election audit is
> planned but has not yet been completed or the deletion of the
> data has been stayed by an order of the court of the Secretary
> of State. Jurisdictions should consult with city, township, or
> county counsel regarding any pending court orders, subpoe-
> nas, or records requests regarding these materials."]*

You and other clerks were clearly instructed to retain ballots and other election materials in sealed ballot bags in a secure place. This is to ensure the chain of custody. However, as the custodian of these records, you are allowed to open the sealed ballot bag to review the ballots yourself. Additionally, you are required to access the ballots if you receive a Freedom of Information Act Request to review the voted ballots from a member of the public. The Bureau has provided detailed instructions (attached) to clerks to ensure the chain of custody is maintained during the process. Chain of custody does not mean you, as the custodian, cannot access the records. It means that you must remain in control of them at all times.

In a recent text message to an election inspector you made the following statement:

> You would be reaching out to all the election inspectors appointed for the November 2021 election to share your concerns about the tabulator.

As you know, Michigan conducted more than 250 audits following the 2020 election, the majority of which were conducted by county clerks of both political parties all across the state. The audits results are publicly available, as is a report by the Michigan Senate Oversight Committee that found that claims of voting equipment being compromised were baseless.

[NOTE: The referenced "audits" which are best classified as "partial recounts" covered 18,000 out of 5,579,317 ballots cast. Per the Deputy AG Erik Grill during oral hearings for the Bailey v Antrim County trial, no audit of the 2020 election has yet to be conducted. The MI Senate Oversight Committee did make such

an assertion, but their report was by no means the result of a professional investigation.[155]]

If you truly have concerns about whether voting tabulators accurately counted ballots, you can review the paper ballots from the November 3, 2020 election in your jurisdiction, which are in your possession. Any other clerk in Michigan can do the same, and any member of the public can inspect the paper ballots by submitting a Freedom of Information Act request.

[NOTE: Concerns with machines go well beyond the accurate counting of ballots. There are statutes on books which prevent poll workers from leaving their duty station until the closure of the polls so that advanced notice of vote tallies and vote tally trends are not released to the public. Likewise, it is necessary to ensure that "unofficial" election reports are not communicated by electronic voting machines prior to the closure of the polls. This requires access to voting system configuration settings and event logs.]

If you truly have concerns about the accuracy or integrity of pollbooks used on election day, you can review the paper record of the electronic pollbook used on election day, which is in the county's possession, and compare it to the Qualified Voter File, to which you have access. Any other clerk in Michigan can do the same. There is no voter information or record on the electronic copy of the electronic pollbook that is not also retained on the paper copy, and it has been standard practice for many years to delete the electronic copy to safeguard the personal identifying information on the file.

[NOTE: The Bureau of Elections has directed the clerks to delete the EPB software and data. This prohibits an investigator from

verifying the assertion that "there is no voter information or re-
cord on the electronic copy of the electronic pollbook that is not al-
so retained on the paper copy". Just because something is supposed
to be true does not mean that it actually is true.]

Under the Michigan Election Law, the Secretary of State is the
Chief Election Officer of this State and "shall have supervisory
control over local election officials in the performance of their
duties under the provisions of this act." MCL 168.21.

[NOTE: Under MCL 168.21, the secretary of state does indeed
have supervisory control over local election officials in the per-
formance of their duties. They can supervise. Poll challengers are
authorized to supervise elections as well. Supervisory authority
does not equate to the authority to prohibit a duly-elected public
official from the performance of their duties.]

The Secretary of State is required by law to "issue instructions"
and "[a]dvise and direct local election officials as to the proper methods of conducting elections." MCL 168.31(1)(a),(b).
County clerks and Boards of Commissioners are required to
comply with the instructions given by the Secretary of State.
Secretary of State v Berrien Co Bd of Election Comm'rs, 373
Mich 526, 530-531 (1964). The Director of Elections is authorized to act at the Secretary's behest "with respect to the
supervision and administration of the election laws." MCL
168.32.

In accordance with my authority under the Michigan Election
Law, you are directed to:
- Permit Hart Intercivic, Inc. to perform preventative main-
  tenance on your voting equipment.

- Conduct Public Accuracy Testing and sign required certificates.
- Conduct all future elections in Adams Township using certified Hart Intercivic, Inc. voting equipment, until such time as the Hillsdale County Clerk chooses a different certified voting system vendor.

[NOTE: Clerk Scott did not refuse to comply with statutory requirements. She merely questioned the state's directives regarding the execution of these statutory requirements.]

Please confirm that you will comply with these instructions no later than Friday, October 22, 2021. If you fail to do so, you will be instructed to refrain from administering any elections in Adams Township and legal action will be taken as necessary to enforce this instruction. Be advised that willfully failing to comply with a lawful order from the Secretary of State is a misdemeanor. MCL 168.931(h).

[NOTE: Clerk Scott was removed from her duties prior to any hearing in a court of law regarding the veracity of such assertions by the MI Bureau of Elections. Therefore she was denied due process of law.]

Sincerely,

Jonathan Brater
Director of Elections

Clerk Scott was subsequently removed by Brater from her oversight responsibility for the election she questioned. The bureau assigned a Hillsdale County election official to oversee the public accuracy test and the subsequent election. Mind you, Ms. Scott had violated no law. No charges had even been filed. There was no hearing to evaluate whether or not the assertions made by Brater in the letter were true. She was removed by state authorities from the duties assigned to her by the citizens of Adams Township for simply voicing her concerns with the election process.

Perhaps the most egregious attack upon a public election official is what happened to the clerk of Mesa County, Colorado, Tina Peters. In an attempt to preserve the integrity of the election records under her responsibility, she engaged a cyber expert to take forensic images of her Dominion DVS Democracy Suite Election Management System before and after her system was to be "updated". As a result, she had a rare image of her election system before and after the system was serviced by private election system vendors. Her findings confirmed what many had suspected.[156] Key information pertinent to the 2020 election needed for a post-election audit was scrubbed from her system in violation of state and federal law.[157]

In return for her attempt to monitor the integrity of election records, she has been accused of helping facilitate breaches in election system security, ignoring election rules and defying orders from the Colorado Secretary of State Jena Griswold. Her home has been raided by the FBI.[158] She has been charged with ten counts related to tampering with voting equipment.[159]

In a statement, Ms. Peters accused Democrats of using the grand jury "to formalize politically motivated accusations" against her.

"Using legal muscle to indict political opponents during an election isn't new strategy, but it's easier to execute when you have a district attorney who despises President Trump and any constitutional conservative like myself who continues to de-

mand all election evidence be made available to the public,"
she said.

She was later arrested allegedly for not providing an iPad cited in a
search warrant.[160] Her legal defense team asserts that she did provide the
iPad but objected when the officers attempted to confiscate property not
on the warrant such as her car keys. She spent time in jail.

In her March 1, 2022, letter to the Board of County Commissioners, she asserts "it appears that our county's voting system was illegally
certified and illegally configured in such a way that 'vote totals can be
easily changed'. We have been assured for years that external intrusions
are impossible because these systems are "air gapped," contain no modems, and cannot be accessed over the internet. It turns out these assurances were false. In fact, the Mesa County voting system alone was
found to contain thirty-six (36) wireless devices, and the system was
configured to allow "any computer in the world" to connect to our EMS
server."[161]

Her letter included a detailed report completed by cyber forensics
experts that highlighted the following critical discoveries:

- Uncertified software installed, rendering the voting system unlawful for use in elections.
- Does not meet statutorily mandated Voting System Standards (VSS) and could not have been lawfully certified for
  purchase or use.
- Suffered systematic deletion of election records (audit log
  files required by Federal and State law to be generated and
  maintained), which, in combination with other issues revealed in this report, creates an unauditable "back door"
  into the election system.
- Violates Voting System Standards (VSS) which expressly
  mandate prevention of the ability to "change calculated
  vote totals". This report documents this non-compliance

from the logged-in EMS server, from a non-DVS computer with network access, and from a cell phone (which may be possible if any of the 36 internal wireless devices in voting system components are deliberately or accidentally enabled and a password is obtained).

- Mandatory VSS "System Auditability" required features are disabled.
- Is configured with 36 wireless devices, which represent an extreme and unnecessary vulnerability, and which may be exploited to obtain unauthorized access from external devices, networks, and the internet.
- Is configured through firewall settings to allow any computer in the world to connect to the Election Management System (EMS) server.
- Uses only a Windows password with generic user IDs to restrict and control access.
- Contains user accounts with administrative access that share passwords, subverting VSS-required user accountability and action traceability controls.
- Uses a self-signed encryption certificate which exposes the system to the risk of undetected compromise or alteration.

Shortly after the release of this letter, a third forensic report on the images she preserved was released. This report revealed evidence of direct manipulation of election result databases. In addition to providing clear evidence of election tampering, this report underscores the importance of going beyond recounting ballots and ensuring that a forensic examination of digital election records is part of any post-election audit.[162]

The attack upon Clerk Peters simply for taking steps to preserve the records under her statutory authority highlights the ongoing election fraud cover-up efforts. Clearly, the Colorado Secretary of State and her political allies sought to make a very public example of Clerk Peters in order to discourage such civic responsibility in the future.

Clerks were not the only targets of censorship. Every day citizens were targeted as well. The law firm Clare Locke has sent out over 150 cease-and-desist letters nationwide, over thirty in Michigan alone, on behalf of their client Dominion Voting Systems.[163] They threatened legal action against individuals who persisted in citing evidence of election fraud.

If this were the most secure election in history, what is there to hide?

Michigan legislators joined in the pursuit of censorship. Intimidation tactics abounded, such as the following Facebook post by Michigan State Representative Cynthia Johnson (D):

> This is just a warning to you Trumpers. Be careful. Walk lightly. We ain't playing with you. Enough of the shenanigans. Enough is enough…. And for those of you who are soldiers. You know how to do it. Do it right. Be in order. Make them pay.

Her only penalty for such action was to be removed from committees. Incidentally, this is the same penalty that I received for informing Michigan Senate Majority Leader Arlan Meekhof on the floor of the Michigan Senate that I did not work for him; I worked for the citizens of Michigan. It is also worth noting that this Facebook post, clearly calling for violence against Trump supporters, was still available on Facebook at the time of this writing.

Such intimidation tactics were not limited to Democrats. The Michigan Senate Oversight Committee featuring Republican State Senators Ed McBroom, Lana Theis, and John Bizon followed her example albeit in a more subtle fashion.

The committee report encouraged the weaponization of state government against those who assert that there was election fraud in the following statement:

The Committee recommends the attorney general consider investigating those who have been utilizing misleading and false information about Antrim County to raise money or publicity for their own ends. The Committee finds those promoting Antrim County as the prime evidence of a nationwide conspiracy to steal the election place all other statements and actions they make in a position of zero credibility.[164]

So much for our First Amendment rights to free speech and the ability to seek redress for grievances.

Legislators, voting system manufacturers, and the Secretary of State were not the only groups threatening legal action. The Michigan Attorney General joined them in an attempt to silence anyone who shared evidence of election fraud. In a July 9, 2021, report by the Epoch Times:

Michigan's attorney general, with assistance from police officers, will investigate people who claimed election fraud happened during the 2020 contest.

A spokeswoman for Michigan Attorney General Dana Nessel told The Epoch Times in an email on Friday that the Democrat will probe people who allegedly made false claims, with help from Michigan State Police.

The spokeswoman said Nessel decided to launch the probes on a request from Republicans in the Michigan Senate.[165]

On the bright side, it is refreshing to see the Democrat Attorney General cooperating with the recommendations of the Republican Senate, albeit it was to pursue the infringement of constitutional rights of citizens.

The federal government also joined the censorship fray.

The example that received the most media attention was a letter from the US Department of Justice to Arizona senate majority leader Karen Fann attempting to prohibit their election investigations in Maricopa County. The deputy assistant attorney general outlined two issues:

> The first issue relates to a number of reports suggesting that the ballots, elections systems, and election materials ... [were] not being adequately safeguarded." The second issue was with canvassers who were knocking on doors "to confirm if valid voters actually lived at the stated address." Their concern with the latter issue is that it might target minorities and be seen as intimidating.[166]

There were less publicized examples of interference, though.

Back in Michigan, Jacky Eubanks, grassroots organizer of canvass activities in Macomb County, submitted her findings to the Macomb County Clerk, Anthony Forlini, who forwarded them to local law enforcement, who forwarded them to the Michigan state police, who then forwarded them to the FBI. The FBI then proceeded to interrogate Jacky Eubanks about her activities. The experience was quite intimidating to a recent college graduate simply attempting to perform her civic duty. The line of questioning gave no indication that the FBI was investigating the voter anomalies discovered by Miss Eubanks.

In the wake of cyberattacks such as the SolarWinds hack, federal authorities treated the malware intrusions as digital crime scenes. They systematically pulled computer logs and copies of files all the while ensuring that the chain of custody for such records was maintained. They eventually identified an "elegant, encrypted little blob of code 'just 3,500 lines long'."[167] Instead of any apparent professional investigation of the digital crime scene known as the 2020 election, federal authorities are investigating the investigators while turning a blind eye to the destruction of records that would be useful in such an investigation.

The FBI is not the only one attempting to intimidate election fraud investigators. The media is as well. On October 13, 2021, Bridge Magazine released a story entitled "Who's at door? It may be Trump loyalists, hunting for Michigan 'ghost voters.'."[168] Stories such as this are designed to discourage canvassing activities that simply seek to validate the data in the statewide voter registration file.

> "Activists loyal to Donald Trump are knocking on doors to talk to Michigan voters about their 2020 ballots in a quixotic quest to uncover fraud in last year's election. They could be coming to your home soon, as organizers seek to expand an effort already underway in a handful of Michigan communities."

> They're on the search for phantom or ghost voters, organizers said Tuesday during a rally at the Michigan Capitol, where they signed up new volunteers while demanding GOP lawmakers order a "forensic audit" of the 2020 contest.
> Federal officials have warned that home canvassing could amount to voter intimidation, and Michigan's top election official is discouraging voters from discussing their ballots with untrained activists.

> "Any effort to violate citizens' privacy or intimidate them by showing up at their doorstep demanding to know how they voted is a desperate attempt to further sow seeds of doubt about election results that were a secure and accurate reflection of the will of the voters," said Tracy Wimmer, a spokesperson for Democratic Secretary of State Jocelyn Benson.

CNN also jumped into the canvasser intimidation game with a story by Fredreka Schouten entitled "Trump loyalists are knocking on voters' doors in the latest quest to find fraud in the 2020 election."[169]

The basic ingredients of such stories are: 1) link election integrity advocates to Trump, 2) re-assert the certified election results, 3) use the word *debunked* or *unsubstantiated*, and 4) accuse election integrity advocates of what they are guilty of (e.g., intimidation). These stories are noticeably void of any substantive reference to or analysis of the core concerns of election integrity advocates (i.e., meddling kids). It is very difficult to get the truth out into the public square when the media is dominated by progressive "news" outlets. In military parlance, progressives have complete air supremacy. Any time one of our planes loaded with the truth attempts a takeoff, they are shot down before they even get a chance to taxi out to the runway.

The media is not only providing cover for fraudulent elections of the past, they are also being proactive. They have taken to scrutinizing the backgrounds of new members of the boards of canvassers for various jurisdictions across the state. On December 3, 2021, *Slate* published a story called "Meet the Trump Fanatics Who Have Taken Over Elections in a Critical Swing State." The title makes it quite clear as to the intended purpose of the article: marginalize.

This rhetoric was taken to new, dangerous heights on February 7, 2022. The Department of Homeland Security issued a Terrorism Advisory System Bulletin entitled "Summary of Terrorism Threat to the U.S. Homeland."

The bulletin cited the following as a key factor contributing to the current heightened threat environment:

1. "The proliferation of false or misleading narratives, which sow discord or undermine public trust in U.S. government institutions:

   • For example, there is widespread online proliferation of false or misleading narratives regarding unsubstantiated widespread election fraud and COVID-19. Grievances associated with these themes inspired violent extremist attacks during 2021.

- Malign foreign powers have and continue to amplify these false or misleading narratives in efforts to damage the United States."

There appears to be collusion between the federal government and the media on the use of the term "unsubstantiated." This collusion has serious implications in light of terrorism investigation practices which eliminate due process protections for Americans. So much for our rights to free speech, the right to seek redress for our grievances, and the due process of law.

The topic of due process also merits attention. When the topic of election fraud evidence comes up, a common assertion is that courts have dismissed all the election fraud lawsuits due to lack of substantive evidence. If the evidence were real, they reason, these cases would have been heard by these judges, many of whom were Trump appointees. Contrary to this narrative, the vast majority of cases that were dismissed were done so on the basis of standing or process concerns, not on the basis of the evidence. In the thirty cases actually reviewed on the basis of the merit of the evidence, twenty-two were ruled in favor of those alleging fraud. In other words, an overwhelming 73% majority of the cases were ruled favorably on the merit of the evidence.[170]

The deliberate misinformation regarding the status of cases in which the election fraud evidence had an opportunity to be presented is even more evidence of a cover up.

Letting people voice their concerns about election fraud is not only supposed to be a right secured under our constitution, it also has a way of exposing who is telling the truth and who is not. In this light, the degree of censorship being promoted by Big Government and Big Media sure seems to indicate they are seeking to cover up not promote the truth. Big Tech has joined them in this pursuit. Social media companies such as Facebook, Twitter, YouTube, and others have all clamped down on posts which expose evidence of election fraud. A brief sample of Big Tech censorship includes:

- Twitter de-platformed a sitting US President but not an Iranian leader promoting terrorism.
- Facebook banned pro-Trump advertising during a presidential campaign.
- Facebook's so-called fact checkers pollute the feeds or users are put in Facebook jail for days or weeks.
- YouTube routinely bans videos on election fraud.
- Yahoo.com even seeded their web searches with derogatory finds for Bernie Sanders.
- PayPal cuts off platforms asserting election fraud.

If claims of election fraud were false, they wouldn't need to be censored. They would be exposed in the public square. This censorship is the type of behavior one finds in the wake of a coup. It is characteristic of a banana republic not a constitutional republic.

The official narrative of those promoting this censorship is that it is necessary to encourage faith in our election system. This narrative is merely the deployment of the misinformation / disinformation strategy conceived of during the preparation phase. In a coup, it is incumbent upon the newly installed regime to promote their propaganda while classifying the truth as misinformation. They rely upon establishing what George Orwell referred to as a "Ministry of Truth" in his classic novel *1984*.

Misinformation and disinformation can take on many forms. As a former legislator, I know firsthand how influential the counsel from trusted staff can be upon the policy direction of a given caucus. During the heat of the discussions regarding policy and legal options available to legislators in the wake of the 2020 election, the Michigan House Republican Caucus and the Michigan Senate Republican Caucus relied heavily upon trusted counsel who made significant employment changes shortly after Joe Biden's inauguration on January 20, 2021. In March of 2021, a senior staffer with the Michigan Senate Republican Caucus,

Amber McCann, left her influential position to serve as the director of legislative affairs for Michigan's Democrat attorney general.[171] A month later, a member of the Michigan House Republican Caucus legal team, whose husband was chief of staff for a Democrat House Minority Leader, abruptly left her position. In August of 2021, senior house republican legal counsel, Hassan Beydoun, left the Republicans in the Michigan house to serve on behalf of the Democrat mayor of Detroit, Mike Duggan.[172]

These employment changes raise important questions concerning what sort of counsel they may have provided Republican legislators during this critical time. Is it any wonder that the Michigan legislature refused to pursue an audit of the election as required under the Michigan constitution?

There is evidence of fifth columnists in action on January 6. The term "fifth columnist" refers to a group of clandestine supporters of an enemy that seek to sabotage efforts within a given faction. The media narrative about the events of January 6 conclude that President Trump exhorted his supporters to storm the Capitol. At the time, many of the stories about January 6 neglected to mention the following facts.

President Trump's speech started at noon and did not end until 1:10 p.m. In President Trump's speech, he stated, "I know that everyone here will soon be marching over to the Capitol Building to peacefully and patriotically make your voices heard"

Protestors featuring pro-Trump clothing and flags head towards the Capitol at 10:58 a.m.

Capitol security was breached at 12:53 p.m.

Remember, Trump's speech did not end until 1:10 p.m.

The US Capitol is a thirty-two-minute walk from the site of President Trump's speech on the Ellipse. Those who attended Trump's speech and then walked to the US Capitol would not have arrived at the Capitol before 1:42 p.m. That is forty-nine minutes after the Capitol security was first breached.

There is a pattern in the media reports about the events of January 6.

Anyone wearing pro-Trump clothing or waving a pro-Trump flag was assumed to be a Trump supporter by members of the media.

While I was not present in DC on January 6, I have been to over 100 pro-Trump events. I have spoken at many of them.

Pro-Trump events, even those protesting our sitting elected officials, feature prayers and people singing God Bless America. Attendees invariably leave the location of the event cleaner than when they found it.

Anti-America events featuring groups such as BLM and Antifa feature vandalism and violence against police. They leave the location of the event in shambles.[173]

The contrast between the fruit of the two ideologically opposed groups could not be clearer.

Did the events of January 6 resemble what happens at a Pro-Trump rally or an Anti-America rally? What was the net effect of storming the Capitol? Was it a Pro-Trump result or an Anti-Trump result?

At 1:05 p.m., Congress commenced their Joint Session to commence a review of the electoral votes submitted by each state.

At 1:12 p.m., Rep Paul Gosar (R-AZ) and Sen Ted Cruz (R-TX) object to certifying the Arizona votes.

At 1:14 p.m., VP-elect Kamala Harris is evacuated by the Secret Service from the DNC Headquarters

At 2:20 p.m., the House is gaveled into recess and starts to evacuate.

At 8:06 p.m., the Senate reconvenes.

At 9:00 p.m. Speaker Pelosi reopens the House debate.

In the dead of night, at 3:24 a.m., Congress completes the counting of the electoral votes ceding Biden a 306-232 victory.

The net effect of the storming of the Capitol was to put a halt to the public discussion of election fraud. Many of us were looking forward to finally having an opportunity for the evidence of election fraud to be heard on the national stage. Instead, the censorship continued. The national discussion of whether or not the electoral college results should be certified was silenced and replaced by a media narrative that President Trump had called for a riot.

No matter how you slice it, the events of January 6 did not lead to a Pro-Trump result. This observation should open the door to the consideration of whether or not Trump supporters were the true instigators behind the storming of the US Capitol.

Have we seen evidence of covert influence operations being used to subvert the results of the 2020 election? Yes.

A whole book could be written on the events of January 6. This is not that book. The ShutdownDC preparations alone could fill a book on the subject. This is not that book either. Instead, I would like to focus upon individuals identified by the media that seem to indicate evidence of fifth columnists at work during the politically charged events of January 6, 2021. For starters, there is video footage available publicly showing groups of people changing their black block wardrobe characteristic of Antifa activists to include pro-Trump paraphernalia prior to marching on the Capitol.[174] There is evidence to suggest that the individuals I would like to focus upon were simply masquerading as Trump supporters. They were well organized and fit the profile of what is referred to as an agent provocateur.

The first of these individuals has been identified by the media as Ray Epps.

An NBC News report on Ray Epps stated,

Epps was seen on video the night of Jan. 5 asking other people to go into the Capitol the next day before others began chanting, "Fed, Fed, Fed" at him. In video from Jan. 6, Epps shouted to those nearby: "OK, folks, spread the word! As soon as the president is done speaking, we go to the Capitol. The Capitol is this direction."[175]

During testimony before the U.S. Senate, FBI agent Jill Sanborn refused to give answers as to who Ray Epps is and whether any agents or informants participated in any capacity in the January 6 Capitol riot.

"Ms. Sanborn, was Ray Epps a fed?" Cruz asked. "How many FBI agents or confidential informants actively participated in the events of January 6th?"
"Sir, I can't answer that," Sanborn said, repeating that the FBI does not go into "sources and methods" in settings like this.
"He then shifted tactics, asking: 'Who is Ray Epps?'
"I'm aware of the individual, sir. I don't have the specific background on him."
Cruz then shared images of Epps from January 5, where his suspicious behavior caught the attention of Trump supporters gathered in Washington, D.C., causing them to chant, 'Fed!'[176]

Republicans, including Representatives Matt Gaetz and Marjorie Taylor Greene, claim Epps was on the FBI's January 6 suspect list but was mysteriously removed six months later after right-wing blog Revolver labeled him a "Fed-protected provocateur." They held a press conference on January 6, 2022, marking the one-year anniversary of the events of January 6, 2021. Media reports after the event chastised them for promoting what the media asserts as "the false claim that the FBI orchestrated the riot."

In contrast to media assertions, speculation regarding FBI agents acting as agent provocateurs is not without merit. FBI agents were recently accused of entrapment in the so-called Governor Whitmer kidnapping plot. On December 27, 2021, Michigan news organization M-Live reported that,

"The government conceived and controlled every aspect of the alleged plot. On September 5, 2020, FBI Special Agent Jayson Chambers texted CHS Dan: 'Mission is to kill the governor, specially,'" the defense attorneys wrote. They said that the informants and undercover agents posed as patriotic Americans to develop the defendants' trust and "radicalize them ... with rousing speeches featuring Antifa, mask mandates and similar topics ... to create an atmosphere of crisis and impending social unrest, all in an effort to motivate the targets to work with CHS Dan, to join him in his plot to kidnap Governor Whitmer."[177]

The net result of the ensuing trial was that two of the defendants in the so-called plot were acquitted and there was a hung jury for the other two.[178]

Oh, and in case you were wondering, Steven D'Antuono, the same Special Agent in Charge at the FBI Field Office in Detroit during the "Governor Whitmer Plot" is now running the DC Field Office overseeing the January 6 investigation.[179] Nothing to see here. These aren't the droids you are looking for.

The involvement of federal employees, including those with significant security credentials, is consistent with the Democracy Defense video evidence provided by Millie Weaver and her informants. Federal employees and contractors were featured prominently in the planning sessions for insurrection-based activities in her videos. These videos would certainly merit further investigation as to what extent is it true that agent provocateurs were being excused from investigation and prosecution due to existing relationships with federal law enforcement officials.

The next individual of interest is John Sullivan (a.k.a. Jayden X). On January 6, 2021, John was in the halls of the US Capitol calling for violent actions. The media narrative for January 6 puts the blame for the events firmly on President Trump and his supporters. In contrast to this narrative, it is important to note that John Sullivan is a supporter of Black Lives Matter and runs a website called Insurgence USA."[180]

On January 1, 2021, he tweeted under the handle @realjaydenx the following:

Chud (slur) Alert: Trump is like the official organizer of J6 (January 6) fash (fascist) rally. When he told PBs (Proud Boys) to "stand down and stand by" he really wasn't kidding. We need numbers to show up No Fascist In DC – March Against Fascism spread the word Comrades!

Trust me. This was not an isolated rant by Sullivan against President Trump and his supporters. This is not exactly the rhetoric one would expect of a Trump supporter in any case. Prior to the election, he openly sold "Made You Look" Black Lives Matter Red Hats with MAGA-style lettering on his website. The hat he donned as he roamed the halls of the US Capitol on January 6, however, was a camo-style Trump 2020 "Keep America Great" hat.

On January 6, 2021, he posted a video of himself and a female friend taken from inside the US Capitol where his friend exclaimed, "You were right. We did it." He responded, "Dude. I was trying to tell you. I couldn't say much... You just have to watch my channel." If you watch his channel, you would have seen him advertising his January 6 "US AGAINST FASCISM" rally meeting at 11 a.m. at the BLM Plaza featuring a communist-inspired fist with rifles in the background which is the logo of the "Fred Hampton Gun Club."[181] Sullivan called on his supporters to wear their "tactical gear" to the January 6 event... which he also sold on his InsurgenceUSA.com website.

This wouldn't be the first time that someone attempted to impersonate Trump supporters to promote a false narrative. Do you recall the trial of Jussie Smollett? On December 10, 2021, he was found guilty on five out of six criminal counts related to his false claims of being a victim of a hate crime attack. During Smollett's trial, Olabinjo Osundairo testified that "He (Smollett) had this crazy idea that two MAGA Trump supporters attack him so he can get the footage and put it on social media so he could show the 'Empire' studio."[182] During his trial, Smollett could be seen raising his fist in a display of communist solidarity. Leftists posing as Trump supporters while doing something unlawful appears to be in vogue.

As a minimum, the actions of John Sullivan is evidence that non-Trump supporters were involved in the storming of the Capitol masquerading as Trump supporters. I would assert, however, that it also indicates that the events of January 6 were part of a well-orchestrated plan that not only included John Sullivan but many others as well.

Both Ray Epps and John Sullivan were detained but later released by police in the wake of the events of January 6. There appears to be a "catch and release" policy within some circles of our law enforcement community when it comes to specific individuals. It is noteworthy that these individuals were indeed "caught" and put into custody. This indicates that there are indeed many officers on the front lines seeking to do their job and enforce the rule of law. It also seems that as soon as a list of the names of those detained by these officers makes its way to the "higher ups", certain suspects were released. While John Sullivan is still on the list of those charged with crimes in the wake of the January 6 events, no charges have been levied against Ray Epps.[183] It would be interesting to know who ordered the release of Ray Epps and John Sullivan from custody while at the same time depriving others not on their "list" of due process of law as required in our US Constitution and detaining them under excessively harsh conditions.[184, 185]

By no means were Ray Epps and John Sullivan the only individuals worthy of further investigation regarding the events of January 6. American journalist Millie Weaver and her informants have done an exceptional job exposing the insurrection plans of a well-organized federation of leftist organizations, many of whom have foreign ties. Video chat sessions for these groups not only provide detailed plans for how to shut down the government, but they also emphasize the need to characterize any actions by Trump supporters as a coup. They have thus far been successful in deflecting the coup narrative away from themselves in large part due to the significant attention they paid to planning and simulating the events of January 6.

Remember, the net effect of the actions of January 6 was to cast a shadow upon the deliberations on the floor of the US House regarding the validity of the electoral votes submitted by the states. This shadow revolved around the false narrative that one of the candidates at the center of the House floor debate had called for a riot at the US Capitol.

The events of January 6 were successful at suppressing a frank and open discussion about election fraud on the floor of the House of Representatives. This was a discussion that many Americans, including myself, were looking forward to after months of having such discussions censored or mischaracterized by the media. The fake "Trump led an insurrection" narrative carried the day on January 6, 2021, and served as the basis of his second impeachment trial. In fact, the agent provocateurs of January 6 were so successful that the insurrection narrative persisted as the basis of a military lockdown of Washington DC that lasted until the end of May. There is no better visual image in support of the assertion that America was the victim of a coup than to see the US Capitol cordoned off by fencing and 26,000 troops.[186]

Most Americans dramatically underestimate the scope of the election fraud that occurred in the 2020 coup. I was among those who drastically underestimated the scope when I commenced my investigations into election fraud. I no longer suffer from this handicap.

Just two weeks after the Inauguration Ceremony for Joe Biden, in an apparent rush to claim credit for the 2020 election victory attributed to Joe Biden, Molly Ball wrote an article for *Time* magazine entitled "The Secret Bipartisan Campaign That Saved the 2020 Election."[187]

Ms. Ball makes some rather startling claims in her article:

There was a conspiracy unfolding behind the scenes, one that both curtailed the protests and coordinated the resistance from CEOs. Both surprises were the result of an informal alliance between left-wing activists and business titans. The pact was formalized in a terse, little-noticed joint statement of the U.S. Chamber of Commerce and AFL-CIO published on Election Day. . . .

Their work touched every aspect of the election. They got states to change voting systems and laws and helped secure hundreds of millions in public and private funding. They fended off voter-suppression lawsuits, recruited armies of poll workers and got millions of people to vote by mail for the first time. They successfully pressured social media companies to take a harder line against disinformation and used data-driven strategies to fight viral smears. They executed national public-awareness campaigns that helped Americans understand how the vote count would unfold over days or weeks, preventing Trump's conspiracy theories and false claims of victory from getting more traction. After Election Day, they monitored every pressure point to ensure that Trump could not overturn the result. "The untold story of the election is the thousands of people of both parties who accomplished the triumph of American democracy at its very foundation," says Norm Eisen, a prominent lawyer and former Obama Administration official who recruited Republicans and Democrats to the board of the Voter Protection Program.

That's why the participants want the secret history of the 2020 election told, even though it sounds like a paranoid fever dream—a well-funded cabal of powerful people, ranging across

industries and ideologies, working together behind the scenes
to influence perceptions, change rules and laws, steer media
coverage and control the flow of information.

Pretty good evidence of a well-organized influence operation don't
you think?

Summary

Thus far, the defense phase of the coup has been very effective. We
have evidence that the following tactics were employed successfully:

- Initial No vote on certification of Wayne County election
  results was reversed after intimidation tactics were successfully employed.
- Rampant Big Media and Big Tech censorship and defama-
  tion of anyone asserting election fraud suppressed communication of evidence to general public.
- Threatening cease-and-desist letters issued to citizens
  speaking out against election fraud.
- Election officials and vendors ordered the destruction of
  election records.
- 104,138 voter records have not been preserved in the state
  voter registration file
- Fake audits were conducted.
- Legislature paralyzed by fear and poor counsel.
- Clerks pursuing investigations threatened by Michigan's
  secretary of state.
- Clerks directed to violate federal law by Michigan's secretary of state.
- Attorneys threatened with disbarment for filing election
  fraud cases.
- Evidence that January 6 was part of a well-orchestrated
  plan executed by agent provocateurs.
- 2020 coup confirmed by coup perpetrators

CHAPTER 7

The Big Picture

Then you have it…the evidence of election fraud that all too many
Americans are led to believe does not exist.

MICHIGAN

We have shown evidence in Michigan that the preparation phase
tactics predicted in our theory of how the election could be stolen were
actually employed successfully as it created and enhanced significant
weaknesses in our mail-in ballot voting processes. We have shown evidence in Michigan that the main attack phase tactics predicted were
actually employed to close the gap on the number of votes required for
victory. We have shown evidence in Michigan that the backup attack
phase tactics predicted were actually employed successfully as the reported vote margin was sufficient to justify awarding Michigan's sixteen
electoral college votes to Joe Biden. We have shown evidence in Michigan that the defense phase tactics predicted were actually employed successfully as the election results have yet to be overturned.

So how does someone ensure victory in a presidential election using this battle plan? Let's zero in on what happens to our key election
records in the chain of custody during each phase.

- Preparation Phase
  - Pre-election projections estimated a record national voter turnout of 145 million. 160 million votes were cast.
  - Former MI Secretary of State estimates that statewide voter registration file featured at least 800,000 ineligible voters
  - Big Tech likely shifted upwards of 12 million votes

- Main Attack Phase
  - Post-election canvassing yielded evidence of 17.6% anomaly rate in pollbook data accounting for a potential 87,000 fraudulent votes in just one of Michigan's 83 counties.

- Backup Attack Phase
  - At 5:00:04 a.m. the cumulative vote count of 4,365,423 votes is reset to zero providing evidence of a digital controller
  - Clear evidence that tabulators were connected to the internet
  - Over 298,000 votes in excess of tabulator capacity were injected into vote tallies
  - Late-night ballot drops after polls closed were counted
  - New pollbooks issued thirteen days after the election

- Defense Phase
  - 104,138 voter records have not been preserved in the state voter registration file
  - Election records needed for a real audit have been deleted

Those behind the 2020 coup have been very successful at discouraging our elected officials from honoring their oaths of office and fulfilling the constitutional right of Michigan citizens to an audit of statewide election results. In the wake of their inaction, citizens from all walks of life have risen up to fill the investigative gap. I refer to these citizens as "meddling kids" hearkening back to the Mystery Inc. crew of Scooby Doo fame. Equipped with not much more than curiosity and determination, these meddling kids have been sacrificing countless hours operating on shoestring budgets to investigate what really happened in the 2020 election. These efforts have met with significant resistance from those complicit with the coup. The conspirators have done their very best to silence any attempt to report out on the fruits of the investigations by these meddling kids.

Thus, the need for this book. The truth cannot be silenced forever.

There is more than enough evidence of fraudulent votes in Michigan to bring into question the reported 154,188 presidential vote margin in favor of Biden.

In other words, there IS evidence of election fraud.

There is evidence of WIDESPREAD election fraud.

There is evidence of SIGNIFICANT election fraud.

The evidence we have presented so far has focused on one state: Michigan. You might be wondering by now about other states. Do we see any similarities between what happened in Michigan and any other states? Let's look at the facts.

ARIZONA

Arizona was the first state in the union to conduct a forensic audit of the election. The vote margin certified in favor of Joe Biden was only 10,457 votes. Canvassing efforts led by Liz Harris discovered 173,104 lost votes and 96,389 phantom voters.

The groundbreaking Arizona audit led by the Arizona State Senate revealed significant breaches in the chain of custody that should call into question the integrity of any vote tallies. For starters, despite attempts to delete internet connection data, forensic analysis revealed undeniable evidence of internet connectivity recovered from "unallocated space" in an EMS server, EMS client workstations, adjudication workstations and other devices instrumental in the management of election results.[1]

Against all common sense and security policies, Remote Access and Terminal Services features of Windows were enabled. The activation of these features combined with internet connectivity is a recipe for remote manipulation of election data by a third party.

In an apparent attempt to cover the tracks resulting from remote control actions, there was also evidence that security logs were deliberately overwritten to prevent examination of election-related data management. In fact, the timing of one of the internet sessions corresponds to execution of a SQL Purge command that resulted in the deletion of the election results database right before Maricopa County was to perform their own audit of the election.

There were significant anomalies related to mail-in ballots as well. One of the most glaring observations featured the application of signature verification stamps to blank signatures by election officials. The audit report concluded that approximately 57,000 ballots should have been disqualified from the official count including the presence of around 17,000 duplicated ballots. Multiple statutory violations were cited in the report and forwarded to the Arizona Attorney General for further investigation and prosecution as warranted. Additional audit report findings are pending.

Obstruction by the Maricopa County Board of Supervisors prevented access to router data which could be used to get to the bottom of who had access to the voting system and when. Very important information. When a report was finally issued on March 23, 2022 by Special Master John Shadegg it asserted that there were no routers or managed devices therefore no splunk logs or "public" internet connections. Many technical experts who have reviewed the report simply saw more evidence of jargon-based word games rather than a substantive investigation.

Electronic routing of election data was not the only suspicious routing activity in Arizona. True the Vote has filed a complaint in Arizona asserting that ballot trafficking occurred during the 2020 general election.

"Acting upon the information provided to us, True the Vote's contracted team of researchers and investigators videoed the testimonies of several individuals regarding the personal knowledge, methods, and organizations involved in ballot trafficking in Arizona. What was described was an organized scheme involving paying individuals to collect and deliver unvoted ballots to centralized locations where the ballots were then marked, sealed, and deposited in absentee ballot drop boxes. The collectors of these ballots were paid between $10 to $40 per ballot.

One of the individuals indicated she was personally responsible for almost 3,000 ballots being placed in a single drop box."[2]

True the Vote proceeded to perform research in an attempt to verify these assertions. In support of this research, they obtained commercially available cell phone data that included geospatial and timestamp data. During the time period studied, they discovered that 202 unique devices made an average of 21 drops each to absentee drop boxes in Maricopa County for a total of 4,242 drops. Surveillance videos of drop boxes in Maricopa County was of insufficient quality to be of any use. Two of the devices tracked in Maricopa County were later identified as making repeated absentee ballot drop box visits during the January 5, 2021, Georgia US Senate runoff election. In Yuma County, they discovered 41 unique devices which made an average of 31 trips each for a total of 1,435 drops. Surveillance video from Yuma County was unavailable which is an apparent violation of USC 52 Section 20701.

Regarding the examination of ballots, there are preliminary reports that indicate a very significant anomaly. The 2.1 million ballots recorded in Maricopa County were supposed to be printed using secure paper technology like that used in paper currency. They were not. This indicates that as many as 2.1 million votes cast in the 2020 election may have been fraudulently cast. Arizona legislators, such as Senator Wendy Rogers and Representative Mark Finchem, have been calling for the decertification of the Arizona election results as a result of these findings. In so doing, the eleven electoral college votes from Arizona would be called into question.

In summary, there were indeed similarities between what was observed in Arizona and Michigan. Most notably, canvassing revealed significant issues with the integrity of mail-in ballots and election officials offered significant resistance to any attempts to demonstrate that the 2020 election was not the most secure election in history.

WISCONSIN

The Wisconsin legislature also launched an investigation of the 2020 election though it has not been officially referred to as an audit. Wisconsin was notably the first state in the union where law enforcement actually filed charges against alleged perpetrators of election fraud. The vote margin certified in favor of Joe Biden was only 20,682 votes.

Like Michigan and Arizona, in Wisconsin there were significant anomalies evident in the processing of absentee ballots and new voter registrations. In 2020, 957,977 Wisconsinites registered to be a new voter. There were 3.68 million registered voters for the 2020 election. That means a whopping 26% of the voters registered were new voters. Of the 957,977 registrations, only 898,421 of the new registrations matched corresponding records used as an integrity check at the Department of

Transportation. Which means that 45,665 or 4.8% of new voters registered with driver's license information that did not match the information possessed by the Department of Motor Vehicles. Which is more than the margin of victory assigned to Joe Biden.

Regarding absentee ballots, the sheriff of Racine County performed an investigation into the handling of ballots in nursing homes. They determined that the Wisconsin Election Commission (WEC) issued directives that violated Wisconsin election law and filed charges to that effect with the county prosecutor.

The Racine County Sheriff's Office was not the only organization performing investigations. True the Vote sifted through terabytes of commercially available cell phone data and video surveillance footage to isolate a manageable set of 138 targeted devices.[3] These targeted devices were limited to those averaging 5 NGO visits and 26 drop boxes during the study period. Their analysis of the data obtained revealed that at least 137,551 ballots were trafficked in a manner that impacted the final vote tally.

On March 1, 2022, former Wisconsin Supreme Court Justice Mike Gableman released his 136-page report[4] to the Wisconsin legislature in his capacity as special counsel. The report featured evidence of the role that Center for Tech and Civic Life played in the manipulation of the election results as well as violations of the law by the Wisconsin Elections Commission. We have already highlighted the large sums of money being funneled by progressive billionaires to organizations such as CTCL. The Gableman Report provides significant insights as to how this money was used to enable private organizations to manipulate public elections.

One of the most alarming mechanisms pertains to electronic voting system security. Throughout the defense phase, clerks who attempt to engage third party technical experts to examine the integrity of their voting systems were threatened with legal action. There was no such rigor applied to access to these same election systems prior to the election as evidence by the lax management of important security credentials by WEC. Per the report, "WEC mass-issued FIDO Keys across the State to counties and municipalities". Under WEC security policies, access to WisVote needs a login name, password, and FIDO key. FIDO is short for Fast Identity Online. The FIDO key is contained in a flash drive that is inserted into a personal computer. FIDO keys should be managed under strict chain of custody requirements. Instead, the WEC appears to have distributed FIDO keys without discretion. In fact, one county clerk received 15 keys but had only requested 2 of these powerful keys.

In an observation likely related to this lack of security key discretion, the report provided evidence of a Brooklyn attorney running Green Bay's election as an "on-site contact" using a hidden wi-fi network. Michael Spitzer Rubenstein, an employee of the National Vote at Home Institute (NVAHI) appears to have leveraged his credentials to run the Green Bay election from his hotel room. In the lead up to the election, his communications with Claire Woodall-Vogg, the Executive Director of the City of Milwaukee Election Commission, show him requesting "absentee data a day ahead of time" so that he "can set things up". Woodall-Vogg appears to have been Rubensteain's connection that opened the door to accessing the election data in Green Bay. He went on to request: '1) Number of ballot preparation teams, 2) Number of returned ballots per ward, 3) Number of outstanding ballots per ward." It may just be me, but it seems he is requesting the information needed to set-up an illegal election night ballot factory. The term "ballot preparation teams" is a huge red flag. Last time I checked, it only takes one person to prepare a ballot when a vote is legally cast. In other communications, Rubenstein is openly requesting instructions for "ballot reconstruction". He references the use of "Quickbase" software which provides "no coding required" process automation scripts. What process was he attempting to automate?

CTCL appears to have played the role of staffing broker. They provided tech savvy personnel experienced with the administration of elections. The Gableman Report features communications from CTCL in which they offered to provide Milwaukee "an experienced elections staff [from the Elections Group] that could potentially embed with your staff". This provides at least some indication that private organizations were at least assisting in the administration of our public elections.

The Gableman Report provided clear evidence of a conspiracy between Big Money, Big Tech, and Big Government to influence the election results. As a result of these findings, special counsel Michael Gableman has called on the state legislature to consider decertification of Wisconsin's 2020 election.[5] Speaker Voss has also acknowledged that these finding demonstrate that there was indeed widespread election fraud in Wisconsin during the 2020 election but has yet to call for decertification.[6]

Wisconsin State Representative Timothy Ramthun has introduced a resolution to recall the state's ten electoral college votes.

GEORGIA

In Georgia, the vote margin certified in favor of Joe Biden was only 12,670 votes. The focus of election fraud investigations in Georgia has, as of this writing, been in Fulton County.

A financial audit of Fulton County's Registration and Elections Department by the Office of the County Auditor during the spring of 2021 revealed several findings specific to private funding of elections. The Registration and Elections Department received three grants: one from the Southern Poverty Law Center and two from the Center for Tech and Civic Life. Key findings include the following:

- The Southern Poverty Law Center (SPLC) gave $85,000 to Fulton County Registration and Elections Department to purchase 25 absentee drop boxes *and* the accompanying surveillance cameras. Fulton County bought 21 drop boxes for around $40,000 but failed to return the remainder of the grant to SPLC.

- The Registration and Elections Department didn't track or note overtime paid out to employees in the amount of $1.9 million.
- Fulton County apparently didn't follow any proper procedures in accepting, spending, or tracking this money. In one instance, the auditor tried to track $4.4 million in spending but could only account for $2.4 million.
- The auditors tried to inventory over 300 of the department's wireless internet routers. Fifteen routers, or 6% of all their routers, vanished without a trace and could not be accounted for.
- There are millions of dollars in invoices for vendor services performed by Dominion.
- The auditors made nine conclusions on the elections department:
  1. Lack of departmental standard operating procedures
  2. Inconsistent procurement procedures
  3. Untimely payment of invoices
  4. Lack of supporting documentation
  5. Improper payment of services
  6. Inadequate safeguarding of assets
  7. Return of unused funds
  8. Obligation not satisfied
  9. Inadequate departmental accountability and oversight of financial transactions

They separately noted that many expenditures were misclassified.

Upon review of the audit findings, the following questions merit explanations:

- Why did SPLC get into the drop box buying game just before the election in September? Was it because they were a major player in the ballot stuffing effort and they recognized that more boxes were needed?

- Where did the $2 million in unaccounted spending go? Was it used to pay ballot traffickers or purchase equipment for ballot factories?
- Why would Fulton County make a last-minute order for almost 1 million absentee ballots four days before the election when most absentee ballots had already been cast? *Note: Fulton County population is just over 1 million people.*

There weren't just financial concerns in Fulton County. There were concerns with the vote count itself. On March 7, 2022, VoterGA released a 15-point analysis that provides evidence that the 2020 Fulton County election results were electronically manipulated.[7] In their analysis of public ballot images, they cited the following issues:

1. 17,724 final certified Fulton votes have no ballot images
2. All 374,128 in-person ballot images for the original count are missing
3. 132,284 mail-in ballot images are missing their authentication files
4. 4,000+ tabulator images have impossible duplicate time stamps
5. 104,994 image files in 1,096 batches have impossible, duplicate time stamps
6. All ballot batches were improperly forced to adjudication to facilitate tampering
7. 10 ballots were impossibly adjudicated in one minute by one user
8. 941 image files were backdated prior to adjudication
9. All 16,034 mail-in image authentication files were added days after scanning
10. Same 12 tabulators closed 148 early voting polls masking identity of scanning tabulator
11. One tabulator serial# impossibly closed two polls in same overlapping times

12. One tabulator was never closed and may have added many illegitimate votes
13. Images in 288 batches have backfilled time stamps out of scanning chronological order
14. 85 closing tapes for 12,024 Election Day ballots are unsigned or missing
15. All but two tabulator closing tapes for early voting are unsigned

Fulton County is only 1 of 159 counties in the state of Georgia.

In DeKalb County, Georgia over 43,000 ballots were processed despite violations of Georgia election law:

"All told, 43,907 absentee ballots deposited in drop boxes in DeKalb County (28,194 absentee ballots whose chain of custody was accounted for on ballot transfer forms that were signed as received by the registrar's designee one day after election workers removed them from drop boxes plus 15,713 absentee ballots whose chain of custody was accounted for on ballot transfer forms for with there was no registrar's designee signature for time or date of receipt) were counted in the certified results of the November 3, 2020 election despite being delivered to the registrar's office in clear violation of the chain of custody documentation of the Georgia State Election Board's July 2020 rule."[8]

And who could forget the video footage of Georgia election officials telling poll watchers to go home after which they proceeded to pull out and count ballots from suitcases hidden under the table. This appears to be a more sophisticated means to prevent oversight than the pizza boxes on the windows at the TCF Center in Detroit.

Clandestine operations are not easy to hide as indicated by additional video footage obtained by True the Vote showing evidence of illegal ballot trafficking operations. True the Vote tracked suspected ballot harvesting mules using commercially available cell phone data. They then proceeded to obtain video surveillance data from government authorities for the drop boxes used to deposit the harvested ballots. The video footage provides clear evidence of ballot harvesting.

> "Under Georgia law, it is illegal for any third party to pick up and drop off ballots for voters, also known as ballot harvesting. According to reports, at least 242 people made over 5,000 ballot drop-offs during the Georgia Senate runoff elections."[9]

Then there is Georgia's version of lawfare reminiscent of the Priorities USA lawsuit against MI Secretary of State Jocelyn Benson.[10] In Georgia, a lawsuit was filed by the Democratic Party of Georgia. In their lawsuit, they claimed that voters aren't told about missing signatures on their absentee ballots until it is too late. In response to the lawsuit, a consent decree was issued that relaxed signature verification requirements for absentee ballots. Once again, the security vulnerability of mail-in ballots was targeted.

President Donald Trump has called for Georgia's 16 presidential electors to be recalled due to 43,000 ballots that are lacking proper chain of custody logs.[11]

NEVADA

The vote margin certified in Nevada in favor of Joe Biden was only 33,596 votes.

Nevada only has four electoral college votes in question, but it does present some of the most damning evidence of vote tally manipulation. Election night reporting reveals there are 19 consecutive vote tally timestamps with Trump locked in at 47.5% of the vote. This would seem to indicate the presence of a digital controller being used to manipulate the vote tally.

Imagine going to Las Vegas and the Roulette wheel shows the same number 19 times in a row. It might just be me, but I'd wager that the casino would have decertified that roulette wheel and investigated what caused this to happen.

PENNSYLVANIA

The vote margin certified in Pennsylvania in favor of Joe Biden was only 81,660 votes. Twenty electoral college votes are in question in Pennsylvania.

We have a live CNN feed that shows negative vote increments for vote tallies that should only be increasing. More evidence of a digital controller manipulating election results.

The national theme of mail-in ballot anomalies was also evident in Pennsylvania. In an election decided by 81,660 votes, the status of 440,781 mail-in ballots was unknown or undeliverable. Against this backdrop, truck driver Jesse Morgan submitted an affidavit in which he swears that as many as 280,000 ballots were stored in a trailer he was hauling. The trailer disappeared with the ballots after an overnight stop.

That is not the only example of ballot trafficking anomalies. There is evidence of the same ballot trafficking that occurred in other states. According to Lehigh County detectives, "at least 288 people deposited more than one ballot" which is a violation of Pennsylvania law.[12] Lehigh County is just one of sixty-seven counties in Pennsylvania.

Just weeks before the election, the Pennsylvania Supreme Court ruled that counties could not reject mail-in ballots if a voter's signature on the outer envelope does not match what's on file.[13] Over 2.6 million mail and absentee ballots were reported to have been cast in Pennsylvania.[14]

On January 28, 2022, the Pennsylvania Commonwealth Court struck down the state's expansive mail-in voting law as unconstitutional calling into question all the mail-in ballots submitted in Pennsylvania during the 2020 election.

Pennsylvania legislators have taken steps to investigate the election results, but they have been met with resistance just as what has happened in other states. Pennsylvania state senate Democrats went so far as to sue the Republican-controlled senate to stop the election investigation. In November 2021, a whistleblower in Delaware County alleged that thousands of ballots were shredded by election officials in order to obstruct investigations. These allegations were supported by corroborating video footage.

Against this backdrop, media outlets such as the *Philadelphia Inquirer* provided cover for the obstruction. They spread stories designed to incite pandemonium over the thought that the government would audit and review voter data.

Perhaps the pièce de résistance, however, is that the official 2020 election results in Pennsylvania showed more votes than voters.[15] The Department of State in Pennsylvania showed that 6,962,607 ballots were cast, yet the SURE system records show that only 6,760,230 total voters actually voted. That equates to a difference of 202,377 more votes cast than voters voting. How does that happen? This is a clear indication of significant election fraud in light of the official presidential vote margin of 81,660 votes.

Registered Democrat, Brian McCaffrey, served as a poll watcher at the Philadelphia Counting Board in the Philadelphia Convention Center. While serving in this capacity on election night, he wrapped up the sentiments of many who have invested time into preserving the integrity of our elections when he said, "The corruption that is going on here. They will not allow us within 30 to 100 feet. This is a coup against the President of the United States of America."

CHAPTER 8

The Aftermath

W as registered Democrat Brian McCaffrey correct? Was it a coup?
Let's shift gears, take a step back and focus on what America looks like in the wake of the election.

Fuel prices jumped when the keystone pipeline project was cancelled as one of the first actions of the Biden administration. Less than a year later, he depleted the strategic petroleum reserve. War drums can now be heard on the horizon as Biden appears to be promoting a war with Russia. Meanwhile our military has been weakened by mandatory vaccines and woke leadership. Business hours have been reduced as employers are finding it increasingly difficult to find employees willing to work. Shelves have become increasingly bare in retail stores as supply chain holes developed. Inflation is on the rise.

The first wake-up call for many, however, was the humiliating manner in which the Biden administration withdrew our military forces from Afghanistan. In addition to leaving almost $85 billion in advanced military equipment with our enemies, we also left as many as 14,000 Americans behind. This was a stark contrast from the America First policy under President Trump.

The scope of the harm done was much more than people left behind and the arming of our enemies, though. America was attempting to build a democracy in Afghanistan. America was attempting to build a nation that secured freedom for all. When America withdrew in the dead of night, the promise of freedom for the Afghanistan people withdrew as well. The rest of the world was watching. In addition to the loss of freedom in Afghanistan, the promise of freedom for others around the world receded as well. The symbol of freedom in the world, America, was now seen as a nation who could not be trusted.

Freedom is now under assault on all fronts in America. For starters, Washington, DC, was under military occupation until the end of May 2021. When was the last time you saw the military being used to enforce the results of an election in America? A strong military presence goes hand in hand with a coup.

We are witnessing the fundamental transformation of America into a nation where the Constitution does not matter anymore.

Let's look at the five freedoms guaranteed to us in the First Amendment found in our Bill of Rights that have been infringed upon by the elite media and politicians.

Freedom of speech. I've lost track of the topics we are no longer allowed to discuss in the public square. The short version of this list is that if it is true, it is banned. It goes without saying that we are not allowed to speak about election fraud without threats of criminal investigation. It goes without saying that if we mention Dominion Voting Systems, we should expect a cease-and-desist letter.

What other topics are banned?

It turns out we are no longer allowed to share information about what our government is doing or the basis of their decisions. Even communicating state supreme court rulings is out of bounds. In the wake of a 7-0 Michigan Supreme Court ruling that ended the unlawful COVID-based state of emergency in Michigan, I attempted to procure a billboard that stated: "The state of emergency is over per a 7-0 MI Supreme Court ruling." No billboard purveyor would take my money. Why? It was too controversial in the wake of non-stop media reports that pushed the narrative that the unanimous decision was a partisan decision.

Social media platforms are rampant with censorship. YouTube took down my post of Catherine Engelbrecht's public testimony before the Wisconsin State Legislature on evidence of election fraud. My election and COVID posts on Facebook are routinely flagged by so-called "Fact Checkers". Payment processing firm PayPal cancelled my business relationship with them because of my posts on the election and COVID.

Freedom of assembly. In 2020 and much of 2021, many people couldn't visit loved ones in hospitals or nursing homes. Rallies in defense of our constitutional rights were classified as "super spreader" events. Travel restrictions for unvaccinated travelers are in effect. American citizens seeking to depart Ukraine in response to State Department warnings were being told that they must be vaccinated against COVID in order to escape to Poland.[1] Poland did not require vaccinations to enter the country. Meanwhile, hundreds of thousands of illegal aliens flood across our Southern border and are distributed all across America courtesy of the American government without such restrictions.

Freedom of religion. In the private sector, workers are being prohibited from employment if they object to being vaccinated on the basis of their religious convictions. Members of the military are being subject to forced vaccinations with experimental vaccines that use aborted fetal tissue.

Freedom to seek redress of grievances. Attempts by individuals such as myself to petition the government to secure rights guaranteed under our Constitution are being ignored, or worse. Parents pushing back against mask mandates or critical race theory curriculum at school board meetings are being ignored or ridiculed, or worse.

Freedom of the press. Many of us may recall how reporter Sheryl Atkinson was spied upon by the Obama administration. Such attempts to suppress the freedom of the press have not stopped. A book by Alex Berenson that was critical of coronavirus lockdowns was banned on

Amazon, the world's largest book retailer. Lou Dobbs, the highest rated show on Fox Business News, was likely taken off of the air in part because of his persistence in investigating 2020 election fraud.

By any objective measure, we are far less free now then we were on November 3, 2020. It is as if our Constitutional rights have been evaporating before our very eyes.

What happens during a coup? Our constitution no longer applies. Candace Owens put it this way:

"Experts" told you if you complied with lockdowns, censorship, masks and vaccinations – life would return to normal.

"Conspiracy theorists" told you Covid was never going to end, and governments would use it to usher in a totalitarian new world order.

Who do you believe now?[2]

America is being destroyed under the Biden administration. Despite a media machine intent upon propping him up at every opportunity, Biden's popularity is among the lowest for an American president in recorded history. After his first year in office, "55% of Americans disapprove of how Joe Biden is handling his job as President and 70% say the country is headed in the wrong direction."[3]

Biden is not even popular in his own residence – the White House. Video shown from an April 5, 2022 White House gathering featuring former President Barack Obama and other Democrat Party dignitaries provides what is perhaps the most eyebrow-raising evidence of all that the 2020 election is suspect.[4] In this video, Joe Biden, the supposed leader of the free world, is shown wandering aimlessly through the crowd while being completely ignored by the attendees. He even went so far as to put his hand on Obama's shoulder in an attempt to distract Obama from his conversation with gushing onlookers. Obama didn't even acknowledge his presence. It was the most pathetic scene that I have ever witnessed for any elected official much less the reported President of the United States. I, like many of you, have been to numerous functions featuring dignitaries. Those in authority are always surrounded by those seeking an audience with them. The video demonstrates that the attendees at a White House function did not see Joe Biden as someone in authority.

One plausible explanation for Joe Biden's dismal approval rating and blatant lack of respect in his own home is that he was selected not elected.

The 2020 election was a coup.

CHAPTER 9

What We Can Do

Proving that a coup occurred is one thing. Fixing it is another. What can we do to make things right? As it turns out, quite a bit.

Let's break down what can be done by the following societal roles:

- Law enforcement
- Judges
- Legislators
- Election Officials
- Citizens

Each of these groups has a unique role. When they all work together towards the same end, we have a functioning society. When they don't, we don't.

LAW ENFORCEMENT

Let's start by addressing what needs to be done by law enforcement. We've shown evidence that state and federal election laws were violated in Michigan. Contrary to the assertions of many people who seek to sweep the 2020 election under the rug and focus on future elections, what makes them think 2022 or any other future election will be any different? For those who assert that we need more election laws, what good are more laws if we don't enforce the laws that are already on the books? The issue in 2020 was not a lack of laws. The issue was a lack of enforcement of the existing laws.

Prosecutors and attorneys general need to prosecute violations of the law without bias. Having laws on the books which are not enforced leads to general disregard for the rule of law. That is why it was a promising development when the Racine County, Wisconsin, sheriff's office filed charges upon investigation of election practices in Wisconsin nursing homes. It is one example of what needs to be done in every county in every state across the nation.

So, what does law enforcement need to do in order to help secure our election integrity? For starters, they need to be trained on election law. The sheer volume of laws on the books can be overwhelming to law enforcement. Prior to each election, law enforcement officers should be briefed on the status of election law. They can't enforce what they don't know. Once they know the law, they can ensure compliance with election laws by *all* parties. That means they need to have boots on the ground in support of the election.

Next, as long as we continue to use electronic voting systems, law enforcement needs to be able to monitor the election record chain of custody in cyberspace.

Lastly, law enforcement officials need to honor their oaths of office and ignore any unlawful directives which may be used to subvert existing statutes designed to preserve election integrity. A prime example of an unlawful order by election officials was the so-called six-foot rule dictated by the Michigan secretary of state, Jocelyn Benson, and the director of the Michigan Bureau of Elections, Jonathan Brater. A court ordered an injunction upon the six-foot rule prior to the election, but this did not prevent some law enforcement officials giving it credence on Election Day.

JUDGES

Before we explore what actions can be taken by judges, let's first review a salient legal principle brought to my attention by Arizona State Representative Mark Finchem which has been upheld in courts of law for centuries in America. This legal principle is expressed as *Ex turpia causa non oritur* action. To my fellow lay citizens, this means that the "right to action" cannot arise out of illegal activity. In context of fraudulent elections, this principle translates to one cannot be allowed to execute the duties of an elected office as the result of a fraudulent election. In a nation which respects the rule of law, our court system must keep this principle at the forefront of their decisions.

Now let's look at how judges can see to it that the rule of law is enforced.

Prioritization

Due to their time sensitive nature, election fraud cases need to be treated in an expedited manner. Remember, our election system is a critical infrastructure component of our constitutional republic. If our electrical grid were to be destroyed, the top priority of government officials would be to restore the electrical grid. Why should elections be any different? Judges need to be willing and able to clear their dockets in order to prioritize election fraud cases. One of the tactics used by lawfare advocates is to slow-walk the wheels of justice in the hopes that the evidence disappears or public interest wanes. Substantive claims of election fraud such as those presented in this book need to be investigated and prosecuted with expediency. As the aftermath of the 2020 election will attest, a significant amount of damage can be done if our election integrity has been subverted.

Injunctions

Judges need to be predisposed to issuing temporary restraining orders that prohibit certification of fraudulent elections until forensic audits have been completed. Judges can order audits. They can decertify and order new elections. They can even designate the lawful winners if the fraud beneficiary is clear from the evidence.

Audits

In Antrim County, Michigan, Judge Kevin Elsenheimer ordered an audit of the 2020 presidential election results. If election officials and legislators refuse to pursue an audit, judges can order an audit to be conducted.

Support Investigations

Judges can support law enforcement officials in the investigation of election fraud by approving lawful requests for subpoenas. Too often, election data needed for fraud investigations is protected from disclosure due to illusory provisions such as those found in many electronic voting system contracts with government officials. Judges need to call out these provisions as illusory and ensure that these provisions are not successful at preventing the discovery of election fraud. The only election information which should not be privy to disclosure under most circumstances are personal voter information such as their social security or driver's license numbers and the actual votes of a voter.

Decertification

The decertification of an election can be ordered as a result of state or federal legal action. State supreme courts would be the ultimate judicial authority for state-based lawsuits. The United States Supreme Court would of course be the ultimate judicial authority for federal lawsuits or lawsuits between the states. Since the states are the primary authority for the execution of elections per the US Constitution, elections are certified by the states, and election processes vary by state, state action would be a logical focus when it comes to the decertification of a given election. However, since the results of federal elections may result in injury to the citizens of states where election fraud was not evident, such states should have standing for consideration of grievances by the United States Supreme Court that would merit decertification of offending state elections. Thus, many of the court actions seeking remedies for fraudulent elections in several of the battleground states are pursuing an audience with the Supreme Court of the United States.

One example of a lawsuit seeking consideration by the United States Supreme Court has been prepared by Texas attorney Kellye Sorelle.[1] While media pundits prefer to mock her for her use of *Lord of the Rings* analogies, I would prefer to provide you with the opportunity to examine the substance of her legal arguments. I have grown tired of media caricatures of public figures mostly because I see them for what they typically are – influence operations.

In her *United States v. The Several States* lawsuit, Ms. Sorelle systematically frames the legal arguments regarding decertification. Though she presented these arguments in a filing for the Supreme Court of the United States, I believe that the logic used has equal merit for legislators to use as the basis for the decertification of the 2020 election in their respective states. State legislators in states without rampant voter fraud could assert many of the same arguments found in Ms. Sorelle's federal brief. State legislators in states featuring rampant voter fraud could replace HAVA citations with citations of their state's election laws in arguments before their state's supreme court.

Let's review her legal argument in favor of decertification.

The following provisions of the U.S. Constitution define the limited authority of the federal government regarding elections:

1. The United States Constitution Article 1 Section 4, Clause 1 states that the respective state legislatures determine the time, places and manner of electing congressional representatives but grants Congress the right to regulate. (Exception being the location for choosing Senators cannot be regulated by Congress).

2. The United States Constitution in article II, Section 1, states that the manner for appointing electors for the President and Vice President are directed by the state legislatures. All of the states failed to comply with their respective legislative directions, codified in state election laws, regarding the choosing of electors and therefore failed to conduct a constitutional selection of the presidential electors.

3. The United States Constitution in article IV Section 4 guarantee our citizens the right to a republican form of government. Without strict compliance to the U.S. Constitution and federal or state election laws, the American people are deprived of their fundamental right to vote and the U.S. government has failed to maintain a republican form of government as required in the United States Constitution.

Congress has leveraged their authority to "regulate" elections of congressional representatives to take the following actions:

1. Help America Vote Act (2002)

   In 2002, after the hanging chad debacle, Congress passed the Help America Vote Act (HAVA). Federal Congressional elections are now regulated through the HAVA which incorporates numerous requirements from the Civil Rights Act of 1964. The states are given a choice in HAVA, the states can choose to adopt the minimum standards in HAVA, which will allow them to seek grants that finances their election equipment, or a state can continue to legislate their own elections, subject only to requirements from the various US Supreme Court cases over voting rights and legal protections.

2. Election Infrastructure Designated as Critical Infrastructure

   In 2017, Election infrastructure was designated as critical infrastructure under the Department of Homeland Security

(DHS) requiring additional security requirements under Cybersecurity and Infrastructure Security Agency (CISA).

3. Securing America's Federal Elections Act (SAFE ACT)
   On June 27th, 2019, the 116th House of Representatives sent to the Senate, H.R. 2722 also known as the Securing America's Federal Elections Act (SAFE ACT), an act designed to protect the civil rights of three hundred and twenty-eight million Americans. The SAFE ACT failed to pass the Senate, however the House committee hearing identified concerns with the electronic voting systems and identified numerous other concerns with our elections, pointing out that systemic fraud was already a substantial risk.

4. Election Security Act
   In 2019 another bill was presented that acknowledged all the security requirements for election critical infrastructure. The bill was the Election Security Act of 2019. This and the SAFE Act discuss the known concerns with our election systems.

Ms. Sorelle went on to cite the following violations of federal law:

1. U.S. Constitution Violations
   The executive branches of several states engaged in significant election modifications that were not authorized by their respective legislatures. The following examples of executive overreach created an environment that promotes fraud:
   • The use of mass mail out of voter's registration cards
   • The mass mail out of mail-in ballots
   • The reduction or elimination of signature requirements to verify a voter's identity
   • The widespread use of unsecure drop boxes
   None of these modifications were created by the state legislatures as Articles I and II of the US Constitution requires. All of them directly violated federal election laws.

2. HAVA Violations

All states opted to adopt the minimum standards and in 2020 (if not in earlier elections), yet states failed to maintain the minimum standards requirement in HAVA for the Congressional race. Evidence provided by the Relator obtained from public sources, including media, testimony and other records, show the conduct of numerous state actors, with support of the media, the political parties and the social media companies, caused the defrauding of the United States Government for all monies received under HAVA through the Election Assistance Commission (EAC) in the 2020 federal election cycle.

Affidavits and Reports by Dennis Nathan Cain and Harry Haury show HAVA 301 violations and other technical violations derived from the election systems being classified as critical infrastructure. Failure by State and Federal actors to comply with numerous provisions of Sections 302 and 303 of HAVA.

3. CARES ACT

Prior to the 2020 election, Congress issued approximately 400 million dollars in federal monies to state actors pursuant to the CARES ACT without lawfully creating a temporary modification to the requirements of HAVA or sponsoring an amendment to the United States Constitution to change the clear requirements of Articles I and II as to elections.

Based upon these arguments, she concludes:

In light of these constitutional and statutory violations, the result is that in all the several states there was no valid—constitutional and lawful—election and therefore no valid, constitutional, or lawful appointment of electors. Because the electors were not constitutionally and lawfully appointed, there could be no proper state certification of those invalid, unconstitutional, unlawful electors, to send to Congress."

She then proceeds to walk through the impacts of such a conclusion:
Furthermore, because the 2020 elections for US Congress itself were neither constitutional nor lawful because they too did not comport with the US Constitution or federal election law, the 117th US Congress (the entirety of the House and 35 seats in the Senate) was also not legitimately seated, and therefore was/is incapable of certifying the state electors for president (or carry out any other congressional powers or duties).

As a result, there was no valid appointment of electors by means of popular vote under established state law, no valid certification of electors by either the states or the US Congress, and therefore no valid transfer of power from Trump to Biden on January 20, 2021.

This means that neither Joseph Biden nor Donald Trump won the election, because the entire election was unconstitutional and therefore null and void from inception. And the same is also true of Kamala Harris and Mike Pence. As this Court has held, and reaffirmed on many occasions, any action, by any branch of government, contrary to the Constitution is null and void from inception. That maxim applies here as well, however painful may be the outcome.

And since there was not, and could not have been, a constitutional transfer of power to Biden, and Trump's term ended on January 20, 2021, both the presidency and vice presidency was vacant at that time and the Speaker of the House would have become the President, except that the current Speaker of the House is herself improperly seated, because her 2020 election, along with that of all other House members, did not comport with the US Constitution and federal election law. And the same problem also applies to the Senators who ran for office in 2020, and were unlawfully declared the winners (despite the unlawful elections) and seated in January 2021, and to their subsequent invalid votes in the Senate, such as their vote for President Pro Tempore of the U.S. Senate, who was putatively Senator Patrick Leahy.

This means that the first person in the line of presidential succession who has a valid claim to a legitimate ability to hold that office would not be Leahy, but in fact would be the prior President Pro Tempore, Chuck Grassley, who would still be President Pro Tempore if the election of Leahy were ruled invalid by this Court because of the illegal election of some 35 U.S. Senators.

This Court Should Declare a Vacancy in the Office of President and Vice President and Trigger the Presidential Succession Mechanisms.

This constitutes a truly unprecedented constitutional crisis that requires immediate action by this Court to remedy. Thankfully, it is not so far gone, or so advanced, that it cannot be remedied.

First, this Court must rule that the offices of the President and Vice President are vacant. Neither Biden nor Harris has any right or authority to either office. And, neither does Donald Trump or Mike Pence, since President Trump's term ended on January 20, 2021, and he was also a candidate in an unconstitutional and unlawful election and therefore cannot be considered the winner either. Contrary to the desires of some Trump supporters, Trump cannot be simply reinstated/or declared to still be President. The constitutional line of succession must be followed when there is a vacancy, even if the vacancy occurred under such extraordinary circumstances which in fact did rob President Trump of a fair election which he most likely would have won had it been constitutionally and lawfully carried out (see below for the one constitutional mechanism by which Trump could regain the Presidency prior to either a new election, or the states appointing electors). The simple fact is, there is now a vacancy in the offices of President and Vice President.

Second, with the massive illegality of the House elections, there is now no current, valid Speaker of the House, but there is a President Pro Tempore of the Senate. Senator Grassley is the last clearly legitimately and constitutionally elected President Pro Tempore of the Senate, elected by an untainted U.S. Senate. Senator Leahy was subsequently "elected," in part, by 35 invalid Senators, and therefore cannot properly be considered a legitimate President Pro Tempore.

Senator Grassley, being the last—and therefore still the legitimate—President Pro Temper of the US Senate, must now step into the office of the Presidency, and then select a Vice President, to serve until a new election can be held in November 2022, or until the states appoint new electors.

The above is the immediate solution to the current Presidential crisis, and as a follow up, the state legislatures could retake their appointment power and appoint electors for whatever candidate they choose to become President. If the state legislatures do not do so, and instead continue to leave the decision of who shall be elected to the offices of President and Vice President in the hands of the people via popular vote, this Court could, and should, order a new election that actually does comply with Article II (being carried out in the manner directed by the state legislatures as established in state law) and also in compliance with federal election law. Any modifications deemed necessary because of Covid 19 would need to be made by the respective state legislatures, not by local or state executive branch officials as happened in 2020. That new election could take place in November of 2022, and still be within the two-year window of the 22nd Amendment in case that becomes a factor for any reason.

And that brings us back to Trump. Once Senator Grassley becomes President, he will select a Vice President. He could, if he chose to, select Donald Trump to serve as his Vice President. Then, if President Grassley were to resign, Donald Trump would become President and could serve as President until a new popular election could be held, or until the state legislatures directly appointed electors. He would be able to run again for President in the new national election so long as he stayed within the two year window of the 22nd Amendment, which he would if the new election were held in November 2022. If Trump won the new November 2022 election, he could still serve four more years, starting in January 2023, even though he served during 2021 and 2022.

Regardless of how it all pans out, what is clear is that there are vacancies in the offices of President and Vice President, and they must be declared and then the proper steps made to fill them, pursuant to the Constitution and existing law. This Court Should Declare Vacancies in All US House Seats and in 35 US Senate Seats (all in contest in 2020), Triggering Emergency Vacancy Appointments by the States Until a Valid Election Can be Held."

According to Attorney Kellye Sorelle's legal argument, the current lawful President of the United States would be current Senator Charles Ernest Grassley. As if that weren't an interesting enough point to ponder, this would open the door to another interesting point to consider especially in light of the breadth and depth of the effort employed to remove Trump from office. In a potentially strange twist of fate, it is conceivable that President Trump could serve ten years as President. The Twenty-Second Amendment of the US Constitution states:

> No person shall be elected to the office of the President more than twice, and no person who has held the office of President, or acted as President, for more than two years of a term to which some other person was elected President shall be elected to the office of President more than once. But this Article shall not apply to any person holding the office of President when this Article was proposed by Congress, and shall not prevent any person who may be holding the office of President, or acting as President, during the term within which this Article becomes operative from holding the office of President or acting as President during the remainder of such term.

What would it take for President Trump to serve ten years? One way is for President Grassley to nominate Donald Trump as his vice president and then step down from the presidency in January 2023. Another pathway would be for Trump to win a court-ordered re-election that would result in the inauguration of a new President in January 2023. Either way, Trump would resume his service as President for a two-year term. He could then run again for President in 2024 thereby earning another four years in office for a total of ten. Imagine the conundrums this would cause for the folks responsible for the Hall of Presidents at Walt Disney World not to mention those afflicted with Trump Derangement Syndrome (TDS).

New Elections

The idea that a judge can order a new election is not mere conjecture. In fact, there are multiple examples of such orders during the 2020 election cycle.

In Aberdeen, Mississippi, a judge ordered a new election for alderman after finding evidence of fraud.[2] There were irregularities in the paperwork for 66 out of 84 absentee ballots cast (78%). The race was decided by only 37 votes. Two notaries were found to be engaged in vote fraud. The judge ordered one of the notaries to be arrested.

In Paterson, New Jersey, a judge ordered a new election for a disputed Paterson City Council seat.[3] The race's winner, Alex Medez, along with sitting council vice president, Michael Jackson, and two other men, Shelim Khalique and Abu Rayzen, were charged with voter fraud. An investigation was launched after the US Postal Service's law enforcement arm notified the state attorney general that hundreds of mail-in ballots were found in a mailbox in Paterson as well as nearby Haledon.

In Eatonville, Florida, nineteen months after Tarus Mack was certified the winner of a 2020 Eatonville Town Council race, a judge ordered that he be removed from his position due to evidence uncovered by his opponent suggesting votes were illegally cast or procured.[4]

Judges have indeed demonstrated their ability to ensure justice is done in the past. It remains to be seen if the evidence of election fraud during the 2020 election will have its day in court.

LEGISLATORS

The purpose of government, per our Declaration of Independence, is to secure the rights of the governed. Legislators play a key role toward that end. Each of them takes an oath affirming their support for their state and the US Constitution. It stands to reason that they need to honor that oath by doing all they can to secure the rights delineated in these constitutions.

Study

Before opining on elections and new bill ideas, responsible legislators should study how the current election system is supposed to work. When I was assigned to serve as vice chair of the Senate Elections and

Government Reform Committee, I did just that as a first order of business. I read the Michigan Election manual and current Michigan election statute. I visited my local clerk's office and walked through the entire election process with her and her team. I diagrammed all the election processes from voter registration to election certification and recounts. I then proceeded to run these diagrams past the state elections director (Chris Thomas at the time) and asked for any revisions that might be warranted.

Why did I do this? When I was a young design engineer with Boeing working on the International Space Station, I gained an appreciation for knowing what you are changing from before you change to something else. The International Space Station is a very complex system. I was responsible for critical life support system components within this system. Any changes to my design could have significant impacts to the operations of other systems as well as my own system. It was critically important to understand whether or not any improvements to my systems would be offset by impacts to other systems.

The same is true for election systems. For example, while ballot drop boxes may make it easier to vote, they also make it easier to stuff the ballot box with fraudulent votes. The benefits of each piece of legislation should be weighed against the risks it introduces. The only way to make these assessments in any substantive way is to understand our current election system, including any mechanisms that could be leveraged to subvert its integrity, before evaluating any proposed changes to this election system.

Communication

Communication is pretty straightforward. It is firmly in the wheelhouse of most elected officials. Most elected officials have no issues giving speeches, but good communication is a two-way street. They need to listen as well. Elected officials are called representatives for a reason. They are supposed to represent those whom they serve. They need to be their voice, especially in an era when those voices are increasingly silenced by the media and Big Tech.

I served as a Michigan state senator for eight years before being termed out in 2018. During my tenure, I served on the leadership team in the Michigan Senate. As a rookie legislator, I learned firsthand the pressures applied to members to "toe the line" on policy stances communicated by leadership. Many times, this pressure results in direct conflict with the pressures applied by my constituents or even my oath of office. There are penalties if you contradict the messaging of the senate majority leader or speaker. There are also penalties if you fail to be responsive to the concerns of your constituents. Failure to comply with the edicts of legislative leadership often results in your legislation being blacklisted, loss of powerful roles as committee chairs, loss of committee assignments, or even loss of staff. I experienced all these penalties during my service in the Michigan Senate because I never forgot for whom I worked. On the flipside, failure to address the concerns of the majority of one's constituents means, you might not get reelected. I say might not, because when you play ball with leadership, it opens the door to significant campaign donations that can be used for campaign ads that mitigate the risk of losing reelection. So, elected officials often reason that it is less painful to ignore their constituents than it is to ignore the legislative power brokers. Suffice it so say, I was not very good at playing ball, but I did sleep very well at night.

You can tell a lot about the character of your elected representatives by what, how, and where they choose to communicate. Do their communications conform to the public statements of the senate majority leader or speaker? Do their press releases or media interviews reveal a different stance on a given issue than what they have shared in personal conversations with you? Ultimately, actions mean more than words, but you can learn a lot about the actions they may or may not be taking on your behalf by the words they share in public.

When it comes to election fraud, any honest elected official should have no issue exposing any examples of election fraud to the public. Remember, they work for us. What message does it send to their bosses when they sign non-disclosure agreements as conditions of getting access to election fraud evidence? Who are they serving when they prevent the disclosure of information pertinent to the integrity of our elections? After all, they serve in their elected positions as a result of an election. Unless they are corrupt, one would think that it would benefit them to expose any evidence of election fraud and share the evidence publicly with media.

Investigation

Many citizens may not think of legislators as being investigators, but they do have significant investigative authority. They rarely seek to leverage this authority, however. The political calculations associated with the decision to pursue investigations often default to the low-risk approach of doing nothing. The gravity of election integrity, however, demands special consideration of using this authority by legislators.

As demonstrated in states like Arizona and Michigan, most, if not all, states have statutory or constitutional provisions that grant investigative authority to the legislature. This authority helps to ensure the checks and balances between all branches of government. If the executive branch fails to execute their duties in accordance with the law, the legislature can investigate regardless of the stance of the judicial branch. This is particularly important on the topic of election fraud since, in the wake of the 2000 "dangling chad" election, the judicial branch is extremely reticent to weigh in on matters related to election outcomes.

While most citizens are limited to filing FOIA requests, which are often denied regarding critical election fraud evidence, legislatures have subpoena authority that can push through most of these restrictions. This subpoena authority is a powerful investigative tool not available to citizen investigators. The legislature can supplement this subpoena authority by designating special commissioners with investigative experience to investigate allegations of election fraud in a professional manner. Upon closure of any such investigation, legislative investigators need to share any findings indicative of election fraud with the public and law enforcement authorities for prosecution.

Decertification

While the authority of the legislature to decertify elections in general varies from state to state, their authority to decertify the electors assigned to the electoral college does not. Under Article II Section 1 of the US Constitution, state legislators have plenary authority regarding presidential elections. That authority includes decertification. Note that this authority does not require the approval of the governor of the respective state as would typically be the case for bills passed into law. This authority belongs solely to the legislature.

In the wake of the evidence of election fraud presented in Arizona, principled legislators such as Senator Wendy Rogers and Representative Mark Finchem have been very vocal in their call for the decertification of the 2020 general election. Former Wisconsin Supreme Court justice and special counsel to the Wisconsin legislature, Mike Gableman, has also called for decertification. If the legislators in battleground states showing significant evidence of election fraud would have the courage to join them in upholding the rule of law, enough presidential electors would be decertified to call into question the positions of president and vice president. In such a circumstance, the down ballot elections would not be impacted.

We would then revisit the process which was interrupted on the floor of the House of Representatives on January 6. If no agreement on the disposition of electors is reached via this process, each state would then have one vote. The current party split in the House by state is 26-23 in favor of Republicans with one tie (Pennsylvania).[5] The vote of 26 states is sufficient to win. Presumably, this would mean that President Trump would be reinstated as president under this scenario. The vice president would be selected by the Senate, however. Unlike the House regarding the presidency, each Senator is given one vote for vice president. The current party split in the Senate is 50-50. Since the sitting vice president would be nullified in a decertified election, there would be no tie breaking vote. It is conceivable that the president and vice president would be from opposing parties in this scenario which has happened before. Prior to the Twelfth Amendment (which was ratified in 1802), the president was the one who received the most electors, and the vice president was whoever came in second. Thus was the case with John Adams and Thomas Jefferson. Will history repeat itself? Only time will tell.

Legislation

And of course, legislators can also pursue legislation. Although, I encourage them not to do so prior to studying the current state of election law in their state. The same Michigan Senate which gave us the Michigan Senate Report, which concluded that they "found no evidence of widespread or systemic fraud in Michigan's prosecution of the 2020 election," introduced thirty-nine election reform bills after the election. The Michigan House introduced another nine bills. I evaluated each one of them against my understanding of how our 2020 election was subverted.[6] My conclusion was that of the forty-eight total bills that were introduced:

- 8 would significantly increase the risk of election fraud
- 1 would slightly increase the risk of election fraud
- 15 wouldn't move the needle one way or another
- 17 would slightly mitigate the risk of election fraud
- 7 would significantly mitigate the risk of election fraud

In other words, a legislature that refuses to acknowledge the existence of significant election fraud introduced more "very bad" bills than "very good" bills. Not a very satisfactory state of affairs in Michigan.

So, what sort of bills would help to mitigate the fraud observed in the 2020 general election? My recommendations are:

- Establish Election Day as a national holiday and eliminate mail-in voting for all but military personnel and the infirmed.

- The benefits of network connectivity for election equipment are outweighed by the risks of election fraud. Prohibit any network connection capability in all electronic voting system equipment. Provide provisions for citizens to monitor and investigate the election equipment to ensure no such connections are present.

- The best way to eliminate the possibility of tampering with electronic voting systems is to go back to paper ballots and eliminate electronic voting equipment altogether.

- Make sure that demonstration of election record chain of custody is required by law prior to certifying election results. Ensure that the certification authority has the authority to conduct an audit of all election records.

- Audit rigor should be defined explicitly in law. Audits must include an investigation of all electronic and physical election records in the chain of custody including the statewide voter registration file, pollbooks, ballots, and vote tallies as a minimum.

- Automatic triggers for the conduct of an audit should be explicitly defined in statute.

- States should enact laws that ensure the explicit protection of all election records (paper and digital) needed for a forensic audit for a sufficient time to ensure that they are available to support the audit.

- Private vendors engaged in support of election operations should be subject to Freedom of Information Act inquiries. Under no circumstances should a vendor's authority supersede that of a duly elected official.

- Require precinct-level results to be presented in a spreadsheet compatible format at least 72 hours before the certification of any vote in order to allow analyses which could identify potential fraud.
- Require the total number of ballots cast to be publicly available immediately upon closure of polls
- It should be mandatory for all poll workers to prominently display their party affiliation while on duty so as to verify compliance with statutes requiring bi-partisan observation of certain election activities. Names must be clearly visible so that poll challengers can easily verify their party affiliation.
- Require 24/7 web-monitoring of election records requiring a chain of custody. In cases where election infractions are identified, the video/audio evidence could be used in court to assist prosecutors.
- Take whatever measures possible to expand transparency of our election processes, not obstruct access to information.
- Take whatever measures possible to empower local clerks and decentralize the management of our election processes.
- If electronic voting systems are still to be used, leverage them to post real-time status data on who has voted, total number of voters, number of ballots cast, number of provisional ballots, etc. Logs of such data can be used in subsequent audits as warranted.
- Require full transparency including ability for any party to examine the source code as a condition for using any electronic voting system.

- Establish election fraud specialty courts. Specialty courts have been used for veteran-specific issues and drug infractions. Many election fraud cases are sufficiently complex to justify specialized courts featuring judges who are subject matter experts on election law and fraud examples.
- Require the use of lot-controlled secure ballot paper technology and prohibit the use of standard stock paper for ballots.
- In order to mitigate the risk of influence operations, Section 230 protections for big tech under federal law should be removed, making them subject to civil liability.
- Photo ID should be required to verify the identity of all voters prior to them being allowed to cast a vote.
- Early voting is used by election fraud enthusiasts to refine their estimates on the number of fraudulent votes needed to ensure victory for their candidate(s). Early voting should be prohibited by law.
- Same day voter registration compromises the integrity of pollbooks and creates chaos during elections. Same day voter registration should be prohibited by law.
- Prohibit the posting of election results until the precinct-level election results have been signed off by election officials (i.e., no more unofficial election results). Unofficial election results can be used by nefarious actors to project how many fraudulent votes are required to sway the election results.
- Prohibit the counting of votes in any precinct which failed to balance their books and demonstrate chain of custody maintenance.
- While poll challengers are able to review voter identification at the polls, they are often prohibited from viewing the verification of absentee voter identity which occurs at clerk offices. Legislators can pass legislation which requires

clerks to enable poll challengers to observe the absentee voter identification process at all times including unannounced inspections.

- Legislation requiring jurisdiction-specific election integrity scorecards to be developed and posted would provide a mechanism for increased oversight in jurisdictions with persistent deficiencies.

- Existing statutes requiring bi-partisan oversight of election processes are difficult to enforce. Lawmakers can pass legislation requiring each jurisdiction to receive party approval of their list of poll workers and their assignments prior to election day.

- Mail-in voting based upon voter registration databases with an average of 20% invalid registrants is a recipe for election fraud. Legislation can be introduced to prohibit mailing of absentee ballot applications and ballots unless specifically requested by a voter.

- Require a website featuring the public display of a downloadable daily log of additions, modifications, and deletions of voter data in the statewide voter registration database.

- Prohibit the use of drop boxes. They enable election fraud via ballot harvesters.

Your state may already have some of these recommendations in law. If so, please ensure they are enforced. If not, please ensure that they are implemented as soon as possible.

ELECTION OFFICIALS

We've examined what elected officials can do. Now let's look at actions that can be pursued by our *election* officials. Election officials include secretaries of state, clerks, and poll workers. While many of these positions are elected offices, it is useful to distinguish election officials from the generic *elected officials* term. Election officials, whether they happen to be elected or not, are responsible for administering elections.

What needs to be done by election officials?

Know the Law

First and foremost, election officials need to read and study election law. In so doing, they will be able to discern whether or not compliance with any directive is consistent with the law or not. If they comply with an unlawful directive, they are complicit with breaking the law. Too many election officials assume that any directive they receive from other election officials, such as the secretary of state, are lawful. Michigan is a prime example of why this is a bad assumption. The Michigan secretary of state issued multiple unlawful directives to clerks across the state. Election officials should only obey directives which are in full compliance with the law. Where there is a conflict in the interpretation of the law, election officials should bias their interpretation in favor of transparency and election integrity.

Monitor Compliance with Election Procedures

Furthermore, election officials need to go beyond knowing the law to actually monitoring compliance of their staff and volunteers with election law. Election officials need to diligently track lot and serial numbers of ballots. Any missing ballots should feature appropriate explanation.

Another solution is for election officials to proactively demonstrate the maintenance of the chain of custody for election records prior to certification including a log of every modification to every critical election record. Failure to demonstrate preservation of the chain of custody would serve as grounds for prohibiting the certification of the precinct's votes.

Promote Transparency

Transparency is critical in order to gain the public trust in the integrity of our elections. Election officials need to take every measure practical to be transparent about how elections are *actually* conducted not simply how they are *supposed* to be conducted.

The fidelity of the voter registration database records for a given jurisdiction should be actively monitored and shared with the public. A dashboard that highlights the number of new voters added, dead voters removed, changes of address, etc., would go a long way toward preserving the integrity of the voter registration database link in our chain of custody.

The public accuracy test for election equipment is a critical event in the preparation for any election. COVID was used as an excuse to limit oversight of this event this past election. There is no reason, however, why the public accuracy test could not be broadcast online for everyone to view. Furthermore, the public accuracy test should be performed on *all* electronic tabulators, not a single demonstration tabulator as is often performed by election officials.

The pre-election walkthrough of election processes would also benefit from improved transparency. Poll workers, poll challengers, poll watchers and citizens at large would benefit from a systematic walkthrough of the election processes to be followed on Election Day.

The chain of custody for each election record should be clearly demonstrated during that walkthrough. In addition to providing an opportunity to cite concerns about the processes *before* the election, poll challengers can use this information to hold poll workers and election officials accountable for executing these processes on Election Day. There is no reason for this walkthrough not to be shared online for all to witness. This approach would mitigate confusion on Election Day.

Conduct Book Audits of Election Processes

The purpose of a book audit is to demonstrate that election standards and procedures comply with established election law. Book audits do not involve looking at election records from a given election. Book audits are best performed prior to an election.

Election officials should periodically execute a book audit of their election processes. This audit could be conducted internally or, preferably, opened to a third-party organization such as the state auditor general. The scope of a book audit should include the following:

1. Evaluate compliance of state statutes with state constitution
2. Evaluate compliance of state election procedures with state statutes
3. Evaluate compliance of local election procedures with state election procedures
4. Evaluate compliance of state statutes with chain of custody requirements
5. Evaluate compliance of state procedures with chain of custody requirements
6. Evaluate compliance of local election procedures with chain of custody requirements
7. Evaluate compliance of state election audit manuals with state election law and state election procedures

Upon completion of these assessments, election officials should provide a report that delineates key findings and corrective actions.

Maintain Integrity of Election Records
One of the primary responsibilities of clerks in general is the maintenance of records. These records not only include deeds, titles, and financial records, they also include election records. The responsibilities for township clerks under Michigan law are delineated in state law: MCL 41.65:

The township clerk of each township shall have custody of all the records, books, and papers of the township, when no other provision for custody is made by law. The township clerk shall file and safely keep all certificates of oaths and other papers required by law to be filed in his or her office, and shall record those items required by law to be recorded. These records, books, and papers shall not be kept where they will be exposed to an unusual hazard of fire or theft. The township clerk shall deliver the records, books, and papers on demand to his or her successor in office.[7]

Custody of records includes the responsibility for maintaining the chain of custody for these records including election records. Election record chain of custody has proven to be problematic for electronic records due to illusory provisions in the contracts between state government and electronic voting system vendors such as the following provision found in the contract between Dominion Voting Systems and the state of Michigan.

4. Prohibited Acts. The Licensee shall not, without the prior written permission of Licensor:

4.1. Transfer or copy onto any other storage device or hardware or otherwise copy the Software in whole or in part except for purposes of system backup.

4.2. Reverse engineer, disassemble, decompile, decipher or analyze the Software in whole or in part.

4.3. Alter or modify the Software in any way or prepare any derivative works of the software or any part of parts of the software.

4.4. Alter, remove or obstruct any copyright or proprietary notices from the Software, or fail to reproduce the same on any lawful copies of the software."

Clerks are faced with the dilemma of whether or not to comply with their statutory responsibilities regarding custody of election records or comply with the illusory provisions of a vendor contract agreed upon by state officials. How are they supposed to maintain custody of the voting equipment and its software configuration state if they are not allowed to analyze the software in whole or part?

To make matters worse, provisions regarding proprietary software have been extended to include examination of configuration settings and logs. Configuration settings and logs are not source code. They are data, often very important data such as network connection settings or security logs. Unfortunately, judges and many election officials often lack the technical expertise to differentiate between software and "configuration data". Vendors take advantage of this ignorance to prohibit clerks from "looking over their shoulders" and monitoring the configuration of the election equipment under their charge. In this environment, it is the vendors, not the election officials, who actually run our elections by unilaterally controlling the configuration of the election equipment that manages the elections.

One prime example of vendor obstruction of clerk duties occurred in Michigan when clerks throughout the state began to investigate how to honor their statutory custody maintenance responsibilities. In an apparent attempt to head off such pursuits, voting system vendor Election Source issued the following communication to local clerks throughout the state of Michigan.

Dear Clerks,

This letter is in response to an inquiry regarding a potential "forensic audit" of the Dominion system currently licensed to you. Any transfer of equipment or software to a third party would be in direct violation of the State of Michigan software license terms and conditions, which govern the use of the voting system and software in your jurisdiction. More specifically, the license terms state, "Licensor grants Licensee a non-exclusive, **non-transferrable** license to use the Software' (emphasis added). Further, the license terms state that the licensee may NOT "Transfer or copy onto any other storage device or hardware or otherwise copy the software in whole or in part except for purposes of system backup."

Any transfer of any component of the voting system to a third party would be a violation of the agreement and Election Source, the State or Dominion may take immediate legal action for such breach of contract.

Both Election Source and Dominion are open to a review of the voting system by an EAC accredited testing laboratory, as previously done during the EAC and State of Michigan certification processes. Any such review must be coordinated with the Michigan Secretary of State.

Should you have any questions please don't hesitate to contact me directly. My cell phone number is below and I am available to you 24/7.[8]

Is there a way to comply with the illusory provisions of the state contract and still comply with the statutory duties of a clerk? First of all, election officials should never sign a contract featuring these provisions, but, if they do, there are ways to mitigate the subversion of their elections.

One potential approach is for election officials to seek out any and all lawful methods to track the configuration changes for election equipment under their charge. Here's one place to start.

Many of the voting systems feature equipment that uses the Microsoft operating system. Below are instructions for collecting non-invasive data on any Windows-based election machines without breaking the seal on the voting equipment. These instructions feature Windows tools that can be accessed by clicking on the Windows icon in the lower left corner of your screen.

Upon clicking the Windows icon, simply type the name of each tool and hit enter on your keyboard.

1. Launch "**Resource Monitor**". Expand all frames as much as possible (especially TCP Connections frame) and take a photo with a camera (or your smartphone).

2. Launch **Device Manager**. Go to View and make sure "Show hidden devices" is active. Expand Ports, Network adapters, and USB Controllers as a minimum and take photos.

3. Launch **Devices and Printers.** Expand the window and take photo of all devices.

4. **Run IPConfig.** Left click on the Windows logo (lower left corner) and type run. Then type IPConfig and take a screenshot of what you find.

5. Launch **Registry Editor** (optional). Go to File and click "Export". Save export to an online folder or USB flash drive. (Only use a USB flash drive if you have verified there is no malware installed on the flash drive.)

None of these actions requires breaking the seals on your voting equipment. None of these actions involves looking at the voting system software or even launching the voting system software. These instructions are fully compliant with the standard provisions of voting system contracts.

These actions will provide you with information that could be analyzed by a tech savvy investigator to determine if there are any basic anomalies such as evidence of internet connections or unauthorized devices. Subpoenas would likely be required in order to get access to much more substantive data.

Conduct a Recount

If the tabulation of votes is suspected to be incorrect, election officials can request a recount of the ballots. As previously mentioned, recounts are limited in scope to simply recounting the votes for a given race. Any anomalies beyond the tabulated results which may be detected are generally not subject to investigation during a recount. That's why audits are necessary if election integrity is a concern.

Conduct an Election-Specific Field Audit

Earlier we discussed the need to perform periodic audits of election procedures to evaluate compliance with state-specific law. Election officials need to take advantage of any investigatory provisions to be found in law. They often won't know about these provisions unless they research the law themselves. If election fraud is suspected, election officials have an obligation to pursue a field audit of election records. Under Michigan Law (MCL 168.870), clerks have the authority to initiate investigations of recounts with full subpoena authority.

Most election fraud audits currently focus upon the ballots. As discussed previously, simple "recounts" are often disingenuously referred to as "audits". It is critical that any election audit go beyond simple ballot recounts and examine the entire chain of custody. The election record chain of custody can be simplified into an evaluation of four basic election records: statewide voter registration file (known as the Qualified Voter File in Michigan), pollbooks, ballots, and vote tallies.

After ballot audits, the next most popular focus of election fraud investigations are the pollbooks. Pollbooks are evaluated by boards of canvassers against ballot counts prior to certification. Post-certification, other organizations and even individual citizens can canvass voters. The purpose of these canvassing activities is to validate the voter data in the pollbook. Canvassing can be thought of as a field audit of the pollbooks. Since pollbook data is supposed to be reflected in the statewide voter registration file after the election, one could also make the case that canvassing provides a field audit of the statewide voter registration file as well. Of course, this assumes that all the pollbook data is accurately reflected in the statewide voter registration file.

A complete audit would also feature an investigation of the statewide voter registration file. During such an audit, the statewide voter registration file would be evaluated against dead voter, census data, or change of address lists. Auditors would examine logs of who updated each voter record, what modifications were made, and when these modifications were made. This information would then be cross-referenced with the data in the pollbook in order to check for any inconsistencies indicative of fraud.

Finally, officials running an audit will thoroughly review the vote tally submittals. As the saying goes, *"Those who cast the votes decide nothing. Those who count the votes decide everything."* Counting the votes is demonstrably more important than casting the votes which begs the question: "Why isn't more attention given to the chain of custody regarding the reporting of election night results?" While election investigations focus upon ballots, pollbooks and statewide voter registration files, a number of vote tally anomalies receive little or no investigatory attention, which begs the questions:

Why did the cumulative vote tally in multiple states suddenly drop to *zero* in the middle of the night?[9]

Why were there multiple examples of negative vote increments reported on election night?[10]

Why were more votes reported than could have possibly been counted during a given time period?[11]

Clearly, an audit of the vote tally records for an election would yield answers to some very important questions—including who the rightful winner of a given race is.

A full forensic field audit would include an audit of each of the election records in the chain of custody listed above. In addition to an audit of election records, I would also recommend an audit of the election finances. Most unlawful activities involve suspect money trails. In the spirit of the old adage "follow the money," I would add an audit of the financial records for suspect jurisdictions. Financial trails such as those featured in this book often provide significant insights as to whether or not there are any attempts to subvert the integrity of our elections. See Appendix B for a more detailed breakdown of what to expect from a full forensic audit.

CITIZENS

Now let's review what citizens can do.

Pray

As we have demonstrated, the 2020 election was not a battle between Republicans and Democrats. It was not even a battle between Trump and Biden. It was a battle between those who seek to fundamentally transform America and those who seek to preserve all that this noble, true, excellent, and praiseworthy about America. The 2020 election was in many ways a physical manifestation of a spiritual battle between good and evil. This battle has persisted in America since we were founded on the fundamental principle that our rights come from God not men. Over the past few decades, the culture in America has drifted away from an appreciation of this principle. Increasingly, we have seen leaders infringing upon our rights as if they were theirs to give and theirs to take away. Prayer will help us recalibrate our nation to the pursuit of this truth.

"If my people, who are called by my name, will humble themselves and pray and seek my face and turn from their wicked ways, then I will hear from heaven, and I will forgive their sin and will heal their land." (2 Ch 7:14)

"Then you will know the truth, and the truth will set you free." (John 8:32)

It has been my personal experience that the most passionate and dedicated investigators into the truths pertaining to the 2020 election are devout Christians. That is not to say that only Christians are performing these investigations, but I believe it is noteworthy that the vast majority of people who have reached out to me regarding their election fraud discoveries clearly understand that Jesus Christ is their Lord and Savior. In fact, many of my phone calls with complete strangers on the topic of election fraud have ended in heartfelt prayer. Prayer is the key to the healing of our nation.

Vote

The 2020 election fraud was difficult to hide because a record number of voters came out to vote. These record numbers broke the algorithms used to shift votes thereby necessitating a backup plan featuring additional election subversion tactics that were easier to detect.

Be a Poll Worker

Serve as a poll worker. Poll workers provide clerks with the extended staff they need to execute election day operations. It is a paid position that requires training and a significant time investment, but if you want to ensure that something is done right, do it yourself. Most clerks are always looking for additional poll workers as many hands makes light work.

Be a Poll Challenger

Another civic service option is to volunteer as a poll challenger. Serving as a poll challenger also requires training but there is no compensation. Certified poll challengers have statutory protections that enable them to challenge election processes which are not executed in a lawful manner. There are also statutory penalties for interference with the duties of poll challengers. Ultimately, the challenges issued by poll challengers are supposed to be captured by poll workers in the pollbooks. The pollbooks are subsequently subject to review by the respective county boards of canvassers prior to certification. If there are significant challenge entries in the pollbook, these challenges may serve as grounds for not certifying the election by a board of canvassers. This is why any interference with the oversight duties of a poll challenger is a serious offense.

Be a Poll Watcher

If you do not have the time available to invest into the training required to be a poll worker or poll challenger, you can still serve as a poll watcher. No training is required, but you have no ability to rectify any election malfeasance you may observe as it is occurring. You are merely, as the name suggests, an observer. What you observe, however, can later be used in support of legal action should the results of the election be challenged.

File Complaints

On the subject of challenging the results, citizens can file formal complaints with law enforcement. For infractions against state election laws, one would typically file a complaint with state or local law enforcement authorities such as county prosecutors, the state attorney general, police, or sheriff. For infractions against federal laws, one would typically file a complaint with federal law enforcement officials such as district attorneys, the US Attorney General or the FBI.

While there is often a statutory duty to prosecute or institute criminal proceedings for the punishment of offenders, you are cautioned to use discretion when submitting evidence of election fraud. Sadly, not all law enforcement authorities execute their duties without bias.

For example, the Michigan attorney general's web page on Election Security and Integrity features the following statement:

"Voting is an opportunity to celebrate our democracy and Michigan voters should expect nothing but a calm, safe and secure process at the polls.

If for any reason you believe you are experiencing voter intimidation, or are witnessing it on Election Day, we encourage you to contact the Michigan Department of Attorney General by calling 517-335-7659 or emailing miag@michigan.gov."

It is worth noting that there was no apparent statement encouraging witnesses of election fraud to submit their testimony to the Attorney General. So what happens when a poll challenger witnesses a violation of election law? What happens when a poll worker refuses to enter a challenge by a certified poll challenger into the pollbook as required by law? Such a situation would likely involve a measure of conflict. After all, anyone "challenging" an illegal vote would be seen as interference with their pursuit of a "calm" process at the polls. Challenges invariably invoke irritation. No one likes to be challenged as evidenced by numerous affidavits regarding the events at the TCF Center in Detroit in the wake of the 2020 election. It would be nice if the Attorney General would show as much appreciation for preventing the intimidation of poll challengers as she shows for the intimidation of voters.

Bottom line? Look before you leap. Ensure that your complaint is filed with a law enforcement organization truly committed to enforcing the rule of law not a political agenda.

Run for Office

Review our list of actions for legislators and election officials. In order to convert this list from a plan to reality, people of integrity need to run for elected office. We need people of integrity serving throughout our government. In addition to state or federal offices, please consider running for school boards, county commissioners, and municipal government.

Form or Join an Election Integrity Organization

Teamwork isn't simply beneficial on the football field or in the workplace. When you work together with others, you can often accomplish much more than you can by yourself. This is why if you want to be effective at protecting the integrity of elections, I recommend joining an election integrity organization. If you don't find one you like, form your own organization and recruit members. Election integrity organizations can be used to share information about elections, expose the true impacts of ballot initiatives via marketing campaigns, train poll challengers, or lobby on behalf of reform legislation. All these efforts require money. The Protect the Results organization formed by Standup America and Indivisible claimed 148 partner organizations. Each of these organizations had significant budgets to fuel their operations all year long. They receive their funding from billionaire progressive activists and political action funds funded by union dues. Conservatives have no such funding streams to counter their efforts. In this light, patriotic citizens need to band together and support political action committees (PACs) and nonprofits that align with traditional American values and promote constitutional governance. It is frustrating knowing we not only have to pay taxes, but we also must pay organizations to lobby for us so that we don't have to pay even more taxes to an out-of-control government. It is even more frustrating when the people we pay to execute the duties of governance fail to do so. Election audits are a case in point. No one ever said that freedom is free.

Investigate

If government authorities are not willing to perform an honest investigation of election integrity, do so yourselves or through an election integrity organization. Information needed in support of your investigation can mostly be obtained via asking clerks or by submitting FOIA requests. This can be expensive, but once again, nobody ever said freedom is free. Once your investigation has been completed, use it as the basis of a complaint that you file with law enforcement and ensure that responsible media outlets are apprised of what was discovered.

Inform Others

When you are in the midst of an information war, there is significant value in becoming a trusted information source for others. Monitor the news shared by media outlets. Go beyond the headlines provided by traditional media outlets. They have earned the title "Fake News" for a reason. Become the fact checker for your personal network of friends and family. In today's internet age, it is easier than ever to become a citizen journalist yourself and share factual news with the public. While facts should be objective in theory, in practice, "fact checker" organizations have been notoriously partisan. There are quite a few of these organizations aligned with the political Left and only one organization of note aligned with the political Right. People are desperate to hear the unvarnished truth from media organizations. Perhaps you would be able to form one that truly is non-partisan.

Prepare and Distribute Election Official Scorecards

Scorecards can be a powerful way to preserve election integrity. They promote civic engagement, accountability by our elected officials, and enable the efficient deployment of limited election oversight resources. You can develop your own scorecard for each jurisdiction that covers the topics which matter most to you. Another option would be to develop and distribute law enforcement scorecards that monitor the performance of prosecutors, sheriffs, and other officers when it comes to enforcing election statutes.

Advocate

Express your right to seek redress of grievances with your elected officials. Become an advocate for election fraud investigations and election reforms. Write letters to the editor. Share information on social media. Join advocacy groups. Contact your elected officials to advocate in favor of true audits or the legislative reforms cited in this book such as a return to hand counts of paper ballots.

Circulate Petitions

If the legislature is unresponsive to the demands of citizens or if the executive branch is not inclined to support election reform legislation supported by the legislature as is the case in Michigan, citizen initiatives are an alternative option that can be pursued as a means of enacting a law. Such initiatives require the collection of signatures. The number of signatures required varies by state, but the common thread is that the citizens do have the means of making their voice heard with or without the support of elected officials.

Canvass

Canvassing is a major component of a full forensic audit of the entire election record chain of custody. Canvassers simply verify the integrity of the election pollbooks. They determine if the voter information captured in the pollbooks is accurate. When one canvasses, one simply asks people which the state says voted in a given election, the following questions:

- Did you vote in the last election?
- If so, how did you vote? By mail or in-person.
- How many registered voters live at this address?
- How many ballots did you receive at this address?

Pretty simple questions. Please note that canvassers DO NOT ASK who you voted for. Canvassers do not validate the vote count. They simply validate the number of people who have voted. If the ballot count does not jive with the number of voters, something is wrong. The information gained through canvassing is one of the best ways to demonstrate evidence of election fraud.

Alternative Media Outlets

How much of the information in this book have you heard previously? If not, ask yourself why not? Coups only survive if they can successfully push their propaganda. Stop supporting media outlets that merely push propaganda and start protesting them. Conversely, support media outlets that give a fair presentation of the facts from both sides of a given issue. Responsible journalists are not afraid of providing you with access to the information sources they use to draw their conclusions. Irresponsible journalists are notorious for not providing access to such information or limit access to controlled snippets.

Remember, ultimately, we are in an information war. We are in a battle over truth itself.

CHAPTER 10

The Question on Everyone's Mind

S o far in this book, we've covered *how* the election was stolen. We've covered *where* the election was stolen. We've covered *what* evidence we have in support of the how and where. We now turn to the question on everyone's mind in the wake of all of this information.

WHO IS BEHIND THE COUP?

Is it Joe Biden? Is it Kamala Harris? Is it Barack Obama? Is it Hillary Clinton?

Is it the Democratic Party? Is it the Republican Party?

Was it Klaus Schwab? Was it George Soros? Was it Bill Gates? Was it Hansjorg Wyss?

Was it a nation state such as Iran or China or Russia?

Was it the current and former intelligence officials who signed a letter right before the election making the false assertion that the Hunter Biden laptop appeared to be part of a Russian disinformation campaign?

Or is it much deeper than any single figurehead?

Was it a shadow organization operating without borders?

Was it all of the above?

In this book, we've provided many clues as to the individuals and organizations responsible for subverting our 2020 election. We have identified many of the organizations involved in planning to preserve election results months before the general public had even cast a vote. Are the individuals leading these organizations responsible for the coup or are the true leaders hidden from public view?

The answer to this question is Important. Ultimately, we need to hold those responsible accountable for their sedition.

Under Title 18 Section 2384 of United States Code, seditious conspiracy is defined as follows:

> If two or more persons in any State or Territory, or in any place subject to the jurisdiction of the United States, conspire to overthrow, put down, or to destroy by force the Government of the United States, or to levy war against them, or to oppose by force the authority thereof, or by force to prevent, hinder, or delay the execution of any law of the United States, or by force to seize, take, or possess any property of the United States contrary to the authority thereof, they shall each be fined under this title or imprisoned not more than twenty years, or both.

Seditious conspiracy is a serious crime. It needs to be treated seriously. We have explored all that we can as "meddling kids." We don't have the financial resources needed to issue FOIA requests for all the data needed to conduct the next level of investigation. We don't have the subpoena authority to access the information that FOIA authorities refuse to divulge.

If you share my passion to get to the bottom of who is responsible for the coup, the only way to do so is to treat each state as a crime scene and perform a full forensic audit in each of the battleground states as a minimum. Ideally, every state in the union would perform a full forensic audit. We need to start treating our election system as the critical infrastructure component it truly is.

CHAPTER 11

Final Thoughts

We have done our best to present factual information you likely may have heard for the first time. Please ask yourself why this is the first time. When you watch the news, are you being educated or are you being manipulated?

Americans have a first amendment protection for freedom of the press for a reason. Our constitutional republic only works when we have informed citizens. We need to provide our citizens with unfettered access to the truth. Clearly, the mainstream media outlets have failed to deliver the truth, especially on the topic of election fraud.

For those who say, "There is no evidence," we've shown you evidence. For those who say, "There is no significant evidence," we've shown you evidence significant enough to overcome the widest reported margin of victory of all of the battleground states: Michigan. This should raise eyebrows on the reported results in other states as well.

Which begs the questions: Why are there people attempting to prevent further discussion of election fraud?

What happens when those who seek to classify claims of election fraud as "misinformation" are the ones deliberately promoting misinformation?

Which side of the election fraud debate is promoting transparency?

Which side of the election fraud debate is promoting censorship?

If the November 2020 election truly was the most secure election in history, why would anyone making this bold statement seek to prevent any investigation that would back up their assertion?

What if this was NOT the most secure election in history?

The information provided in this book is just the tip of the iceberg. There is no lack of evidence. There is no lack of significant evidence. The single biggest challenge in this book was determining what evidence to keep in and what to put in reserve. Now, it is up to you. Upon review of these facts, you can decide for yourself.

Was America the victim of a coup?

Do the facts merit further investigation?

Should we be pursuing substantive, forensic audits of statewide election results?

Why hasn't law enforcement conducted an investigation of the 2020 election with the same digital crime scene investigative vigor as was applied to the SolarWinds hack?

Should we pursue prosecution of those who willfully or neglectfully violated our election laws?

Do these violations merit prosecution for treason for domestic enemies of America?

Do these violations indicate an act of war by our foreign enemies?

Or should we simply stop questioning the integrity of our election system, move on, and continue to supplant our elections with selections?

Much is at stake. The future of an America of the people, by the people and for the people depends upon your decision.

There are some who believe we can postpone this decision. They assert that nothing can be done about the 2020 election and that we need to focus upon the 2022 election. The fact of the matter is that, if we do not address what happened in the 2020 election, we will continue to have selections NOT elections.

Our election system is broken and in dire need of reform.

It goes deeper than that, though.

Our justice system is broken and in dire need of leaders who will enforce the laws we already have on the books.

When a police officer catches a bank robber with loot in hand, does he say "keep the loot but just don't do it again?" No. He arrests them and returns the money to the bank. Why would it be any different for a stolen elected office? Once America ceases to enforce the rule of law, we cease to be a constitutional republic. America is filled with citizens such as elected officials, law enforcement officers and military personnel who took oaths to defend our Constitution and the rule of law.

The evidence is clear. America is the victim of an elaborate coup. We need to hold each of those complicit with the coup accountable for their actions. We need to accomplish this not through the force of arms or violence. We are better than that. America is better than that. That is how those behind the coup like to operate. Plus, they would simply use any use of force as an excuse to take away even more of our God-given freedoms. We need to take a different route. We need to hold them accountable via the relentless pursuit and exposure of the truth.

That is why I wrote this book. That is why I have put my professional life on hold until the truth about the 2020 election has been exposed. All of the other policy issues which we face derive from the fundamental issue of who we elect to represent us in government. The 2020 election is one of the important "kerplunk" sticks that holds up what ails us as a nation. Once we remove this impediment by exposing the truth of what happened, it will allow many of the other policy pieces to fall back into their appropriate position within our nation's constitutional framework.

It is my belief that the only reason that there are so many people that believe that the 2020 general election was the most secure election in American history is that they have not been exposed to the truth. I am convinced that before we gain serious headway in what passes for courts of law in America today, we need to win in the court of public opinion. The media, big tech, and corrupt politicians have been ruthless in their suppression of this information. They have been ruthless in their classification of the truth as misinformation. We need to be equally committed to the dismantling of the election theft plumbing they leveraged so successfully during the 2020 election.

We are in the middle of an information war. If this book reaches as many people with the truth about the 2020 election as I hope it does, me and my fellow meddling kids will likely be on the receiving end of relentless attacks in an attempt to discredit us and the information in this book. We are prepared for the assault. We are prayed up. We have provided you with hundreds of footnotes in this book to back up our assertions. We have created a digital evidence wall depicting graphically how the election fraud evidence fits together. We have also provided you with links to the actual documents, stories, images, or videos referenced in this evidence wall. You can find this information and more at The-2020Coup.com.

When the inevitable attacks are launched, please give me the opportunity to issue a rebuttal to any substantive attack before drawing any conclusions. Simply email any attack claims to questions@letsfixstuff. org. I'll do my best to respond in a timely manner. As time allows, my rebuttals will be posted at The2020Coup.com website for your reference.

The media loves to post one-sided narratives featuring false headlines. We believe it is incumbent upon truth seekers to hear both sides of a given story. To date, whenever I have attempted to issue rebuttals to stories which distort the facts or are maliciously defamatory, the media refuses to print my rebuttals. Why? The mission of all too many in today's media establishment is not the pursuit of the truth. Their mission is to serve as the propaganda arm for the 2020 coup.

These propagandists seek to lull Americans asleep on one of the most consequential issues of our day - election fraud. Despite their best efforts to censor and ridicule us, my fellow meddling kids and I doggedly persist in our pursuit of the truth. As we do so, more and more of their lies will be exposed in the public square.

It is now time for all Americans to stand up to those complicit with the coup before it is too late. This book has equipped you with the information you need to help hold those behind the coup accountable for their actions. You are hereby deputized to share this information and more like it with your network of friends and family members. The more people who know what you now know, the more likely we will finally see justice done so that we can preserve liberty for future generations. Sadly, in today's America, we need to win in the court of public opinion before having a reasonable chance of justice being served in a court of law.

We all need to get out of our comfort zone and stick up for the truth about what happened in the 2020 election regardless of the insults and false accusations. Others before us have sacrificed much more in the cause of liberty.

Evidence Highlights

In this appendix, I have provided evidence highlights organized by each phase of the coup. This is only a small sample of the evidence in support of the case for the coup. For links to additional evidence, please visit **LetsFixStuff.org**.

PREPARATION PHASE

GOAL: Create and expand weaknesses in election system

Ballot proposal 2018-3[1]

The BallotPedia summary of the 2018-3 Ballot Proposal in Michigan is provided in the following table:

Policy	As of 2018	Proposal 3
Secret ballot	Constitution requires legislature to enact laws for secret ballots	Constitution provides a right to use secret ballots
Military/ overseas ballots	Statute provides that military members and overseas voters receive an absentee ballot at least 45 days before the election	Constitution provides that military members and overseas voters receive an absentee ballot at least 45 days before the election

Policy	As of 2018	Proposal 3
Register-to-vote by mail deadline	Statute provides that eligible persons can register to vote by mail until 30 days before an election	Constitution provides that eligible persons can register to vote by mail until 15 days before an election
Register-to-vote in person deadline	Statute provides that eligible persons can register to vote in person at a clerk's office until 30 days before an election	Constitution provides that eligible persons can register to vote in person at a clerk's office during the final 14 days before an election and at the polls on election day
Straight-party ticket voting	No straight-ticket voting	Constitution provides voters with straight-ticket voting option
Automatic voter registration	No automatic voter registration	Constitution provides for the automatic voter registration of eligible persons when interacting with the state regarding driver's license or state ID card, unless the person declines
Absentee voting	Statute provides that specific criteria be met to vote absentee, including at least one of the following: (a) 60 years old or older; (b) unable to vote without assistance at the polls; (c) expected to be out-of-town on election day; (d) in jail awaiting arraignment or trial; (e) unable to attend the polls for religious reasons; or (f) appointed to work as an election inspector in a precinct outside of the inspector's home precinct	Constitution provides that any voter can vote using an absentee ballot (no-excuse absentee voting) during the 40 days before an election
Election results auditing	Statute provides for the auditing of election results	Constitution provides for the auditing of election results

800,000 Ineligible voters

In the wake of the 2020 general election, former Michigan secretary of state and current Michigan state senator Ruth Johnson submitted the following memo to her fellow senate Republican colleagues. Among the assertions made by this former chief election official is that over 800,000 ineligible voters were likely present in the state Qualified Voter File prior to the election.

Memo

From: Ruth A. Johnson
            Chair, Senate Elections Committee
            State Senator, 14ᵗʰ District
To: Senate Republican Colleagues

I have asked for subpoena power several times going back to the spring of 2020 for the Elections Committee to investigate many actions and changes made by Michigan's current Secretary of State Jocelyn Benson which I feel threaten the integrity of our elections, including:

1. Failing to purge records identified through interstate crosscheck as likely no longer eligible to vote in Michigan which have gone through two federal election cycles without activity.

2. Creating an online absentee ballot application which is not signed by a voter as required by law.

3. Instructing clerks to issue absentee ballots to individuals flagged in the QVF to be verified for reasons such as surrendering their license to another state based on a signature comparison alone with no further inquiry to determine the eligibility of the voter.

I feel following the many allegations and concerns surrounding the 2020 November General Election we need a comprehensive audit which is not conducted by the Secretary of State. I have been saying since right after the election that we need an **independent**, third-party review of information to assist the legislature in determining any necessary policy changes that may be needed to ensure the continued integrity of our election processes.

In addition to the review of records subpoenaed by the Senate and House Oversight committees to examine out-of-balance precincts in absentee counting boards, the following issues which have been raised should also be examined by a qualified independent third party:

Forensic analysis of records to include an examination of items such as:

1. Mismatches between between absentee ballot numbers issued to voters and those returned, need to look at change log in computer as well as stubes by absentee counting board and reconciliation to recorded voters.
2. Any evidence of adjudication bias.
3. Specific allegations from affidavits and testimony (e.g., sequential ballots appearing with the same signature all from Goddard Street)

Procedural issues to be examined:

1. Restricting the access of poll challengers to meaningfully observe the absentee counting process.
2. Denying credentialed poll challengers from making good-faith challenges of ballots with identified issues.
3. Not allowing poll challengers to re-enter the counting area and denying the entry of fresh poll challengers to replace those who had left the building.
4. Insufficient number of Republican election inspectors present at absentee counting boards. (Clerk Winfrey and

Daniel Baxter both admitted this is a known issue during the State Board of Canvassers meeting via Zoom. Clerk Winfrey stated that this was due to difficulty recruiting and that some applications for Republican inspectors arrived late, but there seem to be examples of individuals who applied in a timely manner who were not contacted.)

5. Allegations that in some satellite clerk offices, election workers coached and/or intimidated voters to voting for a particular candidate or party.

Other issues to be examined:

1. Groups encouraging college students to register and vote in Michigan even if they maintain primary residence and many vote in another state.

We should also review information regarding other potential election crimes, including working with the Attorney General who is investigating misleading calls made to voters in Detroit, Flint, and Dearborn. We must not tolerate cheating or intimidation of any kind.

For the independent review, I have previously given the name of the Whall Group who assisted me when I was given subpoena power to investigate the Oakland County ISD in the House of Representatives, which resulted in the criminal conviction of the district's superintendent. I am including their contact information again below:

Chris Whall
The Whall Group
(PHONE NUMBER REDACTED)

Bob Norton, the General Counsel at Hillsdale College has also recommended an individual who may be qualified on this front. We could also possibly enlist the help of a clerk(s) with great knowledge of Michigan election processes to assist. My staff and I would be willing to help whoever might be selected as well.

In addition to this independent, comprehensive review, I feel we must also continue to press the Secretary of state to answer for her many actions – and inactions – which are detrimental to election integrity. I estimate that, conservatively, over 800,000 absentee ballot applications were mailed to individuals who are likely not eligible to vote in Michigan. Already, the Secretary of State has received over 500,000 of these applications back as undeliverable. I have also received hundreds of examples of applications ent to non-eligible individueals in my legislature office, including applications sent to those who are underage, non-citizens, moved out-of-state, or deceased.

Examples of further subpoena inquiries to Secretary of State:

1. Asking immediately for the number of records which are being held for "executive review" that would normally have been purged from the Qualified Voter File already, as well as an explanation of why they are being held, what type of review is being done, and when this review will be completed and/or these records removed. (Elections Director Brater stated in the Join Senate Elections/Oversight hearing that he would have to look into this matter, but to date I am unaware of any follow-up on this issue.)

2. Ensuring through appropriate legislative oversight that the 500,000+ returned absentee ballot applications are handled appropriately to put these records in the Qualified Voter File into the countdown process if appropriate so they may be removed after two federal election cycles if these individuals no longer reside at the registered address.

3. Additional information about the programming error that caused non-citizens to be registered to vote when automatic voter registration was rolled out in branches. Including

the dates this programming error was in place, how many individuals who were not eligible due to citizenship were registered, when these individuals were removed from the Qualified Voter File, and how these individuals were notified that they had been incorrectly registered to vote.

Now that the courts have upheld the Secretary of State's authority to send such mailings as lawful (which goes against previous court precedent for clerks that they could not send unsolicited absentee ballot applications), it is even more vital to have a clean Qualified Voter File. When I was Secretary of State, I removed 1 in 6 names on the Qualified Voter File using a variety of techniques to remove individuals who were deceased, moved out-of-state, or non-citizens. But I wasn't using this as a mailing list as our current Secretary of State who has failed to even purge the known and eligible records of individuals who are likely not qualified to vote in our state prior to sending her May mailing.

Prior to the August Primary election, the Secretary of State announced on the Frank Beckmann radio show that she had "invested in signature matching software for the first time to verify and ensure everyone's using the same technology to verify the accuracy of these signatures." However, this statement was simply not true. In fact, this technology was not offered to any clerk in the state for the primary election or for the subsequent general election in November. So in addition to mailing invitations to vote to many individuals she knew to be likely ineligible, the Secretary of State failed to deliver on her promise to offer technology to our local clerks to help detect potentially fraudulent signatures.

The Secretary of state also bragged right after the August Primary Election about the "success"… (that) will serve as our blueprint for the presidential election." However, shortly after this announcement both the Wayne County and State Boards of Canvassers by bipartisan votes directed the Secretary of State to provide greater oversight of election operations in the City of Detroit as the Detroit News reported "after widespread problems counting ballots in the city's primary and ahead of a pivotal presidential election." In fact, 72% of Detroit's Absentee Counting Boards could not be reconciled in August and overall 46% of their precincts (including AV and in-person) could not be reconciled.

70% of Detroit's Absentee Counting Boards could not be reconciled in the November General Election and overall Wayne County had more out-of-balance precincts than all other 82 counties combined. Unfortunately, the issues we are continuing to see in Detroit are not new. My office conducted an audit of Detroit's performance during the November 8, 2016, general election while I was Secretary of State, and we made a number of findings and recommendations for improvement. We must continue to hold both the Secretary of State and local election officials accountable for addressing these issues as the Senate continues its work to ensure that we have safe, secure and fair elections in Michigan that are conducted with the utmost of integrity.

COVID 6-Foot Rule Policy

The Michigan Department of State prepared a document for the November 3, 2020, election covering Polling Place Safety and Accessibility. Among the instructions provided in this addendum to the state election procedures was a COVID-inspired six-foot rule. The rule was leveraged on election night by poll workers to prevent poll challengers from observing their work despite a last-minute court injunction preventing such obstruction.

Michigan Bureau of Elections
Updated 10/28/2020

Please stay at least 6 feet apart while waiting in line and within the polling place. Follow poll worker instructions and marked signs to help maintain social distance. Please wash your hands or use hand sanitizer before and after voting.

6 Feet Apart

Protect the "Results"

The website ProtecttheResults.org was launched months before the 2020 general election was held. What results were they seeking to protect?

Protect the Results has a growing coalition of partners committed to upholding the rule of law and safeguarding the final, legitimate results of the 2020 election. In the event that Donald Trump loses the election and refuses to concede or undermines the results, the Protect the Results partner network will activate their members and take coordinated action to protect our democracy.

Joining our partner network means that your organization is responsible for recruiting Americans who are ready to take action, creating press and awareness opportunities for Protect the Results and helping prepare for a potential post-election crisis. Partners are encouraged to openly exchange ideas, articles, and information to help plan and prepare in case we have to activate the Protect the Results network.

If you are interested in joining the Protect the Results coalition, please fill out this Google Form with contact information for your organization's press, digital, and political/partnerships contacts. Please be sure to upload a transparent .PNG file logo for your organization. Filling out the Google Form does not guarantee that we will be able to take you on as a partner. Someone from Indivisible or Stand Up America will be in touch within 3 business days of your submission.

Please contact partnership@standupamerica.com with any partnership-related questions.

As of October 29, 2020, their list of "Partners" included:

- Standup America
- #MarchForTruth
- 350 Mass Action
- 350 Seattle Action
- AZ AN
- Advance Native Political Leadership
- Arizona Wins
- Bend the Arc Jewish Action
- Black PAC
- Bold New Democracy
- CHISPA AZ League of Conservation Voters
- CPD Action

- Indivisible
- 350 Action
- 350 Action New Hampshire
- 51 for 51
- ATN
- Alliance for Youth Action
- Bay Resistance
- Black Lives Matter
- Bluewave Crowdsource
- CASA in Action
- Color Action Fund
- Care2

- Caring Majority Rising

- Center for Freethought Equality

- Clean Water Action

- CWA

- Count Every Vote! Maryland

- Democracy Matters

- Daily Kos

- Demcast

- Democracy Action

- Democrats.com

- Extinction Rebellion Los Angeles

- Faithful America

- Food & Water Action!

- Friends of the Earth Action

- GMOM

- Health Care Voter

- Indiana Nasty Women

- J Street

- Jobs with Justice

- Let America Vote Action Fund

- Move Texas

- Make the Road Action

- Michigan People's Campaign

- MomsRising.org

- MoveOn

- Center for Biological Diversity Action Fund

- Choose Democracy

- Voting While Black Powered by Color of Change PAC

- Community Change Action

- Courage California

- Demos Action

- @

- 21 Democracy 21

- Democracy Initiative

- End Citizens United (ECU) Action Fund

- Faith in Public Life Action

- Fix Democracy First

- Free Press Action

- Future Coalition

- Greenpeace

- Sing V*&() (Illegible)

- Indivisible Chicago

- JVP Action

- Kairos Fellowship

- Luca Living United for Change in Arizona

- Represent ME Mainers for Accountable Leadership

- March ON

- MIJENTE

- Mormon Women for Ethical Government

- NARAL Pro-Choice America

- NEAT
- National Partnership for Women & Families Action Fund
- The New Georgia Project
- New York Progressive Action Network
- One Fair Wage Action
- Organize Florida
- Our Revolution Organize to Win Massachusetts
- +Action
- Partnership for Working Families Action Fund
- People for the American Way
- Planned Parenthood
- Progress Arizona
- Progress Now Colorado
- Progressive Change Campaign Committee (BoldProgressives. org)
- Progressive Vietnamese Organization (PIVOT)
- Pulso
- A Rebuild the Dream
- Republicans for the Rule of Law
- Ring the Alarm.US
- Rise and Resist
- SEIU
- San Francisco Labor Council

- National LGBTQ Task Force
- New Florida Majority
- New Virginia Majority
- Nextgen America
- One PA
- Our Revolution Organize to Win
- Our Voice Our Vote Arizona
- Poder LatinX
- Peace Action
- People's Action
- Presente Action
- Progress Iowa
- Progress Virginia
- Progressive Democrats of America
- Public Citizen
- Real Justice
- Represent Us
- Resist.St. Louis
- Rise
- Rise
- Showing Up for Racial Justice (SURJ)
- See the Vote, Defeat Trump, Build Our Movements

- ShutdownDC
- Sister District Action Network
- Strong Economy for All Coalition
- Sum of Us
- Supermajority The Power of Women
- Texas Freedom Network
- The Leadership Conference (civilrights.org)
- UNIDOS US Action Fund
- Vote for Respect Powered by United for Respect
- Veterans for Responsible Leadership
- Vote Save America
- Washington Conservation Voters
- Win Black
- Women's March
- Working Families Party

- Sierra Club
- Stand Up Republic
- Suit Up Maine
- Sunrise
- Take On Wall Street
- The Jewish Vote
- Ultraviolet Action
- United We Dream Action
- VPIRG Vermont's Voice
- Vote Pro Choice
- VotoLatino
- Way to Win
- Women for American Values and Ethics
- Workers Defense Action Fund
- Re: Power

Electronic Voting Systems Designed for Internet Connectivity

Contract #071B7700117 between the state of Michigan and Dominion Voting Systems clearly shows how the voting system is designed to work over the internet on Page 114.

NOTE: The "IP" in TCP/IP stands for Internet Protocol.

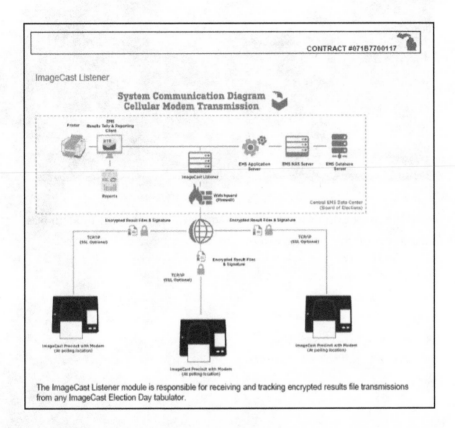

Wireless 4G Modem Chip Embedded on Voting System Motherboard

The Bailey v Antrim County lawsuit featured a court exhibit provided by cyber forensics expert Jim Penrose. The exhibit provided evidence of the installation of a wireless 4G modem installed internally within the enclosure of an ES&S DS200 machine found in a nearby county. This shows that Dominion voting systems were not the only ones designed to connect to the internet. This modem would likely not be detected by the majority of clerks.

The court exhibit went on to provide evidence that the modem was used to communicate with external devices on November 4, 2020.

MAIN ATTACK PHASE

GOAL: Cast a sufficient number of absentee ballots to secure victory in a manner that minimizes the risk of detection.

Ballot Harvesting

Among the evidence presented in the TCF Timeline Report prepared by the Michigan Citizens for Election Integrity (MC4EI.com) is that of the following individual in front of the Detroit Elections Bureau before the election. When asked by poll challengers if the boxes contained ballots, he sped off in his car. He certainly appears to be preparing for ballot trafficking activities.

Machine-based algorithms

In support of the *Bailey v Antrim County* lawsuit, Dr. Douglas Frank compiled a series of analyses of the allocations of ballots to voters in ten counties across Michigan including Antrim County where 7,060 votes were flipped from Trump to Biden between the first and final counts. Dr. Frank shows evidence that irrefutably demonstrated that ballots were allocated to voters with machine-based accuracy. He could predict the 2020 voter turnout with greater than 99% accuracy for any demographic using only the 2010 census records. Does it seem reasonable to you that you could predict the voter turnout for an election ten years into the future by simply knowing the current year census records?

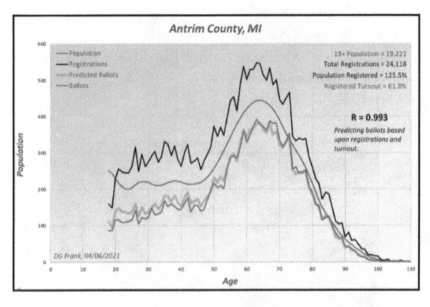

Census.gov provides population estimates for every county in the US in five-year buckets, so a linear interpolation is used to obtain an estimate for each county by single year.

The mathematics only for the Registration Key is discussed here, although an analogous procedure applies to the Population Key, where an interpolated set of the 2019 US Census data for a particular county is used instead of registration data.[2]

The turnout is simply the ratio of the participation to the number of registered voters:

$$t_i = \frac{p_i}{x_i} \qquad (1)$$

Where:

i is an index running from 1 to 83 that corresponds to each year of age from 18 to 100,

x_i is the number of registered voters at each age,

p_i is the number of voters participating in the election at each age, and

t_i the is the registered voter turnout (the fraction of registered voters who participate at each age)

Data from a selected reference county (or small set of counties) is first used to calculate the turnout at each year of age:

$$t_{i,ref} = \frac{p_{i,ref}}{x_{i,ref}} \qquad (2)$$

Once t_i,ref has been determined, it is fitted with a sixth-order polynomial:

$$k(i) = a\,i^6 + b\,i^5 + c\,i^4 + d\,i^3 + e\,i^2 + f\,i^\square + g \qquad (3)$$

where the coefficients a through f are a unique set of constants for every state, and k(i) is referred to as the "key" for that state.

The key is then used to predict the voter participation, $p_{i,pred}$, in a test county:

$$p_{i,pred} = \frac{p_{test}}{\Sigma k_i x_{i,test}} k_i x_{i,test} \qquad (4)$$

Note that this normalization process also conserves ballots. Thus, it is the shape of the distribution that is being investigated, not the scalar values. Accordingly, the Pearson R-coefficient is used as a quantitative measure of the correlation between a predicted distribution and the observed one:

$$R = \frac{\Sigma\left(p_{i,pred}-p_{i,pred}\right)\left(p_{ave,obs}-p_{ave,obs}\right)}{\sqrt{\Sigma\left(p_{i,pred}-p_{ave,pred}\right)^2}\sqrt{\Sigma\left(p_{i,obs}-p_{ave,obs}\right)^2}} \qquad (5)$$

Dr. Frank discovered that each state had its own unique set of co-efficients that was consistent across all counties within a given state. In some states, it was even consistent at the precinct level. In Michigan, the statewide coefficients were as follows:

a =	1.357240E-10
b =	5.337725E-088
c =	8.294682E-06
d =	6.581727E-04
e =	2.820954E-02
f =	6.105048E-01
g =	6.014449E+00

The resulting predictions of voter turnout by age demographic were remarkably accurate.

One has better odds of winning a state lottery six times in a row than for voters to have been allocated to ballots with such precision. As Dr. Frank likes to say, "That's not natural".

Canvassing results

Former Congressional and township clerk staffer Jacky Eubanks formed an organization called the Concerned Citizen Initiative to in-vestigate vote anomalies in Macomb County during the 2020 election. Together, they executed a canvass of Macomb County that identified a 17.6% anomaly rate for the county voter data.

Thursday, November 4, 2021

2020 General Election

Macomb County, Michigan
Canvassing Report

974,917 FRAUDULENT VOTES

Projected in the state of Michigan - 6 times the Biden margin of victory. 154,545 fraud votes projected in Wayne County - greater than the 154,188 it would take to overturn the election. 17.6% fraud rate.

Macomb County was not the only county in Michigan that was canvassed. The following table provides a summary of preliminary results in several other Michigan counties.

COUNTY	REGISTERED VOTERS	VOTES CAST	TURNOUT	# ATTEMPTED CONTACTS	# VOTERS CONTACTED	VOTE ANOMALIES	% ANOMALIES
Berrien	130,487	82,391	63.1%	439	189	6	3.2%
Genesee	343,940	221,360	64.4%	1193	493	45	9.1%
Livingston	160,308	127,197	79.3%	464	184	12	6.5%
Macomb	687,568	494,256	71.9%	NA	1,216	214	17.6%
Ottawa	219,374	168,713	76.9%	NA	478	32	6.7%

Additional counties being canvassed as well.
Data not yet available at time of publication.

Please note that all vote anomaly percentages were greater than the 2.78% margin of victory assigned to Joe Biden. The canvassing results, therefore, are significant enough to demonstrate that the results of the 2020 election are in question.

BACKUP ATTACK PHASE

GOAL: Inject or shift a sufficient number of votes to overcome any deficit due to incorrect voter turnout projections.

Internet Connectivity

Despite repeated objections to the contrary, the workstations at the TCF Center in Detroit were indeed connected to the internet as demonstrated in this photo taken during the pre-election walkthrough. The lower right corner on the computer monitor reveals the "Internet Connectivity" icon displayed on all Windows 10 operating systems.

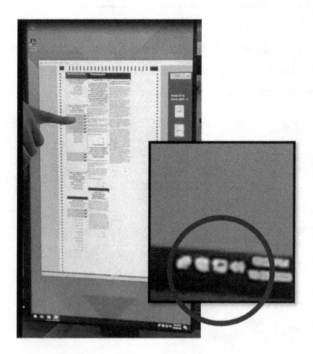

Michigan's "Edison Zero"

At 5:00:04 a.m., the cumulative vote results as reported by Edison Research were reset to zero indicating the presence of a digital controller manipulating the vote results.

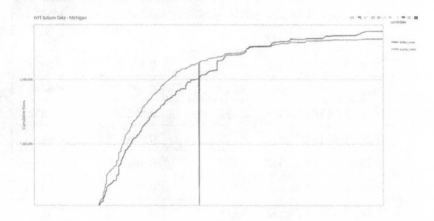

Source of Data: Edison Research feed to NY Times of Michigan Results[3]

2020 GENERAL ELECTION EDISON RESEARCH RESULTS REPORTING FOR MICHIGAN

EEVP	TIMESTAMP	VOTE_SHARE_DEM	VOTE_SHARE_REP	VOTES
1	2020-11-04T01:09:14Z	0.724	0.263	36561
1	2020-11-04T01:13:29Z	0.707	0.281	38469
1	2020-11-04T01:13:52Z	0.589	0.397	54591
1	2020-11-04T01:20:24Z	0.549	0.435	65840
2	2020-11-04T01:20:50Z	0.431	0.552	134852
2	2020-11-04T01:22:30Z	0.429	0.554	136064
3	2020-11-04T01:25:54Z	0.398	0.584	189834
3	2020-11-04T01:26:24Z	0.399	0.583	198052
4	2020-11-04T01:28:36Z	0.413	0.568	216387
4	2020-11-04T01:28:51Z	0.407	0.575	232274
4	2020-11-04T01:32:32Z	0.406	0.575	232460
4	2020-11-04T01:32:51Z	0.402	0.579	254286
5	2020-11-04T01:37:59Z	0.401	0.58	257353
5	2020-11-04T01:39:31Z	0.406	0.576	284659
5	2020-11-04T01:39:54Z	0.405	0.576	285117
5	2020-11-04T01:40:08Z	0.405	0.576	285164
5	2020-11-04T01:41:08Z	0.405	0.576	285529
5	2020-11-04T01:43:02Z	0.404	0.577	289631
7	2020-11-04T01:43:16Z	0.402	0.577	392781
7	2020-11-04T01:43:27Z	0.399	0.579	404321
8	2020-11-04T01:43:55Z	0.4	0.579	433755
8	2020-11-04T01:46:03Z	0.4	0.579	435199
8	2020-11-04T01:46:50Z	0.4	0.579	439375

EEVP	TIMESTAMP	VOTE_SHARE_DEM	VOTE_SHARE_REP	VOTES
8	2020-11-04T01:48:02Z	0.388	0.591	477151
9	2020-11-04T01:50:30Z	0.382	0.597	498880
10	2020-11-04T01:51:17Z	0.397	0.582	550389
10	2020-11-04T01:51:26Z	0.401	0.578	573857
10	2020-11-04T01:51:52Z	0.406	0.568	574417
11	2020-11-04T01:53:23Z	0.404	0.571	641548
12	2020-11-04T01:55:13Z	0.404	0.57	663038
12	2020-11-04T01:56:48Z	0.404	0.57	663321
12	2020-11-04T01:57:38Z	0.405	0.569	671666
12	2020-11-04T01:58:41Z	0.404	0.57	702274
12	2020-11-04T01:59:28Z	0.404	0.57	702415
15	2020-11-04T02:01:11Z	0.384	0.593	876300
16	2020-11-04T02:02:49Z	0.382	0.594	888904
16	2020-11-04T02:04:55Z	0.383	0.594	901077
16	2020-11-04T02:05:31Z	0.383	0.594	906056
16	2020-11-04T02:07:30Z	0.383	0.594	909244
16	2020-11-04T02:07:41Z	0.383	0.593	909862
16	2020-11-04T02:08:04Z	0.384	0.593	931766
16	2020-11-04T02:08:47Z	0.384	0.593	934486
17	2020-11-04T02:10:05Z	0.384	0.593	936292
17	2020-11-04T02:10:51Z	0.384	0.593	954476
17	2020-11-04T02:11:05Z	0.384	0.593	957726
17	2020-11-04T02:11:23Z	0.384	0.593	958809
17	2020-11-04T02:13:39Z	0.383	0.593	959682
17	2020-11-04T02:14:19Z	0.383	0.593	959712

EEVP	TIMESTAMP	VOTE_SHARE_DEM	VOTE_SHARE_REP	VOTES
17	2020-11-04T02:15:54Z	0.384	0.593	968520
17	2020-11-04T02:16:23Z	0.384	0.593	970119
17	2020-11-04T02:19:12Z	0.383	0.594	980979
17	2020-11-04T02:20:21Z	0.383	0.594	985138
18	2020-11-04T02:22:03Z	0.383	0.594	1002101
18	2020-11-04T02:22:31Z	0.383	0.594	1002799
18	2020-11-04T02:23:05Z	0.387	0.59	1015997
18	2020-11-04T02:24:22Z	0.386	0.591	1020643
18	2020-11-04T02:24:33Z	0.386	0.591	1023359
18	2020-11-04T02:25:07Z	0.385	0.592	1032323
18	2020-11-04T02:25:16Z	0.385	0.592	1033098
18	2020-11-04T02:25:49Z	0.385	0.592	1033099
18	2020-11-04T02:28:25Z	0.385	0.592	1033280
18	2020-11-04T02:29:23Z	0.385	0.592	1033523
18	2020-11-04T02:30:54Z	0.387	0.59	1046403
19	2020-11-04T02:31:58Z	0.39	0.587	1058214
19	2020-11-04T02:32:16Z	0.39	0.587	1060349
19	2020-11-04T02:34:27Z	0.39	0.587	1061077
19	2020-11-04T02:35:39Z	0.391	0.586	1095835
19	2020-11-04T02:37:14Z	0.391	0.587	1098388
19	2020-11-04T02:37:34Z	0.391	0.587	1099049
19	2020-11-04T02:38:51Z	0.39	0.587	1100522
20	2020-11-04T02:39:39Z	0.39	0.588	1109685
20	2020-11-04T02:39:43Z	0.39	0.588	1110223
20	2020-11-04T02:40:48Z	0.39	0.588	1110414
20	2020-11-04T02:42:29Z	0.39	0.587	1114156

EEVP	TIMESTAMP	VOTE_SHARE_DEM	VOTE_SHARE_REP	VOTES
20	2020-11-04T02:43:47Z	0.39	0.587	1118593
20	2020-11-04T02:46:01Z	0.39	0.587	1119593
20	2020-11-04T02:47:30Z	0.39	0.587	1123572
20	2020-11-04T02:47:37Z	0.39	0.588	1126627
20	2020-11-04T02:49:58Z	0.39	0.588	1127132
20	2020-11-04T02:50:24Z	0.389	0.588	1132011
20	2020-11-04T02:51:39Z	0.389	0.588	1134704
20	2020-11-04T02:51:51Z	0.389	0.588	1136926
22	2020-11-04T02:53:09Z	0.404	0.577	1255863
22	2020-11-04T02:53:30Z	0.404	0.577	1262790
22	2020-11-04T02:53:48Z	0.404	0.577	1270326
23	2020-11-04T02:54:31Z	0.403	0.578	1281581
23	2020-11-04T02:54:49Z	0.403	0.578	1283379
23	2020-11-04T02:55:48Z	0.403	0.578	1283875
23	2020-11-04T02:57:01Z	0.402	0.578	1288944
23	2020-11-04T02:57:18Z	0.402	0.578	1293253
23	2020-11-04T02:58:08Z	0.402	0.578	1295198
23	2020-11-04T03:00:24Z	0.402	0.578	1298117
23	2020-11-04T03:01:32Z	0.401	0.58	1315455
23	2020-11-04T03:03:52Z	0.401	0.579	1328021
28	2020-11-04T03:04:06Z	0.426	0.555	1565405
28	2020-11-04T03:05:34Z	0.427	0.554	1571959
28	2020-11-04T03:08:17Z	0.427	0.554	1572163
28	2020-11-04T03:09:26Z	0.426	0.555	1575867
28	2020-11-04T03:10:29Z	0.426	0.555	1577983
28	2020-11-04T03:11:08Z	0.426	0.555	1583336

EEVP	TIMESTAMP	VOTE_SHARE_DEM	VOTE_SHARE_REP	VOTES
28	2020-11-04T03:11:37Z	0.426	0.555	1585415
29	2020-11-04T03:13:52Z	0.433	0.548	1618052
29	2020-11-04T03:14:34Z	0.433	0.549	1627212
29	2020-11-04T03:16:05Z	0.432	0.549	1627520
30	2020-11-04T03:16:42Z	0.433	0.548	1710559
30	2020-11-04T03:18:00Z	0.433	0.548	1711403
30	2020-11-04T03:18:31Z	0.433	0.549	1722798
30	2020-11-04T03:20:47Z	0.432	0.549	1724175
31	2020-11-04T03:21:01Z	0.432	0.549	1742721
31	2020-11-04T03:21:31Z	0.432	0.549	1742749
31	2020-11-04T03:22:28Z	0.431	0.55	1783844
32	2020-11-04T03:22:50Z	0.431	0.551	1794800
32	2020-11-04T03:23:56Z	0.432	0.549	1805438
32	2020-11-04T03:24:24Z	0.432	0.549	1806013
33	2020-11-04T03:25:14Z	0.434	0.547	1843163
33	2020-11-04T03:25:49Z	0.434	0.548	1846044
33	2020-11-04T03:26:28Z	0.434	0.547	1852925
33	2020-11-04T03:26:43Z	0.434	0.547	1855440
33	2020-11-04T03:28:00Z	0.434	0.548	1862030
33	2020-11-04T03:29:51Z	0.435	0.546	1876528
33	2020-11-04T03:30:46Z	0.435	0.546	1877030
33	2020-11-04T03:31:40Z	0.434	0.547	1888003
34	2020-11-04T03:32:10Z	0.437	0.545	1945190
34	2020-11-04T03:33:30Z	0.437	0.545	1950083
35	2020-11-04T03:35:53Z	0.436	0.546	1966128
35	2020-11-04T03:36:44Z	0.436	0.546	1968971

EEVP	TIMESTAMP	VOTE_SHARE_DEM	VOTE_SHARE_REP	VOTES
36	2020-11-04T03:36:58Z	0.433	0.549	2017782
36	2020-11-04T03:37:16Z	0.433	0.549	2018739
36	2020-11-04T03:37:34Z	0.433	0.549	2023708
37	2020-11-04T03:38:30Z	0.435	0.547	2074784
37	2020-11-04T03:39:44Z	0.435	0.547	2075111
37	2020-11-04T03:40:09Z	0.435	0.547	2075572
37	2020-11-04T03:40:33Z	0.434	0.548	2080095
37	2020-11-04T03:41:53Z	0.434	0.548	2092325
37	2020-11-04T03:43:01Z	0.434	0.548	2093322
37	2020-11-04T03:44:17Z	0.433	0.549	2095746
37	2020-11-04T03:45:26Z	0.434	0.548	2116843
38	2020-11-04T03:45:58Z	0.435	0.547	2127584
38	2020-11-04T03:46:27Z	0.435	0.547	2130516
38	2020-11-04T03:47:01Z	0.435	0.547	2131214
38	2020-11-04T03:47:55Z	0.435	0.547	2133558
38	2020-11-04T03:49:25Z	0.434	0.547	2134055
38	2020-11-04T03:50:55Z	0.434	0.548	2139776
38	2020-11-04T03:51:08Z	0.434	0.548	2141938
38	2020-11-04T03:51:48Z	0.434	0.548	2143706
38	2020-11-04T03:52:20Z	0.434	0.547	2151723
38	2020-11-04T03:52:46Z	0.434	0.548	2157040
39	2020-11-04T03:54:09Z	0.437	0.545	2193165
39	2020-11-04T03:54:55Z	0.437	0.545	2201439
39	2020-11-04T03:55:07Z	0.437	0.545	2202686
39	2020-11-04T03:56:29Z	0.437	0.545	2203178
39	2020-11-04T03:58:07Z	0.437	0.545	2203693

EEVP	TIMESTAMP	VOTE_SHARE_DEM	VOTE_SHARE_REP	VOTES
39	2020-11-04T03:59:54Z	0.437	0.545	2209087
39	2020-11-04T04:01:28Z	0.437	0.545	2209804
39	2020-11-04T04:02:08Z	0.436	0.546	2220106
39	2020-11-04T04:02:12Z	0.437	0.545	2227998
40	2020-11-04T04:02:34Z	0.436	0.546	2270496
40	2020-11-04T04:02:51Z	0.436	0.546	2275398
40	2020-11-04T04:03:18Z	0.436	0.546	2281314
40	2020-11-04T04:03:25Z	0.436	0.546	2282541
40	2020-11-04T04:03:46Z	0.435	0.546	2291603
40	2020-11-04T04:05:32Z	0.435	0.546	2292906
40	2020-11-04T04:05:58Z	0.435	0.546	2293947
41	2020-11-04T04:06:27Z	0.435	0.546	2295343
41	2020-11-04T04:06:51Z	0.436	0.546	2327829
41	2020-11-04T04:07:07Z	0.435	0.546	2330031
41	2020-11-04T04:07:41Z	0.435	0.546	2330231
41	2020-11-04T04:08:19Z	0.435	0.546	2331090
41	2020-11-04T04:10:35Z	0.435	0.547	2335564
41	2020-11-04T04:11:26Z	0.435	0.547	2347156
42	2020-11-04T04:11:37Z	0.434	0.548	2357750
42	2020-11-04T04:12:11Z	0.434	0.548	2358720
42	2020-11-04T04:12:52Z	0.434	0.548	2404995
43	2020-11-04T04:13:37Z	0.435	0.547	2416902
43	2020-11-04T04:14:53Z	0.435	0.547	2418735
43	2020-11-04T04:15:57Z	0.435	0.547	2420849
43	2020-11-04T04:16:46Z	0.435	0.547	2421440
43	2020-11-04T04:17:39Z	0.435	0.547	2445835

EEVP	TIMESTAMP	VOTE_SHARE_DEM	VOTE_SHARE_REP	VOTES
43	2020-11-04T04:17:56Z	0.436	0.546	2457951
43	2020-11-04T04:19:19Z	0.436	0.546	2462074
44	2020-11-04T04:19:43Z	0.436	0.546	2469219
44	2020-11-04T04:20:51Z	0.436	0.545	2481214
44	2020-11-04T04:21:17Z	0.436	0.546	2483160
44	2020-11-04T04:22:20Z	0.437	0.545	2494704
44	2020-11-04T04:23:51Z	0.437	0.545	2496176
44	2020-11-04T04:23:54Z	0.436	0.545	2498845
44	2020-11-04T04:26:17Z	0.436	0.546	2500232
44	2020-11-04T04:27:34Z	0.436	0.546	2510225
44	2020-11-04T04:29:01Z	0.436	0.546	2513194
44	2020-11-04T04:30:17Z	0.436	0.546	2514725
44	2020-11-04T04:30:38Z	0.436	0.546	2516230
45	2020-11-04T04:31:38Z	0.436	0.546	2521454
45	2020-11-04T04:32:37Z	0.436	0.546	2522328
45	2020-11-04T04:33:14Z	0.436	0.546	2530558
45	2020-11-04T04:34:45Z	0.436	0.546	2532326
45	2020-11-04T04:35:12Z	0.436	0.546	2538168
45	2020-11-04T04:35:25Z	0.435	0.547	2544563
45	2020-11-04T04:36:02Z	0.435	0.547	2544819
45	2020-11-04T04:36:25Z	0.436	0.546	2553616
45	2020-11-04T04:36:59Z	0.437	0.545	2566159
45	2020-11-04T04:37:18Z	0.437	0.545	2569715
46	2020-11-04T04:38:06Z	0.437	0.545	2580027
46	2020-11-04T04:38:42Z	0.437	0.545	2585560
46	2020-11-04T04:38:57Z	0.437	0.545	2591695

EEVP	TIMESTAMP	VOTE_SHARE_DEM	VOTE_SHARE_REP	VOTES
46	2020-11-04T04:39:44Z	0.437	0.545	2594458
46	2020-11-04T04:40:18Z	0.437	0.545	2595825
46	2020-11-04T04:40:37Z	0.437	0.545	2597610
46	2020-11-04T04:42:17Z	0.437	0.545	2597614
46	2020-11-04T04:42:41Z	0.437	0.545	2602716
46	2020-11-04T04:43:00Z	0.436	0.546	2608227
46	2020-11-04T04:43:14Z	0.436	0.546	2609737
46	2020-11-04T04:43:58Z	0.437	0.545	2617275
46	2020-11-04T04:44:05Z	0.436	0.545	2617967
46	2020-11-04T04:44:27Z	0.436	0.545	2618885
47	2020-11-04T04:45:32Z	0.436	0.545	2636460
47	2020-11-04T04:46:11Z	0.436	0.546	2646716
47	2020-11-04T04:48:23Z	0.436	0.546	2650135
47	2020-11-04T04:49:03Z	0.436	0.546	2651380
47	2020-11-04T04:49:42Z	0.436	0.546	2656792
47	2020-11-04T04:50:34Z	0.436	0.546	2658605
47	2020-11-04T04:50:55Z	0.436	0.546	2659532
47	2020-11-04T04:52:00Z	0.438	0.544	2679228
47	2020-11-04T04:52:34Z	0.439	0.543	2689357
48	2020-11-04T04:52:44Z	0.439	0.543	2693947
48	2020-11-04T04:53:33Z	0.439	0.543	2696164
48	2020-11-04T04:53:34Z	0.438	0.543	2701165
48	2020-11-04T04:54:24Z	0.438	0.543	2702364
48	2020-11-04T04:55:34Z	0.438	0.544	2712642
48	2020-11-04T04:55:49Z	0.438	0.544	2714241
48	2020-11-04T04:56:48Z	0.438	0.544	2727984

EEVP	TIMESTAMP	VOTE_SHARE_DEM	VOTE_SHARE_REP	VOTES
48	2020-11-04T04:57:08Z	0.438	0.544	2731448
48	2020-11-04T04:58:37Z	0.438	0.544	2731461
49	2020-11-04T04:58:51Z	0.439	0.543	2750569
49	2020-11-04T04:59:02Z	0.438	0.544	2760695
49	2020-11-04T04:59:50Z	0.438	0.544	2762851
49	2020-11-04T05:01:25Z	0.438	0.544	2764644
49	2020-11-04T05:02:11Z	0.438	0.544	2766881
49	2020-11-04T05:02:20Z	0.438	0.544	2784661
50	2020-11-04T05:02:25Z	0.44	0.541	2828666
50	2020-11-04T05:03:06Z	0.44	0.541	2830283
50	2020-11-04T05:04:15Z	0.441	0.541	2833321
50	2020-11-04T05:05:14Z	0.441	0.541	2837423
51	2020-11-04T05:06:58Z	0.439	0.543	2872225
51	2020-11-04T05:07:29Z	0.439	0.543	2879707
51	2020-11-04T05:09:10Z	0.439	0.543	2884430
51	2020-11-04T05:10:46Z	0.442	0.541	2908393
51	2020-11-04T05:11:44Z	0.441	0.541	2914678
51	2020-11-04T05:12:00Z	0.441	0.541	2916083
52	2020-11-04T05:12:26Z	0.441	0.541	2918790
52	2020-11-04T05:15:48Z	0.441	0.541	2922874
52	2020-11-04T05:16:22Z	0.442	0.54	2952974
52	2020-11-04T05:17:04Z	0.442	0.54	2959093
52	2020-11-04T05:18:06Z	0.442	0.54	2961905
52	2020-11-04T05:18:31Z	0.442	0.54	2964847
52	2020-11-04T05:18:58Z	0.442	0.54	2973481
52	2020-11-04T05:21:00Z	0.442	0.54	2973861

EEVP	TIMESTAMP	VOTE_SHARE_DEM	VOTE_SHARE_REP	VOTES
52	2020-11-04T05:21:48Z	0.442	0.54	2973869
53	2020-11-04T05:22:28Z	0.442	0.54	2977716
53	2020-11-04T05:24:26Z	0.442	0.54	2982315
53	2020-11-04T05:24:30Z	0.442	0.54	2990610
53	2020-11-04T05:24:37Z	0.442	0.54	2992778
53	2020-11-04T05:25:05Z	0.442	0.54	2993598
53	2020-11-04T05:27:02Z	0.442	0.54	3004705
53	2020-11-04T05:28:08Z	0.442	0.54	3005993
53	2020-11-04T05:28:46Z	0.442	0.54	3011175
53	2020-11-04T05:29:02Z	0.442	0.54	3015652
53	2020-11-04T05:29:32Z	0.442	0.54	3015698
54	2020-11-04T05:31:08Z	0.442	0.54	3031975
54	2020-11-04T05:31:38Z	0.442	0.54	3035857
54	2020-11-04T05:31:53Z	0.443	0.539	3052178
54	2020-11-04T05:34:14Z	0.442	0.54	3060282
54	2020-11-04T05:34:25Z	0.442	0.54	3069468
54	2020-11-04T05:34:54Z	0.442	0.54	3076117
54	2020-11-04T05:34:59Z	0.442	0.54	3079380
54	2020-11-04T05:37:14Z	0.442	0.54	3083835
54	2020-11-04T05:37:28Z	0.442	0.54	3084907
55	2020-11-04T05:38:34Z	0.442	0.54	3087539
55	2020-11-04T05:38:54Z	0.442	0.54	3087587
55	2020-11-04T05:39:55Z	0.442	0.54	3088044
55	2020-11-04T05:41:52Z	0.443	0.539	3100918
55	2020-11-04T05:42:11Z	0.443	0.539	3101012
56	2020-11-04T05:43:39Z	0.447	0.535	3155129

EEVP	TIMESTAMP	VOTE_SHARE_DEM	VOTE_SHARE_REP	VOTES
56	2020-11-04T05:44:51Z	0.447	0.535	3163769
56	2020-11-04T05:46:56Z	0.448	0.534	3184301
56	2020-11-04T05:48:44Z	0.448	0.534	3184315
56	2020-11-04T05:49:26Z	0.448	0.534	3186645
56	2020-11-04T05:51:05Z	0.448	0.534	3190726
56	2020-11-04T05:51:44Z	0.448	0.534	3194207
57	2020-11-04T05:52:34Z	0.448	0.534	3205743
57	2020-11-04T05:53:36Z	0.448	0.534	3207289
57	2020-11-04T05:53:51Z	0.449	0.534	3232115
57	2020-11-04T05:53:56Z	0.449	0.533	3237675
57	2020-11-04T05:54:18Z	0.449	0.533	3237871
57	2020-11-04T05:54:33Z	0.449	0.533	3244793
57	2020-11-04T05:56:48Z	0.449	0.533	3248160
57	2020-11-04T05:57:42Z	0.448	0.534	3253831
57	2020-11-04T05:58:01Z	0.448	0.534	3254300
57	2020-11-04T05:58:19Z	0.448	0.534	3255870
57	2020-11-04T05:59:10Z	0.448	0.534	3256723
58	2020-11-04T05:59:48Z	0.448	0.534	3280499
58	2020-11-04T06:00:14Z	0.448	0.534	3285603
58	2020-11-04T06:01:56Z	0.448	0.534	3303286
58	2020-11-04T06:02:49Z	0.448	0.534	3307476
58	2020-11-04T06:06:32Z	0.448	0.534	3308222
58	2020-11-04T06:06:57Z	0.448	0.534	3309219
58	2020-11-04T06:07:13Z	0.448	0.534	3313260
58	2020-11-04T06:08:27Z	0.448	0.534	3313269
59	2020-11-04T06:09:47Z	0.448	0.534	3316681

EEVP	TIMESTAMP	VOTE_SHARE_DEM	VOTE_SHARE_REP	VOTES
59	2020-11-04T06:09:58Z	0.448	0.534	3328250
59	2020-11-04T06:10:48Z	0.448	0.535	3330408
59	2020-11-04T06:12:46Z	0.448	0.535	3330758
59	2020-11-04T06:13:46Z	0.448	0.535	3331621
59	2020-11-04T06:14:34Z	0.447	0.535	3334059
59	2020-11-04T06:14:49Z	0.447	0.535	3339680
59	2020-11-04T06:16:19Z	0.448	0.534	3358823
59	2020-11-04T06:17:49Z	0.448	0.534	3359271
59	2020-11-04T06:18:29Z	0.448	0.534	3368089
60	2020-11-04T06:19:46Z	0.448	0.534	3372030
60	2020-11-04T06:21:56Z	0.449	0.533	3379806
60	2020-11-04T06:23:05Z	0.449	0.533	3379815
60	2020-11-04T06:23:23Z	0.449	0.533	3388545
60	2020-11-04T06:23:48Z	0.449	0.533	3398494
60	2020-11-04T06:24:35Z	0.449	0.534	3401349
60	2020-11-04T06:25:14Z	0.449	0.534	3401361
60	2020-11-04T06:26:17Z	0.448	0.534	3414604
60	2020-11-04T06:26:49Z	0.449	0.534	3421565
60	2020-11-04T06:28:10Z	0.449	0.534	3423444
61	2020-11-04T06:29:51Z	0.449	0.533	3434148
61	2020-11-04T06:31:11Z	0.449	0.533	3439578
61	2020-11-04T06:31:48Z	0.449	0.533	3441317
61	2020-11-04T06:32:54Z	0.449	0.533	3448669
61	2020-11-04T06:33:05Z	0.449	0.533	3452346
61	2020-11-04T06:36:01Z	0.449	0.533	3459769
61	2020-11-04T06:36:46Z	0.449	0.533	3461774

EEVP	TIMESTAMP	VOTE_SHARE_DEM	VOTE_SHARE_REP	VOTES
61	2020-11-04T06:37:22Z	0.449	0.533	3470142
61	2020-11-04T06:38:18Z	0.449	0.534	3475497
61	2020-11-04T06:38:47Z	0.449	0.533	3478398
62	2020-11-04T06:39:22Z	0.449	0.534	3489333
62	2020-11-04T06:39:37Z	0.449	0.534	3495359
62	2020-11-04T06:39:53Z	0.448	0.534	3495962
62	2020-11-04T06:40:06Z	0.448	0.534	3514470
62	2020-11-04T06:40:21Z	0.448	0.534	3514485
62	2020-11-04T06:40:45Z	0.449	0.533	3522733
62	2020-11-04T06:41:46Z	0.449	0.533	3531811
63	2020-11-04T06:42:12Z	0.449	0.533	3544794
63	2020-11-04T06:42:48Z	0.449	0.533	3545674
63	2020-11-04T06:43:38Z	0.449	0.533	3549424
63	2020-11-04T06:44:46Z	0.449	0.533	3553366
63	2020-11-04T06:47:57Z	0.448	0.534	3581471
63	2020-11-04T06:48:41Z	0.448	0.534	3582525
63	2020-11-04T06:48:47Z	0.448	0.534	3587356
63	2020-11-04T06:51:46Z	0.448	0.534	3589112
63	2020-11-04T06:53:50Z	0.448	0.534	3591037
64	2020-11-04T06:54:23Z	0.448	0.534	3597919
64	2020-11-04T06:54:48Z	0.448	0.534	3606490
64	2020-11-04T06:56:47Z	0.448	0.534	3614696
64	2020-11-04T06:58:47Z	0.448	0.534	3616879
64	2020-11-04T07:00:37Z	0.45	0.533	3643075
64	2020-11-04T07:01:46Z	0.45	0.533	3649714
65	2020-11-04T07:03:17Z	0.45	0.533	3656445

EEVP	TIMESTAMP	VOTE_SHARE_DEM	VOTE_SHARE_REP	VOTES
65	2020-11-04T07:03:45Z	0.452	0.53	3689709
65	2020-11-04T07:05:26Z	0.452	0.53	3691717
65	2020-11-04T07:06:46Z	0.452	0.53	3694006
65	2020-11-04T07:07:09Z	0.452	0.53	3698027
65	2020-11-04T07:07:45Z	0.452	0.53	3701034
65	2020-11-04T07:08:46Z	0.452	0.53	3707328
66	2020-11-04T07:09:46Z	0.452	0.53	3711016
66	2020-11-04T07:15:08Z	0.452	0.53	3731784
66	2020-11-04T07:15:59Z	0.452	0.53	3737361
66	2020-11-04T07:16:47Z	0.452	0.53	3739988
66	2020-11-04T07:17:47Z	0.452	0.53	3745052
66	2020-11-04T07:19:18Z	0.452	0.53	3746889
66	2020-11-04T07:20:09Z	0.452	0.53	3749467
66	2020-11-04T07:20:47Z	0.452	0.531	3751208
66	2020-11-04T07:21:56Z	0.452	0.531	3756573
66	2020-11-04T07:22:47Z	0.452	0.531	3757597
66	2020-11-04T07:23:49Z	0.451	0.531	3766173
67	2020-11-04T07:26:09Z	0.451	0.531	3772675
67	2020-11-04T07:26:41Z	0.451	0.531	3780917
67	2020-11-04T07:27:24Z	0.451	0.531	3780919
67	2020-11-04T07:27:48Z	0.451	0.531	3787054
67	2020-11-04T07:29:48Z	0.451	0.531	3791415
67	2020-11-04T07:30:33Z	0.451	0.531	3802678
67	2020-11-04T07:32:07Z	0.451	0.532	3806695
67	2020-11-04T07:33:46Z	0.451	0.531	3809102
67	2020-11-04T07:36:18Z	0.451	0.531	3814267

EEVP	TIMESTAMP	VOTE_SHARE_DEM	VOTE_SHARE_REP	VOTES
67	2020-11-04T07:36:41Z	0.451	0.531	3818589
68	2020-11-04T07:37:47Z	0.451	0.531	3823936
68	2020-11-04T07:38:41Z	0.451	0.531	3828604
68	2020-11-04T07:41:46Z	0.452	0.53	3843273
68	2020-11-04T07:43:47Z	0.452	0.53	3852615
68	2020-11-04T07:44:48Z	0.452	0.531	3876262
68	2020-11-04T07:47:46Z	0.452	0.531	3877624
68	2020-11-04T07:49:09Z	0.452	0.531	3879353
69	2020-11-04T07:50:45Z	0.452	0.531	3882343
69	2020-11-04T07:51:46Z	0.452	0.531	3882746
69	2020-11-04T07:52:48Z	0.452	0.531	3884666
69	2020-11-04T07:54:49Z	0.452	0.531	3887253
69	2020-11-04T07:55:48Z	0.452	0.531	3888991
70	2020-11-04T08:00:57Z	0.455	0.528	3986835
71	2020-11-04T08:03:09Z	0.454	0.528	4004947
71	2020-11-04T08:06:04Z	0.454	0.528	4007034
71	2020-11-04T08:06:36Z	0.454	0.529	4016390
71	2020-11-04T08:11:44Z	0.454	0.529	4021454
71	2020-11-04T08:13:35Z	0.454	0.529	4030157
71	2020-11-04T08:20:05Z	0.454	0.529	4031302
71	2020-11-04T08:20:26Z	0.454	0.529	4043924
72	2020-11-04T08:21:50Z	0.454	0.528	4071108
72	2020-11-04T08:23:08Z	0.454	0.529	4072890
72	2020-11-04T08:23:51Z	0.454	0.529	4078144
72	2020-11-04T08:25:45Z	0.454	0.529	4080673
72	2020-11-04T08:26:36Z	0.454	0.529	4080676

EEVP	TIMESTAMP	VOTE_SHARE_DEM	VOTE_SHARE_REP	VOTES
72	2020-11-04T08:27:47Z	0.454	0.529	4084863
72	2020-11-04T08:33:49Z	0.454	0.529	4090131
72	2020-11-04T08:36:42Z	0.454	0.529	4090508
72	2020-11-04T08:38:32Z	0.454	0.529	4093329
72	2020-11-04T08:43:48Z	0.454	0.529	4095724
72	2020-11-04T08:44:08Z	0.454	0.529	4097222
72	2020-11-04T08:49:12Z	0.453	0.529	4100876
73	2020-11-04T08:50:10Z	0.46	0.523	4156943
73	2020-11-04T08:50:32Z	0.46	0.523	4163471
74	2020-11-04T08:55:47Z	0.46	0.523	4166438
74	2020-11-04T08:56:08Z	0.461	0.522	4177229
74	2020-11-04T08:57:03Z	0.463	0.52	4207367
75	2020-11-04T09:01:14Z	0.464	0.519	4224666
75	2020-11-04T09:03:30Z	0.463	0.52	4227799
75	2020-11-04T09:06:48Z	0.463	0.52	4232157
75	2020-11-04T09:08:13Z	0.463	0.52	4238302
75	2020-11-04T09:13:52Z	0.462	0.52	4243099
76	2020-11-04T09:15:47Z	0.464	0.519	4294021
76	2020-11-04T09:18:51Z	0.464	0.519	4295810
76	2020-11-04T09:20:51Z	0.463	0.519	4297778
76	2020-11-04T09:23:48Z	0.464	0.518	4301386
76	2020-11-04T09:26:49Z	0.464	0.518	4302594
76	2020-11-04T09:33:46Z	0.464	0.519	4304501
76	2020-11-04T09:37:52Z	0.464	0.519	4306766
77	2020-11-04T09:47:49Z	0.463	0.519	4344044
77	2020-11-04T09:48:27Z	0.463	0.52	4345932

EEVP	TIMESTAMP	VOTE_SHARE_DEM	VOTE_SHARE_REP	VOTES
77	2020-11-04T09:49:03Z	0.463	0.52	4345950
77	2020-11-04T09:53:50Z	0.463	0.52	4345952
77	2020-11-04T09:56:35Z	0.463	0.519	4354317
77	2020-11-04T09:57:00Z	0.464	0.518	4365423
0	*2020-11-04T10:00:04Z*	*0*	*0*	*0*
77	2020-11-04T10:00:46Z	0.465	0.518	4383872
77	2020-11-04T10:02:08Z	0.465	0.518	4383922
78	2020-11-04T10:03:43Z	0.465	0.517	4396290
78	2020-11-04T10:11:12Z	0.467	0.516	4439845
78	2020-11-04T10:14:45Z	0.467	0.516	4439859
78	2020-11-04T10:22:15Z	0.467	0.516	4442242
79	2020-11-04T10:33:48Z	0.467	0.516	4449514
79	2020-11-04T10:35:13Z	0.468	0.515	4472601
79	2020-11-04T10:41:47Z	0.468	0.514	4487095
79	2020-11-04T10:42:43Z	0.469	0.514	4498866
80	2020-11-04T10:47:41Z	0.469	0.514	4515533
80	2020-11-04T10:47:47Z	0.469	0.514	4517383
80	2020-11-04T10:49:47Z	0.469	0.514	4525011
80	2020-11-04T10:52:55Z	0.469	0.513	4537220
80	2020-11-04T10:53:51Z	0.469	0.513	4541303
80	2020-11-04T10:56:46Z	0.47	0.513	4544854
80	2020-11-04T11:06:48Z	0.47	0.513	4545797
80	2020-11-04T11:08:35Z	0.47	0.513	4549851
80	2020-11-04T11:13:53Z	0.47	0.513	4552864
80	2020-11-04T11:14:33Z	0.47	0.513	4555784
81	2020-11-04T11:14:48Z	0.47	0.513	4564424

EEVP	TIMESTAMP	VOTE_SHARE_DEM	VOTE_SHARE_REP	VOTES
81	2020-11-04T11:26:47Z	0.47	0.513	4565175
81	2020-11-04T11:31:48Z	0.47	0.513	4574555
83	2020-11-04T11:31:53Z	0.485	0.498	4724327
84	2020-11-04T11:52:08Z	0.485	0.498	4734623
84	2020-11-04T12:03:10Z	0.486	0.498	4752966
85	2020-11-04T12:08:46Z	0.487	0.496	4815774
85	2020-11-04T12:12:57Z	0.487	0.497	4825508
86	2020-11-04T12:14:51Z	0.489	0.494	4866279
86	2020-11-04T12:35:25Z	0.489	0.494	4866299
86	2020-11-04T12:36:47Z	0.489	0.494	4867492
86	2020-11-04T12:44:51Z	0.489	0.494	4868902
86	2020-11-04T12:49:53Z	0.489	0.494	4873736
86	2020-11-04T13:15:47Z	0.489	0.494	4874836
86	2020-11-04T13:23:51Z	0.489	0.494	4883065
87	2020-11-04T13:40:52Z	0.489	0.494	4915925
87	2020-11-04T13:54:47Z	0.489	0.494	4937389
88	2020-11-04T13:59:48Z	0.49	0.493	4963304
89	2020-11-04T14:02:47Z	0.492	0.492	5023632
89	2020-11-04T14:04:48Z	0.492	0.492	5025801
89	2020-11-04T14:05:48Z	0.492	0.491	5048379
89	2020-11-04T14:15:15Z	0.492	0.491	5055174
90	2020-11-04T14:15:50Z	0.493	0.491	5080970
90	2020-11-04T14:23:48Z	0.493	0.491	5095176
90	2020-11-04T14:45:48Z	0.493	0.491	5106890
90	2020-11-04T15:01:49Z	0.493	0.491	5107896
90	2020-11-04T15:23:50Z	0.493	0.491	5108580

EEVP	TIMESTAMP	VOTE_SHARE_DEM	VOTE_SHARE_REP	VOTES
90	2020-11-04T15:32:50Z	0.493	0.491	5110614
90	2020-11-04T15:43:49Z	0.493	0.491	5112648
90	2020-11-04T15:58:49Z	0.493	0.491	5114931
90	2020-11-04T16:07:50Z	0.493	0.491	5121579
92	2020-11-04T16:15:42Z	0.495	0.489	5184544
92	2020-11-04T16:21:48Z	0.495	0.488	5187059
92	2020-11-04T16:24:49Z	0.495	0.489	5201268
92	2020-11-04T16:30:48Z	0.495	0.489	5201437
92	2020-11-04T16:33:49Z	0.495	0.489	5207177
92	2020-11-04T16:36:13Z	0.495	0.488	5217543
92	2020-11-04T16:50:47Z	0.495	0.488	5221380
92	2020-11-04T16:53:48Z	0.495	0.488	5222700
92	2020-11-04T17:00:17Z	0.495	0.489	5235737
92	2020-11-04T17:34:13Z	0.495	0.489	5236020
92	2020-11-04T17:38:48Z	0.495	0.489	5236793
93	2020-11-04T17:42:50Z	0.495	0.489	5252066
93	2020-11-04T17:46:49Z	0.495	0.489	5254215
94	2020-11-04T17:53:12Z	0.496	0.487	5303442
94	2020-11-04T18:23:51Z	0.496	0.487	5291005
94	2020-11-04T18:26:24Z	0.496	0.487	5291155
94	2020-11-04T19:08:47Z	0.496	0.487	5291276
94	2020-11-04T19:13:49Z	0.495	0.488	5329650
94	2020-11-04T19:28:30Z	0.495	0.488	5329728
94	2020-11-04T20:10:47Z	0.495	0.488	5331105
94	2020-11-04T20:23:50Z	0.495	0.488	5335699
94	2020-11-04T20:38:47Z	0.495	0.488	5336392

EEVP	TIMESTAMP	VOTE_SHARE_DEM	VOTE_SHARE_REP	VOTES
95	2020-11-04T20:55:38Z	0.498	0.486	5372494
97	2020-11-04T21:15:13Z	0.498	0.486	5372494
97	2020-11-04T21:37:25Z	0.498	0.486	5389498
97	2020-11-04T23:31:12Z	0.498	0.485	5395016
98	2020-11-05T00:02:49Z	0.501	0.482	5452254
99	2020-11-05T00:29:28Z	0.503	0.481	5472004
99	2020-11-05T01:39:50Z	0.503	0.481	5472595
99	2020-11-05T03:45:20Z	0.504	0.48	5493400
99	2020-11-05T13:34:44Z	0.506	0.478	5515817
99	2020-11-05T21:23:40Z	0.505	0.479	5533144
99	2020-11-06T01:56:40Z	0.505	0.479	5533164
99	2020-11-06T17:46:36Z	0.505	0.479	5533185
99	2020-11-06T18:11:31Z	0.505	0.479	5530389
99	2020-11-06T18:23:36Z	0.505	0.479	5530390

Why would Edison Research format votes for each candidate as decimals rather than integers?

Late-night Ballot Drop

Many poll challengers submitted affidavits of late-night ballot deliveries at the TCF Center in Detroit during the morning of November 4, 2020, after the polls had closed. The Gateway Pundit had to issue a Freedom of Information Act (FOIA) request to obtain video evidence of these assertions. Under MCL 168.765, absentee ballots received after the close of the polls shall be plainly marked with the time and date of receipt and filed in the clerk's office. They are not to be counted.

Ballot Drop At Rear of TCF Center Well After Polls Were Closed

Last Minute Pollbook Drop

One day before the vote by the Wayne County Board of Canvassers on whether or not to certify the county election results, there is evidence that people were attempting to re-synchronize the chain of custody between the vote tallies, ballots, and pollbooks.

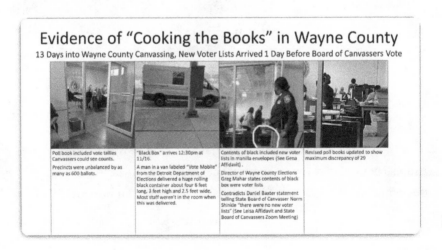

Poll Challenger Interference

During the counting of military ballots at the TCF Center, election officials prohibited viewing of the process by blocking windows with pizza boxes. Poll challengers were prohibited from re-entry to the AV Counting Board inside due to last minute, arbitrary COVID capacity rules.

*Doors at TCF Center During Processing of
Military Ballots*

DEFENSE PHASE

*GOAL: Prevent anyone from overturning the fraudulent
election results*

Fake Audits

In the *Bailey v Antrim County* lawsuit, Judge Kevin Elsenheimer issued a court order for an audit of the 2020 general election to be conducted in Antrim County. The official notice is shown below.

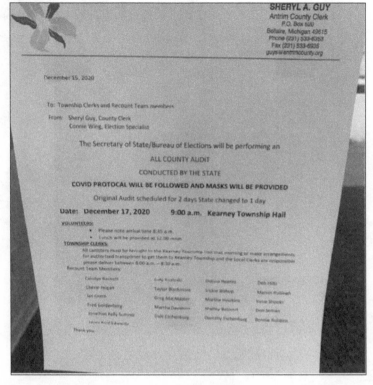

Official Notice by Antrim County Clerk of What She Called An Audit on December 17, 2020

When workers staffing the audit noticed ballot anomalies, they were told they were to simply count the ballots indicating that the audit was simply another recount.

Suspicious ballots highlighted by bipartisan team of election workers

The photo above was taken during the supposed "audit" by election workers. They highlighted suspect ballots for later investigation which never happened.

Records Deletion

The Michigan Bureau of Elections under the authority of the Secretary of State instructed clerks to destroy election records.

STATE OF MICHIGAN
BUREAU OF ELECTIONS
LANSING

MEMORANDUM

DATE: February 12, 2021
TO: County Clerks
FROM: Michigan Bureau of Elections
SUBJECT: Release of Voting Equipment

Please be advised of the following:

RELEASE OF VOTING EQUIPMENT: The security of ballots and election equipment is released as
follows:

Ballots, programs and related materials: The security of all optical scan ballots, programs, test
decks, accuracy test results, edit listings and any other related materials are released.

E-Pollbook laptops and flash drives: The EPB software and associated files must be deleted
unless a post-election audit is planned but has not yet been completed or the deletion of the
data has been stayed by an order of the court or the Secretary of State. Jurisdictions should
consult with city, township, or county counsel regarding any pending court orders, subpoenas,
or records requests regarding these materials.

FEDERAL BALLOT RETENTION REQUIREMENT: If the office of President, U.S. Senator or U.S.
Representative in Congress appears on the ballot (all appeared on the November 3, 2020
general election ballot), federal law requires that all documents relating to the election –
including optical scan ballots and the programs used to tabulate optical scan ballots – be
retained for 22 months from the date of the certification of the election. To comply with the
requirement, the Bureau of Elections recommends that optical scan ballots and the programs
relating to federal elections be stored in sealed ballot bags in a secure place during the 22-
month retention period. The documents subject to the federal retention requirement must not
be transferred to ballot bags for extended retention until after they are released under
Michigan election law as detailed in this memo.

<u>Questions?</u>

If you have any questions, please contact us via email at elections@michigan.gov, or by phone
at (517) 335-3234 or (800) 292-5973.

BUREAU OF ELECTIONS
RICHARD H. AUSTIN BUILDING • 1ST FLOOR • 430 W. ALLEGAN • LANSING, MICHIGAN 48918
www.Michigan.gov/elections • (800) 292-5973

*Letter from MI Bureau of Elections directing Michigan County
Clerks to delete election records that would be valuable in an audit*

This records deletion policy is clearly at odds with USC 52 Section
20701 which states:

"Every officer of election shall retain and preserve, for a period of
twenty-two months from the date of any general, special, or primary
election of which candidates for the office of President, Vice President,
presidential elector, Member of the Senate, Member of the House of
Representatives, or Resident Commissioner from the Commonwealth

of Puerto Rico are voted for, all records and papers which come into his possession relating to any application, registration, payment of poll tax, or other act requisite to voting in such election, except that, when required by law, such records and papers may be delivered to another officer of election and except that, if a State or the Commonwealth of Puerto Rico designates a custodian to retain and preserve these records and papers at a specified place, then such records and papers may be deposited with such custodian, and the duty to retain and preserve any record or paper so deposited shall devolve upon such custodian. Any officer of election or custodian who willfully fails to comply with this section shall be fined not more than $1,000 or imprisoned not more than one year, or both."

Note that the statute specifically references "all records and papers". The Michigan Secretary of State clearly has a unique interpretation of the word "all".

Deplatforming

Multiple social media platforms implemented stringent censorship of individuals asserting election fraud.

YouTube removes videos that address election fraud.

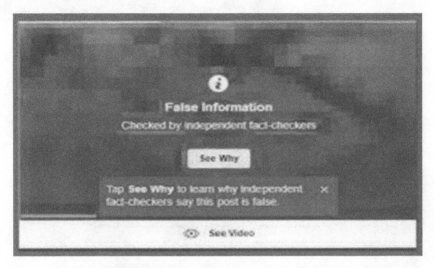

Facebook inserts opinionated 'Fact Checks' into posts that address election fraud or puts the offending user on 'time out' by suspending their account.

You can't use PayPal anymore

After a review of your account activity, we've determined that you're
in violation of **PayPal's Acceptable Use Policy**. As a result, your
account has been permanently limited and you won't be able to
conduct any further business using PayPal. This is permitted under
the **PayPal User Agreement** sections **Restricted Activities** and
Actions We May Take. You must remove all references to PayPal
from your website(s) and/or auction(s), including removing PayPal as a
payment option, the PayPal logo, and the PayPal shopping cart.

Any bank or credit card information linked to your PayPal account
cannot be removed nor can it be used to create a new account. You
can still log in and see your account information but you can't send or
receive funds. If you have funds in a PayPal balance, we'll hold it for up
to 180 days. These funds may be used to satisfy any obligations you
may have under the **User Agreement** and **Acceptable Use Policy**,
including potential liabilities to third parties and to PayPal for each
violation of the Acceptable Use Policy, including liquidated damages.
After that period, we'll email you with information on how to access
any remaining funds.
If there are chargebacks that result in your account balance falling
below zero, you will need to settle the amount owed to PayPal to avoid
further action.
Customers who are permanently limited for violating the **Acceptable
Use Policy** are not permitted to use PayPal services and are not
permitted to open new or additional PayPal accounts

Reference ID: PP-L-282084111229

*PayPal cancels the ability to collect donations for sites such as
LetsFixStuff.org which address election fraud.*

Visible Evidence of Coup

The following photo was taken by Ann Vandersteel (SteelTruth.
com) in the votes. This is the first time that I have ever seen fences
around the US Capitol after an election. It certainly resembles what one
would expect to see after a coup.

The U.S. Capitol after the inauguration ceremony for Joe Biden.

Audit Work Packages

Let's review all of the moving parts that go into a substantive audit of an election in a bit more detail. For convenience, each set of audit activities will be packaged into work packages (WP).

WP-1 PREPARE FOR AN AUDIT

The first work package is focused upon preparation for the audit.

Purpose

The purpose of this work package is to ensure that election records are secured and there is an executable plan for the audit.

Records

The following records should be secured in support of the overall execution of the audit as a minimum:

- Personnel Lists
  - Election Officials
  - Poll Workers
  - Vendors
  - Poll Challengers
  - Poll Watchers

- Governing election laws
- Election procedure manuals
- Disaster Recovery Plan
- Election training materials including audio and video
- List of all election equipment including the vendor, model number, serial number, the name of who certified compliance with the EAC standards, and the warranty service identification tag
- Election Equipment
- Networking Equipment
- Software Configurations
- Hardware Configurations
- Network Configurations
- Network traffic logs
- Machine event logs
- Physical Storage Containers
- Seals
- Seal usage log
- Electronic Storage Media (Portable and Fixed)
- All Security Credentials needed to access all features of the Election and Networking Equipment
- Access to all physical security areas

The following records need to be accounted for in the election record status report and may be requested as part of a subpoena:
- Communications
  - Election officials to/from election officials
  - Election officials to/from vendors
  - Election officials to/from poll workers
  - Election officials to/from public at large including poll challengers and poll workers
  - Election officials to/from law enforcement
- Security Footage

Process

The basic processes for this work package are:

1. Secure all election records needed in support of the audit
2. Catalog the status of all election records needed in support of the audit
3. Prepare the audit workplan
4. Prepare the audit budget
5. Staff the audit

Report

The key contents of any report produced in this work package are:

- Status of records (what, who, where, format, status)
- Organization chart
- Audit Personnel list
- Audit budget
- Milestone plan

WP-2 CONDUCT A STATEWIDE
VOTER REGISTRATION FILE AUDIT

The second work package is focused upon the integrity of the statewide voter registration file.

Purpose

The purpose of this work package is to ensure as a minimum that all of the voters who cast a vote in the election are eligible to vote.

Records

The following records should be secured in support of this work package as a minimum:

1. Statewide Voter Registration File Data

   In an Excel compatible format, request a list(s) of all voters who cast these votes in the 2020 general election that includes the following fields as a minimum:

    a. All name fields

    b. All address fields

    c. Driver's license or state ID number

    d. Last four digits of social security number

    e. Year of birth

    f. Current record status

    g. Affirmative documentation of citizenship

    h. The title/type of affirmative documentation of citizenship presented

    i. Phone number

    j. E-mail address or other electronic contact method

For absentee voters, add the following fields to the list above:

    a. Application date

    b. Application source

    c. Permanent absentee (Y/N)

    d. Date ballot mailed

    e. Date ballot received

2. List of Voters in election (may be different from statewide voter registration database) including the following data as a minimum:

    a. All name fields

    b. Add address fields

    c. Method of voting (in person or absentee)

3. Statewide voter registration file logs

    In addition to this core data, request all database logs pertinent to the modification of voter records within the statewide voter registration file from at least nine months prior to the election through to present day. Logs must include, but not be limited to, the following:

a. The name of each individual who executed an addition, revision, or deletion to the qualified voter file.

b. The location from which an individual described in subdivision (a) executed each addition, revision, or deletion to the qualified voter file.

c. Whether a transaction was an addition, revision, or deletion to the qualified voter file.

d. If a transaction was an addition or revision to the qualified voter file, a detailed description of the records in the qualified voter file that were modified and how these records were modified.

4. Electronic Registration Information Center (ERIC) Communications

   Request copies of each of the following data transmittals specified in the state agreement with the Electronic Registration Information Center (ERIC):

   a. Baseline performance data

   b. Performance data for the activity since the submittal of the baseline data

Per state agreements with ERIC, the following data has been submitted to them on a regular basis:

1. Number of voter registration applications new to the Member's jurisdiction submitted by the voter on a paper form

2. Number of new voter registration applications new to the Member's jurisdiction submitted by the voter electronically

3. Number of updates to a voter's existing voter registration submitted by the voter on a paper form

4. Number of updates to a voter's existing voter registration submitted by the voter electronically

5. Number of records reported from ERIC on In-state Movers report who updated through the jurisdiction's online voter registration system (if available)

6. Election statistics, totals for any federal elections within the period of:

   a. Number of new voters to the Member's jurisdiction who registered and voted on the same day, where applicable

   b. Number of updates to a voter's existing registration submitted on the same day on which they voted, where applicable

   c. Total number of provisional ballots cast

   d. Total number of provisional ballots counted

   e. Total number of provisional ballots uncounted, by reason (if available)

   Note: for context, ERIC will use voter turnout data from the United States Elections Project (www.electproject.org)

7. Number of individuals for whom contact was initiated and invited to register as a result of reports received from ERIC within the period

8. Number of individuals for whom contact was initiated and invited to correct their registration as a result of reports received from ERIC within the period

Process

The basic processes for this work package are:

1. Compare list of voters with state voter registration database

2. Evaluate list of voters for anomalies

   • Check against USPS change of address data

   • Check against death records

   • Check against census records

   • Check for data entry anomalies

THE 2020 COUP

3. Evaluate ERIC submittals for anomalies
4. Compare ERIC submittals with statewide voter registration file records
5. Compare statewide voter registration file voter records with the official statement of ballots cast

Report

The key contents of any report produced in this work package are:

- Summary of differences between list of voters and statewide voter registration database
- Number of ineligible voters who voted organized by the reason for their ineligibility
- Number of voters (ineligible, eligible) added by user account, organization
- Number of voters (ineligible, eligible) who registered on election day
- Key findings
- Corrective Actions
  - Election Official Actions
  - Legislative Actions
  - Judicial Actions
  - Law Enforcement Actions

WP-3 CONDUCT A POLLBOOK AUDIT

The third work package is focused upon the integrity of the pollbooks.

Purpose

The purpose of this work package is to determine whether or not ballots were distributed only to eligible voters.

Records

The following records should be secured in support of this work package as a minimum:

- Provide a list of all pollbooks used including the following information as a minimum:
  - Type
    - Electronic
    - Paper
  - Designated precinct or counting board
  - Timestamp for statewide voter registration file configuration used for pollbook
  - Name of individual who loaded or printed pollbook
- Electronic pollbooks including all journal data (e.g., poll challenger challenges), and transaction logs
- Paper pollbooks including all journal data (e.g., poll challenger challenges), and logs tracking modifications to the pollbooks
- Ballot envelopes
- Returned absentee ballot applications
- Returned absentee ballot application envelopes
- Canvass reports
- Personnel
  - Provide a list of all personnel with access to pollbooks including the following information as a minimum:
    - Name
    - Assignment
    - Party affiliation
    - Shift times
    - Assigned station
  - Provide a list of all individuals authorized to examine the hardware configurations for all pollbook equipment including the following information as a minimum:
    - Name
    - Organization

- Qualifications
- Event log (list of events pertaining to the activation or modification of the equipment)

Process

The basic processes for this work package are:

1. Examine Pollbooks
   - Compare general election pollbooks with current QVF status
   - Evaluate pollbook journal entries for anomalies
2. Examine Ballot Envelopes
   - Compare ballot envelope counts
     - With absentee ballot count
     - With absentee voter count
     - With absentee vote tally (if counted separately from poll-based ballots)
   - Evaluate ballot envelopes for anomalies
     - Same signatures
     - No signatures
     - Ballot envelope markings to differentiate party affiliation of voter
3. Canvass

   Canvassing is a subset of a complete pollbook audit. Canvassing will help to validate or invalidate the data captured in the pollbooks. Canvassers are effectively auditing key entries in the pollbook. When one canvasses, one simply asks a registered voter simple questions designed to verify the data in the pollbook. Sample questions include the following:
   - Did you vote in the last election?
   - If so, how did you vote? By mail or in-person.
   - How many registered voters live at this address?
   - How many ballots did you receive at this address?

Pretty simple questions. Please note that canvassers DO NOT ASK who did you vote for.

Canvassers do not validate the vote count. They simply validate the number of people who have voted. If the ballot count does not agree with the number of voters, something is wrong. The information gained through canvassing is one of the best ways to demonstrate evidence of mail-in ballot election fraud.

Report

The key contents of any report produced in this work package are:

- Number of registered voters
- Number of votes cast
- Number of voter anomalies identified during review of pollbooks
- Number of voter anomalies detected during canvassing
- Key findings
- Corrective Actions
  - Election Official Actions
  - Legislative Actions
  - Judicial Actions
  - Law Enforcement Actions

WP-4 CONDUCT A BALLOT AUDIT

The fourth work package is focused upon the integrity of the ballots.

Purpose

The purpose of this work package is to determine the integrity of any ballots cast and that the votes cast on the ballots were accurately tabulated.

Records

The following records should be secured in support of this work package as a minimum:

- All Ballots
  - Provisional but not verified
  - Spoiled
  - Cast
  - Blanks
  - Other
- All Ballot Stubs
- All Ballot Images
  - No tabulation errors
  - Tabulation errors
    - Pre-adjudication version
    - Post-adjudication version
- Ballot Logs
  - For each ballot delivered or printed in support of the election, provide the following information as a minimum:
    - Source (vendor, printed on demand)
    - Date issued to voter
    - How issued to voter
      - At poll
      - Via mail
    - Status
      - Cast at poll
      - Cast absentee
      - Mailed but not returned
      - Provisional but not verified
      - Spoiled
      - Not Used

- Adjudication Logs
  - For all adjudicated ballots, provide the following information as a minimum:
    - Timestamp of adjudication
    - Error description
    - What equipment was used to support adjudication
    - Adjudication method (manually or via automatically via software)
    - Name of individuals who adjudicated the ballot
    - Name of any election officials or vendors who provided technical support during adjudication process
- Ballot Printer Information
  - Ballot specifications
  - Printer equipment list
  - Vendor list
  - Orders
  - Receiving (how many, from where, how received, vendor, vendor personnel)
  - Distribution (how many, to where, how delivered, vendor, vendor personnel)
- Public Accuracy Test Reports and Supporting Materials
- Personnel
  - Provide a list of all poll inspectors, poll workers, election officials and vendors affiliated in any way with the processing of ballots cast including the following information as a minimum:
    - Name
    - Assignment
    - Party affiliation
    - Shift times
    - Assigned station

- Provide a list of all individuals who tabulated ballots including the following information as a minimum:
  - Name
  - Party affiliation
  - Shift times
  - Assigned Station
- Provide a list of all individuals who adjudicated ballots including the following information as a minimum:
  - Name
  - Party affiliation
  - Shift times
  - Assigned Station
- Provide a list of all individuals authorized to issue ballot-related requests (e.g. new orders, change ballot configuration) featuring the following information as a minimum:
  - Name
  - Organization
  - List of requests (what was requested, when, status of request, fulfillment of request)
- Provide a list of all individuals authorized to examine the hardware configurations for all voting system equipment including the following information as a minimum:
  - Name
  - Organization
  - Qualifications
  - Event log (list of events pertaining to the activation or modification of the equipment)
- Tabulator Specifications
- Purchasing Logs
  - Orders

- Receiving (when, how many, from where, how received, vendor, vendor personnel)
- Distribution (when, how many, to where, how delivered, vendor, vendor personnel)
- Hardware specifications for each piece of equipment
- Maintenance Logs
    - Software audit of each piece of equipment
    - Service log for each piece of equipment (when, pickup timestamp, drop-off timestamp, list of services provided, who provided service, under what contract)

Process

The basic processes for this work package are:

1. Conduct high speed scan of all ballots cast
2. Evaluate ballot scans using automated tools
3. Compare ballot images to physical ballots
4. Evaluate ballots meriting physical examination by audit personnel
5. Examine vote counts based upon ballot scans

Report

The key contents of any report produced in this work package are:

- Number of absentee ballots without crease marks
- Number of absentee ballots without valid signatures on the ballot envelopes
- Number of absentee ballots completed by machines
- Number of absentee ballots cast without any record of a ballot being mailed
- Number of ballots cast on non-standard paper
- Number of absentee ballots requiring adjudication
- Number of ballots stored in unsecured ballot containers

- Number of ballot measures requiring ballot updates within 30 days of election
- Number of unbalanced precincts by municipality
- Key findings
- Corrective Actions
  - Election Official Actions
  - Legislative Actions
  - Judicial Actions
  - Law Enforcement Actions

WP-5 CONDUCT A VOTE TALLY AUDIT

The fifth work package is focused upon the integrity of the vote tally reporting.

Purpose

The purpose of this work package is to ensure that certified vote tally is accurate.

Records

The following records should be secured in support of this work package as a minimum for each precinct, county and state as applicable:

- Certified election results
- Electronic equipment log (model number, serial number, installed software, hash data for configuration, Mac address, IP address, connected equipment)
- Precinct tabulator configuration data memory cards
- Precinct tabulator ballot image memory cards
- Precinct tabulator vote tally memory cards
- Precinct tabulator workstation event logs
- Adjudication workstation event logs
- Adjudication workstation ballot change logs
- Adjudication workstation ballot images before adjustment

- Adjudication workstation ballot images after adjustment
- Election management server event logs
- Election management server file transfer configuration settings
- Election equipment network configuration map
- Network traffic logs for all electronic equipment from time of equipment certification to certification of election results
- Event logs for all electronic equipment from time of equipment certification to certification of election results
- Election results databases (precinct, county, state)
- Election results database transaction logs
- Unofficial Electronic data transmittals (timestamps, content, sending IP address, receiving IP address)
- Official electronic data transmittals (timestamps, content, sending IP address, receiving IP address)
- Printed statements of votes with poll inspector signatures
- Election equipment chain of custody logs
- Statements of votes chain of custody logs
- Memory card chain of custody logs
- Cast Vote Records including timestamps

Processes

The basic processes for this work package are:

1. Evaluate Electronic Vote Tally Data for Anomalies
   - Precinct to county tally comparison
   - County to state tally comparison
   - Evidence of chain of custody violations
   - Evidence of third party connections
2. Evaluate Paper Vote Tally Data for Anomalies
   - Precinct to county tally comparison
   - County to state tally comparison
   - Evidence of chain of custody violations

3. Compare Electronic Vote Tally Data to Paper Vote Tally Data
    *   Precinct comparison
    *   County comparison
    *   State comparison
4. Compare Vote Tallies to Number of Votes Cast
    *   Precinct comparison
    *   County comparison
    *   State comparison
5. Evaluate vote tally logs for timing anomalies
6. Evaluate programmable or configurable components
    *   Confirm configuration complies with certified configuration
    *   Evaluate any configuration changes since certified configuration had been delivered
    *   Evaluate if any malware is present and its actions
    *   Evaluate any network connections and ascertain what was data was transferred by whom and when

Report

The key contents of any report produced in this work package are:

*   For each precinct:
    *   Number of votes cast for each race from ballots
    *   Total number of votes for all ballots
    *   When was tally complete?
    *   Who approved tally?
    *   How was tally transferred?
    *   To whom was tally transferred?
    *   When was tally transferred?
    *   When was tally received?
*   For each municipality
    *   Number of votes cast for each race from ballots
    *   Total number of votes for all ballots

- When was tally complete?
- Who approved tally?
- How was tally transferred?
- To whom was tally transferred?
- When was tally transferred?
- When was tally received?
- For each county
  - Number of votes cast for each race from ballots
  - Total Number of votes for all ballots
  - When was tally complete?
  - Who approved tally?
  - How was tally transferred?
  - To whom was tally transferred?
  - When was tally transferred?
  - When was tally received?
- For the state
  - Number of votes cast for each race from ballots
  - Total number of votes for all ballots
  - When was tally complete?
  - Who approved tally?
  - How was tally transferred?
  - To whom was tally transferred?
  - When was tally transferred?
  - When was tally received?
- Key findings
- Corrective Actions
  - Election Official Actions
  - Legislative Actions
  - Judicial Actions
  - Law Enforcement Actions

WP-6 CONDUCT A FINANCIAL AUDIT

The sixth work package is focused upon the integrity of the election financials.

For each election jurisdiction subject to an election audit, a financial audit should be prepared. If conducting a statewide election audit, each jurisdiction subject to the audit would be responsible for providing a financial report specific to their jurisdiction. Local municipalities would submit their report to county authorities. County authorities would supplement the data provided by municipalities within their jurisdiction with a county-specific financial report. County officials would submit their complete financial report to state officials. State officials would supplement the aggregate report of the counties with a state-specific financial report.

Purpose

The purpose of a financial audit is to determine if the financial management of elections is accurately recorded and if the financial transactions are consistent with the information evaluated in other audit work packages.

Records

The following records should be secured in support of this work package as a minimum:

- General Ledger including all income and expense transactions for all accounts related to election administration under authority of pertinent jurisdiction
- All Purchase Orders
- All Invoices
- All Contracts

Process

The basic processes for this work package are:

1. Review all income transactions and validate source
2. Review all expense transactions and validate receipt of services or products associated with the expense
3. Prepare financial reports

Report

The key contents of any report produced in this work package are:

- Income Statement
- Balance Sheet
- Key findings
- Corrective Actions
  - Election Official Actions
  - Legislative Actions
  - Judicial Actions
  - Law Enforcement Actions

WP-7 COMMUNICATIONS

The seventh work package is focused upon the integrity of the audit communications.

Purpose

The purpose of this work package is to establish a clear and consistent communication protocol and messaging for the audit.

Records

The following records should be secured in support of this work package as a minimum:

- Periodic audit status reports from each work package
- Final reports from each work package

Process

The basic processes for this work package are:
- Conduct stakeholder briefings
- Conduct press briefings
- Evaluate election record chain of custody
  - Evaluate WP-2 vs WP-3 findings
  - Evaluate WP-3 vs WP-4 findings
  - Evaluate WP-4 vs WP-5 findings
  - Evaluate WP-6 findings against all other work packages
- Prepare final report

Reports

The core work product of this work package is a consolidated audit report featuring a roll-up of each of the other work package reports. The key components of this report include:
- Executive Summary
  - Number of vote anomalies
  - Determination of whether or not anomalies were significant enough to change election results
  - Corrected election results (if determinable)
- WP-2 Report
- WP-3 Report
- WP-4 Report
- WP-5 Report
- WP-6 Report
- Key findings
- Corrective Actions
  - Election Official Actions
  - Legislative Actions
  - Judicial Actions
  - Law Enforcement Actions

APPENDIX C:

Manual vs. Electronic Voting Systems

O ne of the election reforms cited in this book is the need to re-turn to manual voting systems particularly for the all-important tabulation of election results. We used to have manual counts of ballots in America. Invariably, however, whenever the topic of returning to manual counts comes up there is vocal opposition. The primary reasons given for such opposition are that it would take too long in larger jurisdictions or that it would cost too much. Let's address each of these arguments.

In Michigan, the larger versus smaller argument is essentially null and void. Every precinct in Michigan is capped by state law at 2,999 active registered voters.[1] Typically, only around 1,500 voters actually vote in a given precinct. The tabulation of votes from each ballot occurs in precincts. Precincts are the basic building blocks of our elections. They are all about the same size. That means that precinct workers in large cities such as Detroit, Michigan, count the votes on roughly the same number of ballots as those in smaller townships such as Ontonagon, MI. There are 503 precincts in Detroit and only 1 in Ontonagon. So, in Detroit, 503 precinct tallies need to be aggregated as opposed to the one and done process in Ontonagon. The ballots, however, have already been counted at the precinct level. So, the "takes longer for large cities to count" narrative falls flat.

Do manual elections cost too much? Let's look at the primary cost drivers for electronic and manual elections. Manual systems are much less complex than electronic voting systems. Consequently, there are fewer security vulnerabilities. Any fair comparison of electronic versus manual voting systems must ensure that sufficient rigor has been applied to mitigate the security vulnerabilities of the electronic system to the same level as a manual system. Such an analysis would require a much more rigorous certification and security approach for electronic voting systems than currently in place. On the other hand, one needs to account for the observation that electronic systems should be able to tabulate the votes faster than a manual account. Any analysis would therefore need to address the labor cost incurred when providing a sufficient number of personnel to tabulate votes during relatively the same time period as an electronic tabulator. Labor costs are simply the product of effort (e.g., man hours) and hourly rate. There is likely more effort required to manually count the ballots. One can account for this effort by adding additional personnel until the total duration for electronic vs manual counting are roughly equal. Once you have addressed the resource requirements needed to put electronic and manual voting systems on equal footing regarding security and speed, you are ready to perform an apples-to-apples comparison of their costs. I recommend that any such analysis include the cost factors in the following table as a minimum:

TYPE	PRE-ELECTION	ELECTION DAY	POST-ELECTION

Electronic	• Material cost
	  • Hardware
	  • Software
	  • Networking equipment
	• Cost of certification*
	  • Federal
	  • State
	  • County
	  • Local
	• Training costs
		• Technical specialists	• Cost of maintenance & upgrades
			• Storage costs
			  • Physical
			  • Digital
			• Monitoring costs

Manual	• Training costs • Poll workers	• Poll workers	• Not applicable

Notes

Chapter 1: Most Secure Election in History?

1   "Joint Statement from Elections Infrastructure Government Coordinating Council & the Election Infrastructure Sector Coordinating Executive Committees," Cybersecurity and Infrastructure Security Agency, November 12, 2020, https://www.cisa.gov/news/2020/11/12/joint-statement-elections-infrastructure-government-coordinating-council-election.

Chapter 3: Security Threats to Our Election System

1   Kevin Monahan, Cynthia McFadden and Didi Martinez, " 'Online and vulnerable': Experts find nearly three dozen U.S. voting systems connected to internet," NBC News, January 10, 2020, https://www.nbcnews.com/politics/elections/online-vulnerable-experts-find-nearly-three-dozen-u-s-voting-n1112436.

2   "Critical Infrastructure Security and Resilience Note," Cybersecurity and Infrastructure Security Agency, July 28, 2020, https://www.cisa.gov/sites/default/files/publications/cisa-election-infrastructure-cyber-risk-assessment_508.pdf.

Chapter 4: Investigative Tools

1   "Let's Audit the MI Auditor General Report on Elections", https://letsfixstuff.org/2022/03/lets-audit-the-mi-auditor-general-report-on-elections/

2   "Michigan's Freedom of Information Act," Prepared by the Office of the Attorney General, January 2017, https://www.michigan.gov/documents/ag/FOIA_Pamphlet_380084_7.pdf.

3   CISA Critical Infrastructure Security and Resilience Note, July 28, 2020.

Chapter 5: The Theory

1   Per the U.S. Constitution states are the primary authority for the conduct of elections. This has not stopped the federal government from passing statutes that explicitly or implicitly infringe upon this authority.

Chapter 6: The Evidence

1   "Official 2020 General Election Results", https://mielections.us/election/results/2020GEN_CENR.html

2   "Michigan Proposal 3, Voting Policies in State Constitution Initiative (2018)", BallotPedia, https://ballotpedia.org/Michigan_Proposal_3,_Voting_Policies_in_State_Constitution_Initiative_(2018).

3   "Who Funded Statewide Ballot Campaigns?" Michigan Campaign Finance Network, https://mcfn.org/ballotproposals and "Sixteen Thirty Fund (1630 Fund)," Influence Watch, https://www.influencewatch.org/non-profit/sixteen-thirty-fund/.

4   Priorities USA v. Benson, https://www.govinfo.gov/app/details/USCOURTS-mied-3_19-cv-13188

5   Jerry Dunleavy, "Steele dossier funder Marc Elias testified before John Durham's grand jury," *Washington Examiner*, January 25, 2022, https://www.washingtonexaminer.com/news/steele-dossier-funder-marc-elias-testified-before-john-durhams-grand-jury.

6   Hillary Clinton Lawyer Marc Elias Press Release, April 21, 2020, "ANOTHER VICTORY FOR VOTING RIGHTS. Michigan Secretary of State Revises Signature Match Process as a Result of a Federal Lawsuit."

7   Beth LeBlanc, "Judge rules Benson's ballot signature verification guidance 'invalid'", Detroit News, March 15, 2021, https://www.detroitnews.com/story/news/politics/2021/03/15/judge-rules-secretary-state-bensons-ballot-signature-verification-guidance-invalid/4699927001/.

8   Ken Haddad, "Michigan voters to receive application to vote by mail for August, November elections," *Click On Detroit*, May 19, 2020, https://www.clickondetroit.com/news/politics/2020/05/19/michigan-voters-to-receive-application-to-vote-by-mail-for-august-november-elections/.

9   Riley Beggin, "Michigan GOP lawmakers claim Jocelyn Benson's absentee ballot mailings illegal," Bridge Michigan, June 24, 2020, https://www.bridgemi.com/michigan-government/michigan-gop-lawmakers-claim-jocelyn-bensons-absentee-ballot-mailings-illegal.

10   Communications discovered during course of investigation in support of Bill Bailey v. Antrim Country.

11   Communications revealed during deposition in Bill Bailey v. Antrim County.

12   Ibid.

13   "Post-Election Audit Manual," Michigan Department of State Bureau of
      Election, January 2020, page 3.
14   Bailey v. Antrim County, Exhibit Lenberg #8
15   Bailey v. Antrim County, Exhibit 10 Lenberg
16   Bailey v. Antrim County, Exhibit Cyber Ninjas #1
17   Bailey v. Antrim County, Exhibit #10 Penrose
18   Ibid.
19   Noted by Adams Township Clerk Stephanie Scott.
20   Bailey v. Antrim County, Exhibit #10 Penrose
21   "The SolarWinds Cyber-Attack: What You Need to Know," Center
      for Internet Security, March 15, 2021, https://www.cisecurity.org/
      solarwinds/#Who-What-When-Where.
22   Allen Zhong, "Trump Says Voting Machines May Have Been Breached by
      SolarWinds Hack During Election," Epoch Times, December 19, 2020,
      https://www.theepochtimes.com/trump-says-voting-machines-may-have-
      been-breached-by-solarwinds-hack-during-election_3625553.html?utm_
      source=ai&utm_medium=search.
23   Cerberusftp, "Security Vulnerabilities," https://www.cvedetails.com/
      vulnerability-list/vendor_id-10990/product_id-19703/Cerberusftp-Ftp-
      Server.html.
24   Voting System Test Laboratories, Pro V&V, U.S. Election Assistance
      Commission, https://www.eac.gov/voting-equipment/voting-system-test-
      laboratories-vstl/pro-vv. Voting System Test Laboratories, SLI Compliance,
      U.S. Election Assistance Commission, https://www.eac.gov/voting-
      equipment/voting-system-test-laboratories-vstl/sli-compliance-division-
      gaming-laboratories.
25   Voting System Test Laboratory Program Manual Version 2.0, https://www.
      eac.gov/sites/default/files/eac_assets/1/1/Voting%20System%20Test%20
      Laboratory%20Program%20Manual.pdf
26   Ibid, 25
27   Sean Lyngaas, "Election commission hires 2 tech experts for testing
      and certification program," CyberScoop, May 21, 2019, https://www.
      cyberscoop.com/election-commission-hires-2-tech-experts-testing-
      certification-program/.
28   US Election Assistance Commission, "State Requirements and the Federal
      Voting System Testing and Certification Program," page 30, https://www.
      eac.gov/sites/default/files/eac_assets/1/1/State%20Requirements%20
      and%20the%20Federal%20Voting%20System%20Testing%20and%20
      Certification%20Program.pdf.

29   EAC Testing & Certification Program, August 11, 2021, V1.0, Page 7.

30   Requirement 1.1.A.17 under Voting System Hardware Technical
      Requirements in Dominion Contract with the State of Michigan, Exhibit 2
      (Page 2 of 25).

31   Bailey v Antrim County, Cyber Ninjas Exhibit #1

32   Lv Wenge, et al., "Tuning Digital PID Controllers for Discrete-Time
      System by Election Campaign Optimization Algorithm," Institute of
      Electrical and Electronics Engineers, August 3, 2010, DOI: 10.1109/
      MACE.2010.5536508.

33   *Zero Days*, dir. Alex Gibney, Showtime Documentary, 2016.

34   Tripp Adams, et al., "Michigan Election Security Commission Report,"
      October 2020, https://www.michigan.gov/documents/sos/ESAC_Report_
      Recommendations_706522_7.pdf.

35   "Election Administration and Voting Survey 2020 Comprehensive Report,"
      U.S. Election Assistance Commission, August 2021, https://www.eac.gov/
      sites/default/files/document_library/files/2020_EAVS_Report_Final_508c.
      pdf, Table 3, page 153.

36   Voting Age Population Analysis, Anonymous but based upon verifiable data
      sources

37   Public Interest Legal Foundation v Jocelyn Benson, https://
      publicinterestlegal.org/cases/pilf-v-benson-2/

38   Letter from former MI SoS and current MI State Senator Ruth Johnson to
      MI Senate Colleagues

39   Glen Sitek v Jocelyn Benson, https://www.thomasmoresociety.org/wp-
      content/uploads/2020/08/EIF-v-Benson-002.pdf

40   "Are Ballot Image Audits Useful?", https://letsfixstuff.org/2021/12/are-
      ballot-image-audits-useful/

41   Emma-Jo Morris and Gabrielle Fonrouge, "Smoking-gun email reveals how
      Hunter Biden introduced Ukrainian businessman to VP dad," *New York
      Post*, October 14, 2020, https://nypost.com/2020/10/14/email-reveals-how-
      hunter-biden-introduced-ukrainian-biz-man-to-dad/.

42   Natasha Bertrand, "Hunter Biden story is Russian disinfo, dozens of former
      intel officials say," *Politico*, October 19, 2020, https://www.politico.com/
      news/2020/10/19/hunter-biden-story-russian-disinfo-430276

43   Wendell Husebø, "15 Media Personalities Claimed Hunter's Laptop
      Emails Were Likely Russian Propaganda Before New York Times
      Admitted," *Breitbart*, Mar 17, 2022, https://www.breitbart.com/the-
      media/2022/03/17/15-media-personalities-claimed-hunters-laptop-emails-
      were-likely-russian-propaganda-before-new-york-times-admitted/.

44 Rich Noyes, "SPECIAL REPORT: The Stealing of the Presidency, 2020,"
    MRC NewsBusters, November 24, 2020, https://www.newsbusters.org/
    blogs/nb/rich-noyes/2020/11/24/special-report-stealing-presidency-2020.

45 Michael S. Schmidt, "Hunter Biden Paid Tax Bill, but Broad Federal
    Investigation Continues," *New York Times*, March 16, 2022, https://www.
    nytimes.com/2022/03/16/us/politics/hunter-biden-tax-bill-investigation.
    html.

46 Tripp Adams, et al., "Michigan Election Security Commission Report,"
    October 2020, https://www.michigan.gov/documents/sos/ESAC_Report_
    Recommendations_706522_7.pdf.

47 Bailey v. Antrim County, MIOC Bulletin.

48 Department of Homeland Security Threat Pre-Election Assessment, https://
    www.dhs.gov/sites/default/files/publications/2020_10_06_homeland-threat-
    assessment.pdf

49 Report of the Select Committee on Intelligence United States Senate on
    Russian Active Measures Campaigns and Interference in the 2016 U.S.
    Election, Pg 3.

50 King v Whitmer, https://www.michigan.gov/documents/ag/172_opinion_
    order_King_733786_7.pdf

51 Peter Schweizer, "Chinese elite have paid some $31 million to Hunter
    and the Bidens," New York Post, January 27, 2022, https://nypost.
    com/2022/01/27/chinese-elite-have-paid-some-31m-to-hunter-and-the-
    bidens/.

52 "Now or Never Democracy", Brennan Center, https://secure.brennancenter.
    org/secure/now-or-never-democracy?ms=gad_brennan%20center%20justic
    e_573687137435_1717766584_67680376459&gclid=CjwKCAiAyPyQBh
    B6EiwAFUuakgEAdgqzFO2IlwoydfMYZ0qw2253S4Oz1e483_n-V7bCm-
    W3IuyZRhoCVI4QAvD_BwE

53 ACLU Voter Suppression Narrative, https://www.aclu.org/issues/voting-
    rights/fighting-voter-suppression

54 League of Women Voters Voter Suppression Narrative, https://www.lwv.org/
    voting-rights/fighting-voter-suppression

55 Millie Weaver, "Revenge Of The Kraken!" MillennialMillie.com, December
    26, 2020, https://www.millennialmillie.com/post/revenge-of-the-kraken.

56 Millie Weaver, "Guess Who Counted the Votes", https://rumble.com/
    vb0sq5-guess-who-counted-the-votes-millennial-millie-mirror.html

57 Millie Weaver, "BREAKING: The 100 Day Siege Begins!" MillennialMillie.
    com, August 1, 2020,https://www.millennialmillie.com/post/breaking-the-
    100-day-siege-begins.

58   Millie Weaver, "Feds Plan Internal Coup Narrative", https://rumble.com/
      vbj8q1-feds-plan-internal-coup-narrative-full-zoom-call-millennial-millie-
      mirror.html

59   Millie Weaver, "Election Night Coup D'état Plot Exposed!"
      MillennialMillie.com, November 2, 2020,https://www.millennialmillie.
      com/post/election-2020-coup-plot-exposed.

60   Morsi assumed the office of Egyptian President following the resignation of
      Hosni Mubarek as a result of the Egyptian Revolution of 2011. Morsi was
      later deposed in a coup after he issued a new constitution that granted him
      unlimited authority and implemented Sharia Law throughout Egypt.

61   PsyOp: The Steal, Millie Weaver, https://www.millennialmillie.com/post/
      psyop-the-steal

62   Millie Weaver, "Feds Plan Internal Coup Narrative - FULL ZOOM CALL,"
      Millennial Minnie, December 1, 2020, https://rumble.com/vbj8q1-feds-
      plan-internal-coup-narrative-full-zoom-call-millennial-millie-mirror.html.

63   Wayback Machine snapshot of ProtecttheResults.com, http://web.archive.
      org/web/*/protecttheresults.com

64   "Center for Tech and Civic Life (CTCL)," Influence Watch, https://www.
      influencewatch.org/non-profit/center-for-tech-and-civic-life/.

65   "Center for Election Innovation & Research," Influence Watch, https://
      www.influencewatch.org/non-profit/center-for-election-innovation-
      research/.

66   "The Michigan Center for Election Law and Administration," Influence
      Watch, https://www.influencewatch.org/non-profit/the-michigan-center-
      for-election-law-and-administration/.

67   Alan MacLeod, "Documents show Bill Gates has given $319 million to
      media outlets to promote his global agenda," Grayzone, November 21,
      2021, https://thegrayzone.com/2021/11/21/bill-gates-million-media-
      outlets-global-agenda/.

68   "EXPOSED: Who's REALLY Running the Biden Administration," Glenn
      TV, EP 171, https://www.youtube.com/watch?v=DDfaZcNi8lQ.

69   Robert Epstein is a senior research psychologist at the American Institute
      for Behavioral Research and Technology in California. Epstein, who holds
      a doctorate from Harvard University, is the former editor-in-chief of
      Psychology Today and has published 15 books and more than 300 articles
      on internet influence and other topics. He is currently working on a book
      called "Technoslavery: Invisible Influence in the Internet Age and Beyond."
      His research is featured in the new documentary "The Creepy Line." You
      can find him on Twitter @DrREpstein.

70   Epoch Times, "10 Ways Big Tech Can Shift Millions of Votes", https:// www.theepochtimes.com/10-ways-big-tech-can-shift-millions-of-votes-in-the-november-elections-without-anyone-knowing_2671195.html

71   "Facebook admits the truth: 'Fact checks' are really just (lefty) opinion," New York Post, December 14, 2021, https://nypost.com/2021/12/14/facebook-admits-the-truth-fact-checks-are-really-just-lefty-opinion/.

72   State of Michigan Dominion Contract (Contract 071B7700117), Prohibited Acts, Page 140

73   Affidavit of Dr. Phil O'Halloran

74   Cushman v Benson, https://electionlawblog.org/wp-content/uploads/MI-Carra-20201023-complaint.pdf.

75   Detroit Leaks video originally posted at BigLeaguePolitics.com.

76   U.S. Elections Project, Early voting statistics, https://electproject.github.io/Early-Vote-2020G/MI.html

77   Official 2020 General Election Voter Turnout Results, https://mielections.us/election/results/2020GEN_CENR_TURNOUT.html

78   Nathaniel Rakich and Jasmine Mithani, "What Absentee Voting Looked Like In All 50 States," FiveThirtyEight, February 9, 2021, https:// fivethirtyeight.com/features/what-absentee-voting-looked-like-in-all-50-states/.

79   Former Chesterfield Township Clerk Staffer, Jacky Eubanks, presentation on February 12, 2022 Election Integrity Workshop in Howell, MI.

80   Affidavit, Former MI State Senator and Certified Microsoft Small Business Specialist Patrick Colbeck

81   Election Summary Report, General Election Detroit, Michigan, November 3, 2020, https://detroitmi.gov/sites/detroitmi.localhost/files/2020-11/November%202020%20Election%20Summary%20Report%20Signed%20Copy.pdf.

82   Philip O'Halloran, "TCF Timeline: The 2020 General Election in Detroit," Michigan Citizens for Election Integrity, August 2021, https://mc4ei.com/wp-content/uploads/2022/01/TCF-Timeline-Report-2020-Detroit-General-Election.pdf.

83   Voter records show that 170 year Jason Daniel Lemoyne voted in the 2020 General Election, https://voterrecords.com/voter/21575028/jason-daniel

84   Bailey v Antrim County Expert Testimonies, https://www.depernolaw.com/uploads/2/7/0/2/27029178/all-expert-reports.zip

85   See Appendix A for additional canvassing figures

86   O'Halloran, "TCF Timeline.", MC4EI.com

87   Elissa Salamy, "Georgia opens investigation into ballot harvesting claims,"
      The National Desk, January 5, 2022, https://thenationaldesk.com/news/
      americas-news-now/georgia-opens-investigation-into-ballot-harvesting-
      claims.

88   O'Halloran, "TCF Timeline.", MC4EI.com

89   CD Media Staff, "BREAKING: Evidence To Soon Be Presented To Citizens
      Grand Jury Of Interstate Conspiracy To Manufacture/Harvest Counterfeit
      Ballots For Use In 2020 Election, Creative Destruction Media, July 21,
      2021, https://creativedestructionmedia.com/investigations/2021/07/21/
      breaking-evidence-to-soon-be-presented-to-citizens-grand-jury-of-interstate-
      conspiracy-to-manufacture-harvest-counterfeit-ballots-for-use-in-2020-
      -election/.

90   "BREAKING: Updated Massive AZ Ballot Fraud Operation Uncovered",
      https://americascivilwarrising.org/breaking-updated-massive-az-ballot-
      fraud-operation-uncovered-ballots-flown-on-private-korean-air-flight-into-
      phoenix-airport-says-facebook-whistleblower-ryan-hartwig-videos/

91   Affidavit, Mellissa Carone, November 9, 2020.

92   Bailey v Antrim County, ASOG Report

93   O'Halloran, "TCF Timeline.", MC4EI.com

94   Debra Heine, "IT Contractor Who Worked With Dominion on Election
      Day in Detroit: 'What I Witnessed at the TCF Center Was Complete
      Fraud'," *American Greatness*, December 1, 2020, https://amgreatness.
      com/2020/12/01/it-contractor-who-worked-with-dominion-on-election-
      day-in-detroit-what-i-witnessed-at-the-tcf-center-was-complete-fraud/.

95   O'Halloran, "TCF Timeline.", MC4EI.com

96   Niraj Warikoo and Joe Guillen, "Detroit election officials project: Voter
      turnout highest in 20 to 30 years," *Detroit Free Press*, November 3, 2020,
      https://www.freep.com/story/news/politics/elections/2020/11/03/detroit-
      voter-turnout-highest-decades-election-officials/6152193002/.

97   Election Summary Report, General Election Detroit, Michigan, November
      3, 2020, https://detroitmi.gov/sites/detroitmi.localhost/files/2020-11/
      November%202020%20Election%20Summary%20Report%20Signed%20
      Copy.pdf

98   William A. Galston, "Election 2020: A once-in-a-century, massive
      turnout?" Brookings, August 14, 2020, https://www.brookings.edu/blog/
      fixgov/2020/08/14/election-2020-a-once-in-a-century-massive-turnout/.

99   O'Halloran, "TCF Timeline.", MC4EI.com

100   Ibid, 34.

101   Ibid, 35.

102 "The Case for Decertification of Michigan Election Results", https://
     letsfixstuff.org/2021/01/the-case-for-decertification-of-michigan-election-
     results/
103 MCL 168.765a, http://legislature.mi.gov/(S(lspxe3xgmfm4ne5jborkfc2o))/
     mileg.aspx?page=getObject&objectName=mcl-168-765a.
104 MCL 168.931, http://legislature.mi.gov/(S(lspxe3xgmfm4ne5jborkfc2o))/
     mileg.aspx?page=getObject&objectName=mcl-168-931.
105 See Appendix A for Michigan election night reporting data from Edison
     Research
106 "The SolarWinds Cyber-Attack: What You Need to Know," Center
     for Internet Security, March 15, 2021, https://www.cisecurity.org/
     solarwinds/#Who-What-When-Where.
107 Bailey v. Antrim County, 357838 (COA, 2021).
108 Marking Ballots presentation at DefCon, August 9, 2019.
109 King v. Whitmer, Russ Ramsland Affidavit, https://www.mied.uscourts.gov/
     PDFFIles/PelDoc49.pdf.
110 The Navarro Report, Page 4, https://peternavarro.com/the-navarro-report/.
111 2020 Presidential Election Fraud Video produced by JohnWayne_FightOn
     compiling live broadcasts showing negative vote increments.
112 Bailey v Antrim County, Lenberg Exhibit
113 Mary Folts Affidavit captured via email on November 9, 2020.
114 "EXCLUSIVE: Suspicious Vehicle Seen Escorting Late Night Biden Ballot
     Van at TCF Center on Election Night" by The Gateway Pundit, https://
     www.thegatewaypundit.com/2021/02/exclusive-suspicious-vehicle-seen-
     escorting-late-night-biden-ballot-van-tcf-center-election-night-video/.
115 O'Halloran, "TCF Timeline.", MC4EI.com
116 August 17, 2021, Petition for Manual Recount Based on Malfeasance and
     Fraud, Tom Joe Barrow, Detroit Mayoral Candidate.
117 Wayback Machine Freep.com article, "Gateway Pundit Video Doesn't Show
     Election Fraud in Detroit", http://web.archive.org/web/20210206022546/
     https://www.freep.com/story/news/local/michigan/detroit/2021/02/05/
     gateway-pundit-video-doesnt-show-election-fraud-detroit/4411975001/
118 O'Halloran, "TCF Timeline.", MC4EI.com
119 Ibid.
120 Ibid.
121 O'Halloran, "TCF Timeline," MC4EI.com.
122 Tresa Baldas, et al., " 'Get to TCF': What really happened inside Detroit's
     ballot counting center," Detroit Free Press, November 23, 2020, https://

www.freep.com/story/news/local/michigan/detroit/2020/11/06/tcf-center-detroit-ballot-counting/6173577002/.

123 O'Halloran, "TCF Timeline," MC4EI.com.

124 Tresa Baldas, et al., " 'Get to TCF'.

125 Tresa Baldas, et al., "'Get to TCF': What really happened inside Detroit's ballot counting center," *Detroit Free Press*, November 23, 2020, https://www.freep.com/story/news/local/michigan/detroit/2020/11/06/tcf-center-detroit-ballot-counting/6173577002/.

126 Grant Hermes, "New videos falsely claim fraud in Detroit on 2020 election night," Click on Detroit, February 8, 2021, https://www.clickondetroit.com/news/politics/2021/02/09/new-videos-falsely-allege-election-fraud-in-detroit-on-2020-election-night/.

127 MCL 168.765, http://legislature.mi.gov/(S(ft431nue3wvuypzbjxb0x34v))/mileg.aspx?page=getObject&objectName=mcl-168-765

128 Devon Link and Ashley Nerbovig, "Fact check: Videos showing crowd locked out of Detroit TCF Center with windows obstructed are missing context," USA Today, November 10, 2020, https://www.usatoday.com/story/news/factcheck/2020/11/10/fact-check-videos-crowd-locked-out-detroit-center-lack-context/6195038002/

129 Ibid.

130 Wayne County Board of Canvassers canvassing report, 2020 general election.

131 Official MI 2020 General Election Results, https://mielections.us/election/results/2020GEN_CENR.html

132 "Presidential election in Michigan, 2020," BallotPedia, https://ballotpedia.org/Presidential_election_in_Michigan,_2020.

133 Louis Avallone, letter to Michican's secretary of state and Bureau of Elections director, November 1, 2021.

134 Michigan Public Act 116 of 1954, 168.509q § f, http://www.legislature.mi.gov/(S(5xy2xiiv4ihe4cbibo3eozn4))/mileg.aspx?page=getObject&objectName=mcl-168-509q&highlight=precinct

135 February 12, 2021, MI Bureau of Elections Directive to County Clerks to Destroy Records, "Release of Voting Equipment". See Appendix.

136 "Preventative Maintenance? Yeah Right", https://letsfixstuff.org/2021/07/preventative-maintenance-yeah-right/

137 Dan Firnbach, "Antrim County Election Results Corrected After Issue Skewed Initial Results," 9&10 News, November 6, 2020, https://www.9and10news.com/2020/11/06/antrim-county-election-results-corrected-after-software-issue-skewed-initial-results/.

138 December 15, 2020 MI Senate Testimony of John Poulos

139 March 4, 2021, Antrim County Commissioner meeting video, https://
     youtu.be/bFtXbt0M_wg.

140 National Intelligence Council, 10 March 2021, Foreign Threats to the
     2020 US Federal Elections, https://www.dni.gov/files/ODNI/documents/
     assessments/ICA-declass-16MAR21.pdf

141 Peter Schweizer, "Chinese elite have paid some $31 million to Hunter
     and the Bidens," New York Post, January 27, 2022, https://nypost.
     com/2022/01/27/chinese-elite-have-paid-some-31m-to-hunter-and-the-
     bidens/.

142 "DNI Ratcliffe Releases Report Showing China Interfered with the 2020
     Election", https://event201.com/dni-ratcliffe-releases-report-showing-china-
     interfered-with-the-2020-election/.

143 December 15, 2020, John Poulous MI Senate Oversight Committee
     transcript

144 Senator Edward McBroom, et al., "Report on the November Election in
     Michigan," Michigan Senate Oversight Committee, June 23, 2021, https://
     www.misenategop.com/oversightcommitteereport/.

145 Ibid.

146 M.L. Elrick, et al., "What persuaded the GOP members of Wayne
     County Board of Canvassers to reverse course,: Detroit Free Press,
     November 20, 2020, https://www.freep.com/story/news/local/michigan/
     wayne/2020/11/19/wayne-canvassing-board-monica-palmer-william-
     hartmann/3770140001/.

147 Rod Meloni, "A closer look at Wayne County canvassers Monica Palmer and
     William Hartmann," NBC's Local 4 News, November 19, 2020, https://
     www.clickondetroit.com/video/news/2020/11/19/a-closer-look-at-wayne-
     county-canvassers-monica-palmer-and-william-hartmann/.

148 Julie Mack, "6 reasons that allegations of Michigan election fraud defy
     common sense," MLive, November 22, 2020, https://www.mlive.com/
     public-interest/2020/11/5-reasons-that-allegations-of-michigan-election-
     fraud-defy-common-sense.html.

149 Mike Wilkinson, Mansur Shaheen, Paula Gardner, "Trump, who now
     claims fraud, got more votes in Detroit than most Republicans," Bridge
     Michigan, November 5, 2020, https://www.bridgemi.com/michigan-
     government/trump-who-now-claims-fraud-got-more-votes-detroit-most-
     republicans.

150 "Facebook admits the truth: 'Fact checks' are really just (lefty) opinion, New
     York Post, December 14, 2021, https://nypost.com/2021/12/14/facebook-
     admits-the-truth-fact-checks-are-really-just-lefty-opinion/.

151   How 'do your own research' hurts America's Covid response, CNN,
      September 9, 2021, https://www.cnn.com/videos/business/2021/09/19/
      how-do-your-own-research-hurts-americas-covid-response.cnn.
152   Ethan Siegel, "You Must Not 'Do Your Own Research' When It Comes
      To Science," *Forbes*, Jul 30, 2020, https://www.forbes.com/sites/
      startswithabang/2020/07/30/you-must-not-do-your-own-research-when-it-
      comes-to-science/?sh=118e7a4e535e.
153   Doug Gould, Mesa County, CO Forensic Analysis Report #2, https://
      static1.squarespace.com/static/620c3af99f21b965e2cbef44/t/62268289
      a0e00c56951c5044/1646690974087/mesa-county-forensic-report-no.-
      2+compressed+1.1.pdf
154   See MI Bureau of Elections memo directing deletion of records in Appendix
      A: Defense Phase
155   "MI Senate 2020 Election Report #BigLie", https://letsfixstuff.org/2021/06/
      mi-senate-2020-election-report-biglie/
156   Frankspeech broadcast on Tina Peter's Office Being Raided, https://
      frankspeech.com/tv/video/tina-peters-office-being-raided-and-corrupt-
      secretary-state
157   Doug Gould, Mesa County, CO Forensic Report #1, September 15,
      2021, https://www.tinapetersforcolorado.com/s/Mesa-EMS-Server-Image-
      Forensic-Report-No-1-09-15-21.pdf
158   Madelynn Fellet, "FBI raids homes of Mesa County Clerk and Recorder
      Tina Peters and Lauren Boebert's former campaign manager, NBC 11
      News, November 17, 2021, https://www.nbc11news.com/2021/11/17/fbi-
      raids-homes-mesa-county-clerk-recorder-tina-peters-lauren-boeberts-former-
      campaign-manager/.
159   Maggie Astor, "Colorado County Clerk Indicted in Voting Security Breach
      Investigation," *New York Times*, March 9, 2022, https://www.nytimes.
      com/2022/03/09/us/politics/tina-peters-colorado-election.html.
160   Ernest Luning, "Mesa County Clerk Tina Peters arrested by Grand Junction
      police for resisting search warrant," Colorado Politics, February 8, 2022,
      https://www.coloradopolitics.com/elections/2022/mesa-county-clerk-
      tina-peters-arrested-by-grand-junction-police-for-resisting-search-warrant/
      article_702b156e-8914-11ec-ae7c-13181b203440.html.
161   Doug Gould, Mesa County, CO Report #2, February 28, 2022, https://
      www.tinapetersforcolorado.com/s/mesa-county-forensic-report-no-2-
      compressed-11.pdf.
162   Jeff O'Donnell, Mesa County, CO Forensics Report #3, https://www.
      tinapetersforcolorado.com/s/mesa-forensic-report-3-signed-1.pdf

163 Copies of cease-and-desist letters submitted by Clare-Lock to me as well as my response can be viewed at ExposeElectionFraud.com.

164 MI Senate Oversight Committee Report on the 2020 Election, https:// committees.senate.michigan.gov/testimony/2021-2022/Senate%20 Committee%20on%20Oversight%20Report%20on%20the%20 November%202020%20Election%20in%20Michigan,%20adopted.pdf.

165 Zachary Stieber, "Michigan Attorney General, Police to Probe People Who Made Election Fraud Claims," *Epoch Times*, July 9, 2021, https://www. theepochtimes.com/michigan-attorney-general-police-to-probe-people-who-made-election-fraud-claims_3894132.html?utm_source=ai&utm_medium=search.

166 US Dept of Justice Civil Rights Division email letter to Arizona state senator Karen Fall, May 5, 2021, https://www.justice.gov/crt/case-document/file/1424586/download.

167 Dina Temple-Raston, "A 'Worst Nightmare' Cyberattack: The Untold Story Of The SolarWinds Hack, *All Things Considered*, April 16, 2021, https:// www.npr.org/2021/04/16/985439655/a-worst-nightmare-cyberattack-the-untold-story-of-the-solarwinds-hack.

168 Jonathan Oosting, "Who's at door? It may be Trump loyalists, hunting for Michigan 'ghost voters'," Bridge Michigan, October 13, 2021, https://www. bridgemi.com/michigan-government/whos-door-it-may-be-trump-loyalists-hunting-michigan-ghost-voters.

169 Fredreka Schouten, Trump loyalists are knocking on voters' doors in the latest quest to find fraud in the 2020 election, CNN, January 18, 2022, https://www.cnn.com/2021/12/18/politics/trump-supporters-knock-on-doors-in-search-for-2020-fraud/index.html.

170 Election Integrity Info list of 2020 election court cases, https://election-integrity.info/2020_Election_Cases.htm.

171 Press Release announcing Amber McCann's new position with Attorney General Dana Nessel, https://www.michigan.gov/som/0,4669,7-192-47796-553781--,00.html

172 Sarah Rahal, "Duggan appoints Hassan Beydoun as senior advisor, counsel," *Detroit News*, August 24, 2021, https://www.detroitnews.com/story/news/local/detroit-city/2021/08/24/detroit-mayor-duggan-appoints-hassan-beydoun-senior-advisor-general-counsel/5573261001/.

173 Seattle, Kenosha, Portland, Minneapolis, Provo.

174 "Who Was Behind The Insurrection At The US Capitol?" Millennial Millie Mirrors, January 7, 2021, https://rumble.com/vcjaqx-who-was-behind-the-insurrection-at-the-us-capitol-millennial-millie-mirror.html.